The Smithsonian Guides to Natural America
THE NORTHERN ROCKIES

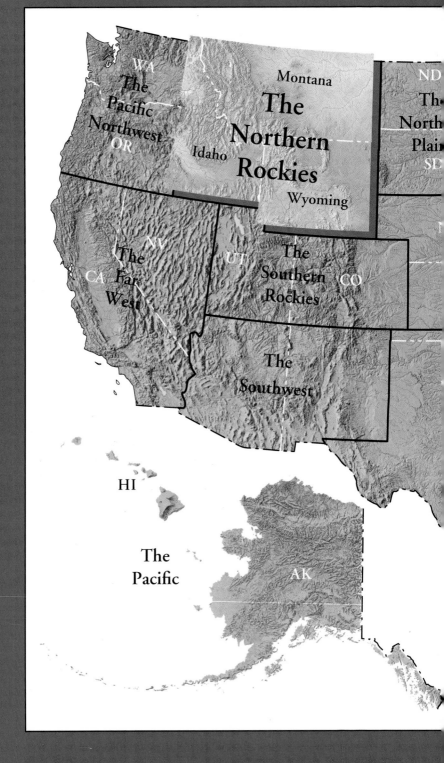

WA
The Pacific Northwest
OR

Montana

The Northern Rockies

Idaho

Wyoming

ND
The North Plai
SD

NV
The Far West

CA

UT

The Southern Rockies

CO

The Southwest

HI

The Pacific

AK

MN

WI

MI

The
Great
Lakes

IA

The
Heartland

IL

IN

OH

MO

KY

Central
Appalachia

TN

AR

The
South
Central
States

MS

AL

LA

The
Southeast

GA

SC

FL

Northern
New
England

ME

VT

NH

NY

The
Mid–Atlantic
States

MA
CT RI

Southern
New
England

PA

NJ

MD DE

WV

VA

The
Atlantic
Coast

NC

THE NORTHERN ROCKIES
IDAHO – MONTANA – WYOMING

THE SMITHSONIAN GUIDES TO NATURAL AMERICA

THE NORTHERN ROCKIES

IDAHO, MONTANA, AND WYOMING

TEXT BY

Jeremy Schmidt and
Thomas Schmidt

PREFACE BY

Thomas E. Lovejoy

SMITHSONIAN BOOKS • WASHINGTON, DC
RANDOM HOUSE • NEW YORK, NY

Front cover: Snake River, Grand Teton National Park, Wyoming
Half-title page: American bison, Yellowstone National Park, Wyoming
Frontispiece: Bob Marshall Wilderness, Montana
Back cover: Cougar and cubs, Montana; wildflowers, Idaho; bighorn sheep, Wyoming

THE SMITHSONIAN INSTITUTION
SECRETARY I. Michael Heyman
COUNSELOR TO THE SECRETARY FOR
BIODIVERSITY AND ENVIRONMENTAL AFFAIRS Thomas E. Lovejoy
ACTING DIRECTOR, SMITHSONIAN INSTITUTION PRESS Daniel H. Goodwin

SMITHSONIAN BOOKS
EDITOR IN CHIEF Patricia Gallagher
SENIOR EDITOR Alexis Doster III
MARKETING MANAGER Susan E. Romatowski
BUSINESS MANAGER Steven J. Bergstrom

THE SMITHSONIAN GUIDES TO NATURAL AMERICA
SERIES EDITOR Sandra Wilmot
MANAGING EDITOR Ellen Scordato
PHOTO EDITORS Mary Jenkins, Sarah Longacre
ART DIRECTOR Mervyn Clay
ASSISTANT PHOTO EDITOR Ferris Cook
ASSISTANT PHOTO EDITOR Rebecca Williams
ASSISTANT EDITOR Seth Ginsberg
COPY EDITORS Helen Dunn, Karen Hammonds
FACT CHECKER Jean Cotterell
PRODUCTION DIRECTOR Katherine Rosenbloom

Library of Congress Cataloging-in-Publication Data
Schmidt, Thomas
    The Smithsonian guides to natural America. The Northern Rockies—
  Idaho, Montana, and Wyoming / text by Tom and Jeremy Schmidt;
  preface by Thomas E. Lovejoy
      p. cm.
    Includes bibliographical references (p. 254) and index.
    ISBN 0-679-76312-0 (pbk.)
    1. Natural history—Idaho—Guidebooks. 2. Natural history—
Montana—Guidebooks. 3. Natural History—Wyoming—Guidebooks.
4. Idaho—Guidebooks. 5. Montana—Guidebooks. 6. Wyoming—
Guidebooks. I. Schmidt, Jeremy. II. Title.

QH105.I2S35 1995   95-5255
508.78—dc20   CIP

Manufactured in the United States of America
98765432

How To Use This Book

The SMITHSONIAN GUIDES TO NATURAL AMERICA explore and celebrate the preserved and protected natural areas of this country that are open for the public to use and enjoy. From world-famous national parks to tiny local preserves, the places featured in these guides offer a splendid panoply of this nation's natural wonders.

Divided by state and region, this book offers suggested itineraries for travelers and briefly describes the high points of each preserve, refuge, park, or wilderness area along the way. Each site was chosen for a specific reason: Some are noted for their botanical, zoological, or geological significance, others simply for their exceptional scenic beauty.

Information pertaining to the area as a whole can be found in the introductory sections to the book and to each chapter. In addition, specialized maps at the beginning of the book and each chapter highlight an area's geography and geological features as well as pinpoint the specific locales that the author describes.

For quick reference, places of interest are set in **boldface** type; those set in **boldface** followed by the symbol ❖ are listed in the Site Guide at the back of

the book. (This feature begins on page 261, just before the index.) Here noteworthy sites are listed alphabetically by state, and each entry provides practical information that visitors need: telephone numbers, mailing addresses, and specific services available.

Addresses and telephone numbers of national, state, and local agencies and organizations are also listed. Also in appendices are a glossary of pertinent scientific terms and designations used to describe natural areas; the author's recommendations for further reading (both nonfiction and fiction); and a list of sources that can aid travelers planning a guided visit.

The words and images of these guides are meant to help both the active naturalist and the armchair traveler to appreciate more fully the environmental diversity and natural splendor of this country. To ensure a successful visit, always contact a site in advance to obtain detailed maps, updated information on hours and fees, and current weather conditions. Many areas maintain a fragile ecological balance. Remember that their continued vitality depends in part on responsible visitors who tread the land lightly.

CONTENTS

PREFACE

There is a map in Captain John C. Frémont's *Report of the Exploring Expedition to the Rocky Mountains* of 1842 (four years before the Smithsonian's establishment) that appeals to my vicarious sense of nineteenth-century wanderlust. So from time to time I pull the volume off the shelf and gently, ever so gently, unfold the fragile map and gaze with fascination at the names and the features...and mostly the blank space. It is reminiscent of most maps of the Amazon until relatively recently: rivers, vast, largely undisturbed areas, and a sprinkling of names and outposts.

That is not the way maps of these three states of the Northern Rockies—Idaho, Montana, and Wyoming—look today, but much of the region's natural wonder and beauty is still there. Indeed, I don't feel a summer is complete without a visit to the Rockies—northern or farther south. I like to lie in my sleeping bag under the brilliant fretwork of stars and really feel as though I were part of the Milky Way and the universe.

Here is the home of the world's first national park and one of the most famous—Yellowstone. The signal beauty of its natural features led to this designation, and it was their representation in watercolor by Thomas Moran (in sketches today held by Tulsa's Gilcrease Museum) that persuaded Congress to take such a precedent-setting step. Appropriately, the Smithsonian's National Museum of American Art displays Moran's oil *Grand Canyon of the Yellowstone*, a Brobdingnagian canvas that dwarfs the viewer and in many ways epitomizes America's fascination with the wilderness and the natural (see pages xiv–xv).

In Yellowstone graze bison that are part of one of the first conservation efforts in this country. When the enormous herds had been reduced nearly to naught, American zoologist William Hornaday arranged for a few specimens to be brought to the nation's capital in 1886 and exhibited at the U.S. National Museum. On May 10, 1888, several live bison were purchased and an old photograph reveals them grazing on the Mall with the Smithsonian Castle looming in the background. Those

---

PRECEDING PAGES: *In Grand Teton National Park, sunrise glances off the snowcapped peaks soaring above the quiet oxbows of the Snake River.*

animals were among the progenitors of the current national bison herd, including the animals in Yellowstone today. They also constituted the beginning of the Smithsonian's National Zoological Park.

The Northern Rockies and Yellowstone continue to make conservation history as surely as Old Faithful performs. This is one of the regions of the country where it has become apparent that designating a protected area may not be enough to preserve it. Rather, it is now clear that the Yellowstone beloved by Moran and so many others can survive undiminished only if it is approached as part of the greater Yellowstone ecosystem. Many of its species—the most obvious being the grizzly—cannot continue to exist there unless they are part of a larger functioning ecosystem. The problem, of course, is that human activity and development have splintered the greater Yellowstone ecosystem and inadvertently imperiled this great wonder of the world.

The biology of habitat fragmentation happens to be my own personal line of research, full of fascinating turns and surprises. The "solution," however, is complex because we need to restore connections within the landscape, to guide human activity away from fragmentation, and to take an ecosystem-management approach in decision making. It is an awesome responsibility in which the power and responsibility are themselves widely dispersed.

I am nonetheless optimistic because Yellowstone is important to so many people. Enormous fires occurred in Yellowstone in 1988, revealing the error of suppressing natural cycles of fire until the accumulated tinder was overwhelming. Equally edifying is the great concern that emanates from those living around Yellowstone who depend upon it economically. Yellowstone has become substantially integrated into the surrounding social matrix.

The Northern Rockies are also home to spectacular rivers and wonderful wildlife. The River of No Return (the Salmon) remains etched in my mind in part because it is the second deepest gorge in North America and also because of its bighorn sheep and the curious American dipper (formerly called the water ouzel), which walks along the bottom of streams and nests behind waterfalls with nonchalant impunity. The Snake River Bird of Prey Area explodes with raptorial acrobatics, Grays Lake, with the stately dances of cranes.

OVERLEAF: *Thomas Moran's 1872* **Grand Canyon of the Yellowstone** *(detail) helped persuade Congress to establish the first national park.*

Idaho's Redfish Lake tells the sad story of so many of the once-plentiful salmon stocks of our northwestern rivers. In 1993, when I served as Science Advisor to the Secretary of the Interior, only four adult salmon made it back to spawn; like so many other salmon populations, this one was the victim of multiple factors, including hydroelectric dams, deforestation, and overfishing at sea.

Yet Idaho also offers an encouraging story of conservation progress. It was the first state where the relevant managing agencies pooled their data about plants and animals in a computerized geographic information system (GIS) that could then be subjected to the national Gap Analysis Project, directed by the U.S. Biological Survey. This provides enormous efficiency and flexibility in conservation planning.

Just in the nick of time, we are learning that nature harbors a welter of magical molecules capable of generating human benefit and wealth through biotechnology. The most wonderful of these molecules to date is an enzyme from the little bacterium *Thermus aquaticus*, which occurs in the hot springs of Yellowstone National Park. The enzyme is part of a reaction that magnifies genetic material geometrically, making the polymerase chain reaction possible. It is at the heart of diagnostic medicine today, makes the human genome project possible, and its discovery was recognized by the 1993 Nobel Prize for Chemistry. Visitors to Yellowstone Park learn not only about geology and nature, but also about the story of the little bacterium with the amazing enzyme. From Moran to molecules, natural America in the Northern Rockies is extraordinary indeed.

—*Thomas E. Lovejoy*
Counselor to the Secretary for
Biodiversity and Environmental Affairs,
SMITHSONIAN INSTITUTION

RIGHT: *Amid charred trunks, magenta fireweed and yellow arnica colonize a newly sunny area, opened up by Yellowstone's fierce 1988 fires.*
OVERLEAF: *Where the Rockies meet the prairies and bison once roamed, a rancher moves cattle over the rolling grasslands near Choteau, Montana.*

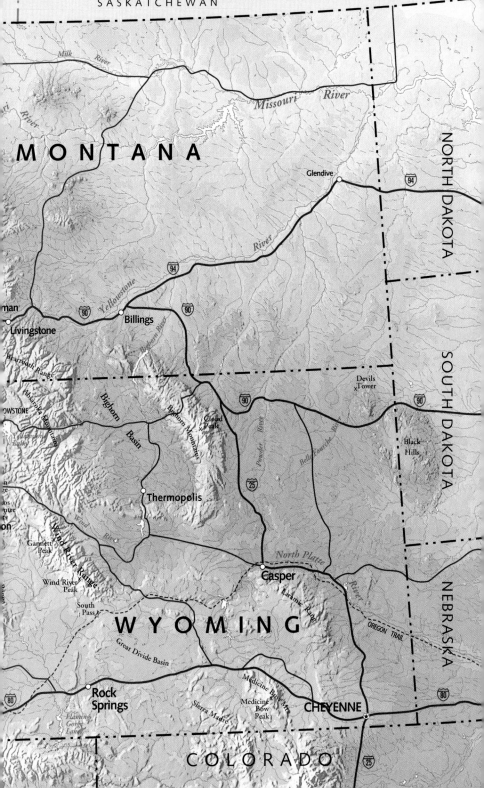

Milk *River*

Missouri *River*

M O N T A N A

NORTH DAKOTA

River

Glendive

94

River

Yellowstone

90

90

man

Livingstone

90

94

Billings

Bighorn *River*

SOUTH DAKOTA

Beartooth *Range*

90

Devils
xTower

90

Absaroka *Mountains*

Bighorn

Bighorn
Mountains

Cloud
xPeak

Powder *River*

Belle *Fourche* *River*

Black
Hills

OWSTONE

Basin

25

Thermopolis

Wind *River*

Gannett
xPeak

Wind River
Range

Wind *River*

North Platte

25

Casper

Laramie *Range*

River

NEBRASKA

Wind River
xPeak

South
Pass

W Y O M I N G

OREGON TRAIL

Great Divide Basin

80

Medicine *Bow* *Mtns.*

80

Rock
Springs

Sierra Madre

Medicine
Bow
xPeak

CHEYENNE

*Flaming
Gorge
Lake*

25

C O L O R A D O

INTRODUCTION:
THE NORTHERN ROCKIES

S cratched from the eroding badlands of southern Wyoming, Rock Springs is the sort of place that gets tucked into the back of tourist brochures. It's a parched town of truck stops, mini marts, and cloverleaf exits that wrap around clusters of faded mobile homes and dusty horse corrals. It's an oasis of cold beer, cheap diesel, and chicken-fried steak—a place where you're never far from the drone of the interstate and where a stiff wind kicks up clouds of dirt mixed with potato-chip bags and faded candy-bar wrappers. For many visitors to the Northern Rockies, though, this forlorn outpost of asphalt, concrete, plastic, and neon is also a gateway to the promised land.

Just a few miles north of town, you can stand on a battered slope of sun-baked clay, kick aside a used oil filter, and gaze across a vast desert landscape to the shimmering ramparts of the Wind River Mountains. Heavily laden with snow through early summer, the Winds are the first step of the Northern Rockies. They shoulder up from the sands of Wyoming's Great Divide Basin, a desert region enclosed by a split in the Continental Divide. A depression with no drainage and precious little water to drain, the basin marks a lull in the alpine theatrics of the Rocky Mountains.

I n Wyoming, Idaho, and Montana, the Rockies are the main story and the backdrop for a tremendously diverse landscape that also includes short-grass prairie, high plains desert, fields of sand dunes, great marshes, tracts of hardened black lava, volcanic cones, canyons, buttes, and mesas. Starting with the Wind River Mountains and comprising many other subranges, the Northern Rockies tumble toward the Arctic through Grand Teton, Yellowstone, and Glacier national parks. Not simply a narrow crest, the mountains swell. They expand across Idaho and spill onto the plains, until they are hundreds of miles wide with thousands of individual summits.

They aren't just the Rockies. They are the Tetons, the Sawtooths, the

---

PRECEDING PAGES: *The Absaroka Range, mauled by glaciers, looms over a lush corridor of cottonwoods, willows, and aspens that line the stony Yellowstone River in Montana's Paradise Valley, north of Gardiner.*

Beartooths, the Greens, the Gravellys, the Rubys, the Sapphires, the Bitterroots, the Tobacco Roots, the Bridgers, the Bighorns, and the contorted, mostly unnamed mass of ridges that make up central Idaho. Each constituent range tells its own unique creation story, reflected in different rocks, different shapes, and characteristic skylines. Yet despite regional differences, all the peaks of the Northern Rockies share common beginnings—the Sevier and Laramide orogenies, pleasingly named but wrenching geologic events that began, respectively, about 144 and 70 million years ago and forced much of western North America skyward.

The region records a violent geologic history. Some geologists hypothesize that a meteorite landing in southeastern Oregon 17 million years ago formed a large crater and cracked the crust of the earth. Lava flowing from the crater over millions of years built up the Columbia Plateau between the Rocky and Cascade mountains. According to another theory, a crack in crustal rocks allowed molten rock to surge upward. That plume of molten rock forms a hot spot in the earth's underlying mantle, which is located beneath today's Yellowstone National Park in northwestern Wyoming. As the continent slowly shifted westward, part of its surface passed over the hot spot, much like a sheet of plastic moving over a flame. Just as a line of melted plastic shows where the sheet passed over the flame, so the earth's surface is marked by its passage over the hot spot—most notably in southern Idaho's vast Snake River Plain.

Periodically, the hot spot burns through to the surface and causes a volcanic explosion. Large eruptions occurred 2 million and 1.3 million years ago, the latter creating northeastern Idaho's Island Park caldera, or collapsed crater. Then, 600,000 years ago, a cataclysmic explosion—one of the largest eruptions known to have occurred anywhere on earth—blew the central part of Yellowstone sky high and created the famous Yellowstone caldera. The hot spot still lies restively below the park, producing its geysers, hot springs, and boiling mud pots.

In some eras, whole mountain ranges were formed during the Sevier orogeny, when rocks were folded and thrust eastward, sometimes stacking up against each other as they came to rest. During the Laramide orogeny huge slabs of rock were lifted and tilted along tremendous faults, forming the Wind River and Bighorn ranges in Wyoming. Over millions of years when the climate was dry, many of the ranges almost vanished beneath their own erosional debris. Then long, moist eras gave rise to new rivers that cleared much of the debris, opening valleys among the summits. During the ice ages, huge sheets of ice smoothed the northern plains and rounded some of the peaks. The continental glaciers were joined by smaller alpine glaciers that gouged broad U-shaped valleys; carved arêtes, cirques, and horns in the mountains; and piled up moraines that now contain the waters of high country lakes.

L andforms vary throughout the region. In southwestern Montana, · broad valleys separate compact mountain ranges, and the mountains often top out in great slabs of smooth, naked rock. Northwestern Wyoming is primarily volcanic, punctuated by fault-block mountains like the jagged Tetons, which burst from a flat valley floor to heights of 13,000 feet above sea level. (Fault blocks occur where large blocks of the earth's surface are raised.) In northern Montana, the mountains seem somehow bulkier, heavier, an impression reinforced by the broad horizontal lines of colorful sedimentary rock and deep glacial valleys. Jagged peaks of the Sawtooths and the Bighorn Crags rise above central Idaho, while in the Idaho Panhandle, rounded summits sink into the lush covering of northwestern rain forest.

Ice shaped the mountains; water draws us to them. Melting from the high snowfields, water pools in alpine lakes, nourishes wildflowers and trout, flows through every mountain valley, twists across small meadows in threads just a foot wide, or thunders through boulder piles, filling the air with cool, rainbowed mist.

This compelling high-country landscape, beautiful enough on its own, also contains the animals that in most people's minds define wild spaces. Although it has been chased off the plains by the growth of towns and roads and agriculture, the grizzly bear still finds a home in the high country of Glacier and Yellowstone national parks and in the remote stretches of wild land in western Montana. Mountain goats, with their shaggy covering of white fur, bound through the highest meadows and pick their way across broad rock faces. Bighorn sheep knock heads every autumn on the flanks of the mountains. Black bears roam the bands of dense forest, looking for roots and grubs in the trunks of fallen spruce trees. Elk and deer graze in the meadows and prairies or in isolated openings in the forest created by forest fires. Moose wade through the bogs and backwaters and willow-choked

RIGHT: *A two-toned bull elk shares winter quarters with a bighorn sheep in Yellowstone National Park. Each year, thousands of elk, bighorns, and bison migrate to crucial winter range along the Yellowstone River.*

bottomlands of the mountain rivers. There are legions of smaller but no less interesting mammals—beavers, marmots, pikas, pack rats—even squirrels that fly and shrews that walk on water.

And then there are the birds—hundreds and hundreds of different birds. Big ones drifting overhead, sweeping down on inattentive rodents, combing the thermals beneath swelling thunderheads—bald eagles, golden eagles, prairie falcons, marsh hawks, ospreys, and dozens more. Small birds flit through the trees or disappear into streamside brush, flashing bits of color as they go and trailing a seemingly infinite variety of calls from the squawks and giggles of sparrows to the oratorios of meadowlarks.

B eyond the ranges stretch the plains. Prairie grassland sweeps across eastern Wyoming and Montana and breaks against the base of the mountains. Where great numbers of bison wallowed in the dust, pronghorn (sometimes called antelope) still nibble at the sagebrush, and the wind, blowing unimpeded, forces all living things to keep a low profile. The prairies are a big landscape where the views are long and lonely. In summer, anvil-shaped thun-

LEFT: *High in Glacier National Park, Lunch Creek splashes over ancient sedimentary stone ledges flanked by wildflowers and dwarfed subalpine fir trees. Pollock Mountain caps this glacial basin, which is frequented by grizzly bears, mountain goats, and bighorn sheep.*

derheads dance across the parched ground on lightning legs, stirring up clouds of dust and bearing the promising smell of newly moist earth.

Ironically, even these great open spaces owe their character, in part, to the mountains. In rising, the Rockies lifted the whole region higher and tipped the water of ancient seas from the plains. Rich tropical forests and swamps disappeared in the cooler, dry conditions, and a newly evolved family of plants—the grasses—took their place.

In modern times, the mountains continue to deprive the plains of abundant rainfall; by blocking Pacific moisture they create a rain shadow on the eastern, or downwind, slope. Even the rivers that flow on the prairies come largely from the mountains, running in precious ribbons through dry hills and badlands. Far from barren, the prairies are among the most intensely developed lands of the West. There are dams along the rivers, irrigation canals, open-pit coal mines, gas and oil wells, and the region's largest cities—though even these are infrequent and small in comparison to urban areas elsewhere. Folks who live here would not exactly call the place lonely; but the word might seem apt to those unaccustomed to driving miles without seeing a house or another car.

In places, the land is arid enough to qualify as true desert. These are high deserts battered by wind, beaten by the sun in summer, and frozen by intense cold in winter. The Red Desert in Wyoming's Great Divide Basin is a collage of sand dunes, colorful rock formations, badlands, escarpments, and sagebrush flats. Parts of the Bighorn Basin look more like southern Utah. And most of Idaho's Snake River Plain, all the way from Idaho Falls to Hells Canyon, seems better suited to cacti than cattle.

Some of the country's wildest rivers crash through the Northern Rockies, bounding down from their headwaters in the mountains and carving the deepest gorges on the continent before stretching out across the prairies and deserts. The Salmon, the Snake, the Selway, the Bitterroot, the Clarks Fork rivers (both in Montana—where it's the Clark Fork—and in Wyoming), the Payette, the Clearwater, and others rank among the finest white-water runs in the country.

Other rivers, some hardly less turbulent, are famous for their fish or their history. On the eastern side of the divide, most waters eventually find their way to the Missouri River, which sweeps across the Great

---

RIGHT: *In Idaho's White Knob Mountains, a verdant green Copper Basin teems with prairie wildflowers in early summer. Part of an arid region, this lush landscape will bake to a light brown by mid-August.*

ABOVE: *Members of the 1871 Hayden Survey gaze west over Wyoming's Sweetwater River from Devils Gate, a landmark on the Oregon Trail.*

Plains to the Mississippi in a grand southeastward arc. Along the way, it collects the North Platte, the Bighorn, the Powder, the Stinking Water (now more agreeably called the Shoshone), the Yellowstone, the Sun, the Teton, the Milk, the Marias, and others written into western history by the adventures of the mountain men who trapped their headwaters for beaver.

The rivers guided and sustained Native Americans and their animals with water, forage, and game. The streams were sinuous oases filled with waterfowl, pronghorn, elk, bison, deer, and a variety of smaller mammals. On their banks, the grass grew sweet, and dense thickets of cottonwoods provided welcome shade from the sun-hammered plains.

Beginning 150 years ago, these rivers also marked the way for generations of emigrants who came West by wagon or horseback along the Oregon Trail and its various branches. Crossing the Continental Divide at South Pass, Wyoming, the emigrants forded or floated or swam the Green River. Rather than accompany it through Flaming Gorge into the forbidding southwestern canyon lands, the wagons followed rivers and streams heading northwest, along the flat, volcanic

The photo was taken by William H. Jackson, whose images of the Yellowstone area helped persuade Congress to establish the first national park.

barrens of the Snake River Plain westward to Oregon, to the great Columbia River, and inevitably, the Pacific Ocean. Pumping in clear and mysterious from the north came rivers rarely followed—the Salmon (called ominously the River of No Return), the Clearwater, the Selway, the Flathead, and the Bitterroot. Those rivers emerged from deep forests of white pine, cedar, hemlock, and Douglas fir, a well-watered land far different from the rain-shadowed plains of the eastern slope.

Happily for visitors interested in the natural scene, large areas of the Northern Rockies are protected to some degree and made available to the public as national parks, monuments, national forests, wild rangeland, recreation areas, designated wilderness areas, wildlife refuges, wild and scenic rivers, and state parks. These are the subjects of this book. They include the largest wilderness areas outside Alaska. One of them, the Frank Church–River of No Return Wilderness Area, forms the nucleus of some four million acres of continuous wilderness in central Idaho—but even such a huge area can lie secluded in the immensity of the Northern Rockies.

13

I
D
A
H
O

SOUTHERN IDAHO

Whether seen on maps, from the air, or on the ground, southern Idaho seems out of place. This broad, flat arc covered with sagebrush and lava resembles nothing else in the region. Mountains tumble down from the north—the Centennials, the Lemhis, the Lost River Range, and the turmoil of ridges and peaks that surround the Sawtooths—only to stop abruptly on the edge of the Snake River Plain, as if it were forbidden territory. Across the plain, however, on its southern edge, mountains pick up again and march off into Nevada and Utah. Obviously, something happened here. It looks as if a giant thumb had smeared a flat track 400 miles long and 30 to 125 miles wide across an otherwise rugged land. The Snake River Plain is indeed a track, but instead of being caused by pressure from above, it is the result of events not far below the surface.

Geologists report that the plain records the slow migration of the continent over a hot spot in the underlying mantle. The hot spot is a weak zone, a plume of near-molten rock that periodically burns through to the surface and causes a volcanic explosion. Such an event occurred 600,000 years ago in what is now Yellowstone National Park.

PRECEDING PAGES: *Idaho's Henrys Fork River crashes over Lower Mesa Falls and sweeps beneath nearly vertical cliffs southwest of Yellowstone.*
LEFT: *Rarely visited, the Owyhee Uplands in southwest Idaho sprawl over a forbidding terrain of rumpled high desert cut by spectacular chasms.*

The catastrophic explosion, far larger than any volcanic eruption in historic times, created the famous Yellowstone caldera, a collapsed crater measuring about 28 by 47 miles. The same sort of eruptions occurred 1.3 and 2 million years ago in generally the same area. Geologists find that similar events can be traced back millions of years all the way across Idaho into Oregon.

Although the hot spot appears to have moved across the state, Idaho has in fact been moving, along with the rest of the continent, crumpling, twisting, and bubbling as it passes over the hot spot. According to one theory, the hot spot originated when a meteorite landed 17 million years ago in southeastern Oregon. The impact shattered crustal rocks, releasing pressure and allowing molten rock to surge upward. It set off a violent and continuing chain of events. Currently the hot spot lies restively beneath Yellowstone, where the ground is measurably rising from underground pressure. By this interpretation, the Snake River Plain is a trough created by a series of titanic explosions. The theory helps explain why no mountains survive here: Whatever existed before was blown sky high. Alternate theories hold that the trough is a depression caused by faults or down folding and subsequently filled with lava.

Another catastrophic event has left its erosional mark on the land—the great Bonneville flood, which moved boulders, carved new canyons, and left high water lines where rivers have not flowed since. Late in the last ice age a large body of water filled the Salt Lake Basin, which then as today had no outlet. Called Lake Bonneville by geologists, this ancient inland sea rose until it finally overflowed the basin rim in southeastern Idaho at Red Rock Pass, near Malad Summit on Interstate 15 near the town of Journey. Once the outlet stream was established, it quickly sliced 300 feet into soft sediments, releasing a volume of water comparable to that found in Lake Erie. Following what is now the channel of the Portneuf River, the flood slammed into the Snake River near today's Pocatello and swept downstream carrying huge loads of sand, gravel, and boulders. Estimates of maximum flows range as high as 40 million cubic feet per second; by comparison, modern summer flows on the Snake are usually just a few thousand.

In geologic terms, today's Snake River is relatively young. It appears not to have existed two or three million years ago in the dry times preceding the ice ages. Only after precipitation increased did water begin

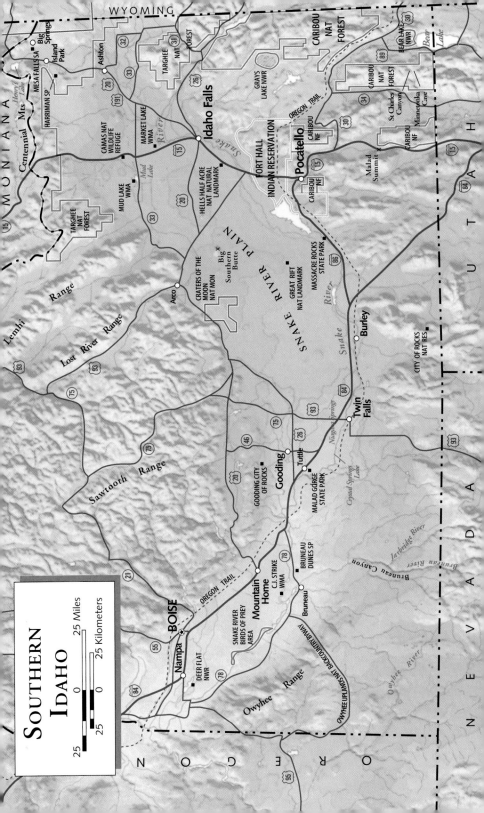

ABOVE: *Salmon fishermen show off their catch in the 1920s. Immense chinook and sockeye salmon were once plentiful in Idaho's major rivers, but a series of hydroelectric dams have virtually wiped them out.*

to flow into existing low areas—in this case, along the edge of the south-sloping Snake River Plain.

This chapter follows the river, its plain, and the region's continuing volcanic story. It begins in the eastern corner of the state, in the high country in the shadow of Yellowstone, a land of pines and deep-snow winters where the Snake collects most of its water. The route proceeds southwest, toward the town of Gooding, through lower elevations. Vegetation grows thinly on dry, sun-baked ground. Enormous recent lava flows lie fresh and jagged, forming some of the most forbidding terrain on earth, difficult even to walk across. Summers are hot. Winters are cold. With nothing to stop it, the wind can blow furiously. Whatever lives here must run fast, dig burrows for shelter, or fly. Or, like sagebrush, it must be unusually tough.

Next we follow the Snake River Valley west to Nampa, turning south into the intriguing and little-known southwestern corner, a challenging place of desert mountains and deep, pristine river canyons. Here flow the Jarbidge, the Owyhee, the Bruneau, and other streams hidden beneath the surface of a sagebrush ocean that few people ever explore closely.

Heading east again, the route runs north of the Utah and Nevada borders, where a slice of Great Basin topography is characterized by parallel ranges with open valleys slung between them. This is the classic landscape of Nevada, the so-called basin and range. We end in Idaho's southeastern corner, which supports a number of rivers, lakes, and wildlife refuges. By no coincidence, this is also the most densely populated part of the state.

HEADWATERS COUNTRY: NORTH OF IDAHO FALLS

We begin our journey through southern Idaho on the edge of Yellowstone—on the rim, as it were, of the current volcano—at **Island Park,** an area of streams, reservoirs, and lodgepole-pine forest in the **Targhee National Forest❖.** Although this is the head of the Snake River Plain, the main stem of the Snake River rises some distance away in the Teton Wilderness, near the southeastern corner of Yellowstone, and flows through Grand Teton National Park before entering Idaho. The major drainage here is a tributary of the Snake called the Henrys Fork, which begins as a small stream flowing out of Henrys Lake to the north and becomes a full-fledged river when it meets the bountiful flow from **Big Springs.**

Located four and a half miles east of the town of Macks Inn, the springs are among the 40 largest in the United States, producing a constant volume of 120 million gallons of water per day at a constant temperature of 52 degrees Fahrenheit. The crystal-clear water flows over gravel beds between bright-green clumps of water plants, creating conditions ideal for trout. Five game-fish species are found here: brook, cutthroat, and rainbow trout and coho and kokanee salmon. The water is so clear and the fish so numerous (no fishing, wading, or boating is allowed at the springs or for half a mile downstream) that visitors can watch fish as they would birds, with binoculars. Also here is the **Big Springs National Water Trail,** a four-mile float trip starting about a mile below Big Springs and limited to hand-carried light craft.

OVERLEAF: *At Harriman State Park, a placid Henrys Fork River glides across the flat floor of a large volcanic crater. Meadows, marshes, and lodgepole forests attract tundra swans, otters, moose, and ospreys.*

ABOVE: *Purple lupine, sticky geranium, and red paintbrush bloom in an Idaho meadow. A semiparasite, paintbrush muscles in on the roots of surrounding plants, penetrating the tissue in order to steal food.*

On the way south from Island Park, numerous roads branch eastward, climbing into the foothills, following streams into the wild lands of the Yellowstone plateau, an area known for its waterfalls. Falls River is named for superb waterfalls in the Bechler region of Yellowstone National Park. Other forest roads lead into the Teton foothills, ending at quiet forest campgrounds and trailheads of the **Jedediah Smith Wilderness❖.**

Downstream, beyond the Island Park Reservoir, the Henrys Fork breaches the wall of the **Island Park Caldera,** a collapsed volcano whose rim appears as a dark line of forested hills to the northwest. Across the caldera floor, the river rolls in wide bends through a restful landscape of meadows, marshes, and lodgepole pines. The caldera's peaceful nature today belies a violent past—1.3 million years ago, a volcano exploded here with stupendous force. Having emptied itself, it collapsed to form a caldera 20 miles across (another volcano with the same general magma source exploded 2 million years ago in the area and again 600,000 years ago in the heart of

ABOVE: *A great gray owl returns to its young with a carry-out snack. Owls descend silently upon prey thanks to a serrated wing feather that eliminates the vortex noise of air flowing over a smooth surface.*

Yellowstone). These eruptions, hurling hundreds of cubic miles of pulverized rock into the atmosphere, are simply the most recent actions of the hot spot that warms the ground in Yellowstone. It promises to perform again in, we hope, some far distant future.

At the caldera's center, **Harriman State Park❖** was a 1977 gift from the Harriman family (of railroading fame) to the state of Idaho. It is simply a splendid place. For 75 years, the Railroad Ranch, as it was called, was a hunting reserve, working ranch, and private retreat for several wealthy eastern families, including the Guggenheims and the Harrimans. As part of the transfer to state ownership, some 10,000 acres of adjoining national-forest land was designated a wildlife reserve, creating 16,000 acres of protected habitat.

The entrance road off Route 20/191 ends near the old ranch headquarters, where there is a visitor center offering history displays and information on trails. This is a park for walking, horseback riding, or mountain biking, and despite its compact area, it encompasses a tremendous variety of habitat and wildlife. Terrain varies from forest to meadow, from flat to hilly. Water is plentiful in several lakes, spring-fed streams, and six miles of the Henrys Fork. Wildlife includes trumpeter swans, Canada geese, muskrats, beavers, otters, minks, weasels, mule deer, pronghorn, moose, and elk. Bald eagles, ospreys, common mergansers, kingfishers, and people in rubber waders with fly rods all patrol the river, known as one of the West's finest trout fisheries. To keep it that way, the stretch from Island Park Dam to Riverside Campground—some 20 miles—is mostly designated fly-fishing only, catch and release. This is surely one of the prettiest rivers in the country.

About a mile north of the entrance to Harriman, the **Mesa Falls Scenic Byway** (on Forest Road 294, which becomes Route 47 near the falls) takes off to the east, making a worthwhile 27-mile detour on the way to Ashton. For a few miles, the road crosses the flat caldera floor. Things get interesting where the Henrys Fork cuts through the southern rim of the caldera, forming a lovely canyon and two impressive waterfalls, Upper and Lower Mesa Falls, now included in the **Mesa Falls Scenic Area❖.** Private property until 1986, the site is now operated jointly by Targhee National Forest and the Idaho Department of Parks and Recreation. A system of walkways leads to the edge of **Upper Mesa Falls,** a wide, beautifully formed curtain of water dropping 100 feet over a ledge of more erosion-resistant rock. A short distance downstream, **Lower Mesa Falls** drops 70 feet.

At Ashton, the **Teton Scenic Byway** (a clearly marked auto trail that follows sections of Routes 32, 33, 31, and 26) runs through rolling hills covered with wheat, barley, and potatoes, with the unmistakable crest of the Teton Mountains visible on the eastern horizon. In July the fields are green seas. Most afternoons, black-bellied thunderstorms stride across the country on legs of lightning, enveloping the peaks, dropping gusts of cold air and hail. By late August, the wheat has turned golden. It shimmers in the wind. Combines ride the hills like strange yachts on giant ocean swells, and travelers use up roll after roll of film.

At Swan Valley the Teton Byway meets the main stem of the Snake River (here called the South Fork) and follows it to Idaho Falls. Like the Henrys Fork, this river is loaded with trout and popular among anglers. For 60 miles below Palisades Dam it flows through forested hills, rock-walled canyons, and bottomlands thick with cottonwood trees and associated plants. Idaho's largest nesting population of bald eagles is found here, along with a great variety of other birds and wildlife. With no rapids, and enough public access points to allow for flexible planning, the South Fork ranks high among area float trips.

North of Idaho Falls off I-15 are several wildlife areas located in an extensive wetland region. The **Camas National Wildlife Refuge❖** is a 10,578-acre complex of ponds, lakes, upland meadows, and cottonwood groves that provides good bird-watching from a system of roads built on dikes. In the spring up to 100,000 ducks pass through on their way to northern breeding grounds. Some stay here; nesting residents include mallards, blue-winged and cinnamon teal, redheads, shovelers, lesser scaups, Canada geese, white-faced ibis, herons, and trumpeter swans. Also present, depending on the season, are sandhill cranes, American bitterns, snowy egrets, double-crested cormorants, and more—in all, 177 feathered species.

Nearby, the **Market Lake Wildlife Management Area❖** is another important spring migration site. Thousands of waterfowl, including a large number of snow geese and perhaps 150,000 northern pintails, visit three large marshes in the spring. At the center of **Mud Lake Wildlife Management Area❖**, just off Route 33, is a shallow 2,000-acre reservoir built and managed more for irrigation than wildlife; nevertheless it remains important as a stopover for the same migrant species that use Market Lake. Roads at both sites provide good bird-watching access.

WEST FROM IDAHO FALLS TO GOODING

In eastern Idaho water is plentiful, but suddenly everything changes dramatically: As we head west from Idaho Falls on Route 20 in the black, volcanic heart of the Snake River Plain, the water literally goes underground. Rivers and streams flowing out of mountain ranges to the north (one is aptly named the Lost River Range) vanish into the porous volcanic rock. So does moisture from rain and melting snow (some of this water reappears as springs in the walls of Snake River Canyon near Hagerman).

West of Idaho Falls, Route 20 passes through potato and wheat fields for a few miles. Then, suddenly, plowed fields give way to sagebrush and lava rock, a black and prickly landscape that defies travelers, farmers, and engineers alike. A close-up look can be had at **Hell's Half Acre Natural Landmark❖**, 20 miles west of Idaho Falls on Route 20.

Acres must be pretty big in hell, because this 142,000-American-acre lava flow covers some 222 square miles. Here, the lava spread out horizontally rather than piling up to form a high cone. The most recent vent, which spewed lava 2,000 years ago, rises 4.5 miles to the south. It is 95 to 200 feet wide and 730 feet long, and it contains 13 pit craters created when some of the lava receded back into the vent. From that high point the lava slopes down to the east; Interstate 15 south of Idaho Falls cuts through the same flow.

The Bureau of Land Management has marked two trails. One goes south to the main vent and requires a full day of walking. The other is a short loop. Even a 100-yard walk imparts an appreciation for the rugged terrain and for the impressive ability of plants and animals to make a living on seemingly inhospitable ground. There is beauty to be found here, and delicacy. Ferns grow in cracks 10 feet deep. Numerous little caves formed by lava collapse provide shelters, harboring cool air, damp moss, and perhaps the bones of some animal that climbed in for shelter from the heat or cold. Rodents thrive here, hiding in the numerous rock crevices and caves; but as the occasional owl pellet shows, their world is not completely secure. (Owls regurgitate the bones of their prey in pellet form.)

Dominating the horizon farther west are three large buttes created 300,000 to 600,000 years ago by eruptions of rhyolite. The one farthest south, Big Southern Butte, is a Kilimanjaro-like mountain standing 2,800 feet above the brooding lava fields to an altitude of 7,500 feet above sea level. Travelers watching the butte can easily miss the narrow trench, often dry, that marks the course of the Big Lost River. Not very big, and definitely lost, this river cuts across Route 20 near a rest stop, wanders toward the northeast, and vanishes into the ground.

Informative exhibits and park rangers make **Craters of the Moon National Monument❖,** a geologist's own junkpile of the strange and fascinating, one of the best places for developing an appreciation of this formidable landscape. Off Route 20 some 15 miles southwest of Arco, the monument encompasses part of a 643-square-mile lava flow, the

---

LEFT: *At Hell's Half Acre, a thunderhead broods over the vast lava flow. Rain falling on the Snake River Plain, however, percolates quickly through volcanic soils, leaving little moisture for plants and animals.*

largest of three to emerge from a 62-mile line of weakness called the Great Rift. Neither the rift nor the lava fields are connected with the Yellowstone hot spot, which this area passed over millions of years ago. Rather, the rift was caused by the same tensional forces that built—and continue to build—the basin-and-range topography characteristic of Nevada and southern Idaho. It's all very new: Activity here is thought to have begun only about 15,000 years ago. There is evidence of at least eight distinct eruptive periods separated by centuries of inactivity. During that time, 40 different lava flows emerged from 25 separate vents along the rift. The most recent activity occurred about 2,000 years ago, and although the rift is currently quiet, another eruption is possible. Such an event would give scientists a chance to see firsthand how this landscape was created.

Craters of the Moon during an eruption must have been an impressive sight. Clouds of ash darkened the sky, steam explosions hurled blobs of molten lava into the air, fine airborne cinders rattled down in a parody of rain, and patches of ground, semiliquid, moved like hot taffy. In places, breaks in the black, hardening crust revealed an incandescent river. The problem would have been where one could stand to watch it happening.

The apparent freshness of the landscape makes imagining easier. As demonstrated by stopping points along the monument's seven-mile loop road and several excellent nature trails, lava can assume an amazing range of shapes and textures. Among the most dramatic are lava tubes, which run like subway tunnels beneath the surface. Averaging about 6 feet across, lava tubes can be as little as half an inch or as big as 50 feet in diameter and quite long. A tube is formed when the surface of a lava flow cools but the lava keeps moving beneath until it drains away, leaving an empty, tunnel-like shell. Miles of such tunnels wind beneath the surface of the monument; a few, including the enormous **Indian Tunnel** (30 feet high and 50 feet wide), can be entered through collapsed portions of their roofs.

Visitors soon learn to recognize the difference between Hawaiian-named ʻaʻa and pahoehoe lava flows (the former is rough and broken while the latter has a smooth, ropy surface) and to understand how spatter cones, cinder cones, volcanic bombs, lava tubes, tree casts, ice caves, and other features came into being. A wider perspective can be

ABOVE: *Overlooking the volcanic terrain at Craters of the Moon National Monument, a lone limber pine grows atop Inferno Cone, one of a distinct chain of cinder cones that rises from the Snake River Plain.*

had by climbing **Inferno Cone,** a short, steep walk from the loop drive. From this high point, a distant line of cinder cones reveals the alignment of the Great Rift.

Yet all is not lava. Despite harsh conditions, softer things manage to survive. Here, wind builds up the soil, bringing it from surrounding areas; caught by irregularities in the landscape, it collects in crevices and other sheltered areas. Much of the 15 to 20 inches of precipitation that falls on average each year evaporates or quickly sinks through the porous lava, but a critical portion is trapped by the same crevices, where thirsty roots can find it.

The plants that thrive grow like those in Japanese gardens—carefully placed, standing separate, and shaped by the environment as if by a meditative gardener. The most common tree is the stout, flexible limber pine. Shrubs include rubber rabbitbrush, big sagebrush, antelope bitter-brush, syringa, and cinquefoil. There are fields of grass—including bluegrass, wheatgrass, bottlebrush squirreltail, and needlegrass—and depending on moisture and season, generous displays of wildflowers: buckwheat, blazing star, desert parsley, paintbrush, bitterroot, arrow-

31

leaf balsamroot, monkeyflower, prickly pear cactus, and others. Owls roost in shady places like lava tubes. Raptors scour the rough ground for rodents. There are mule deer, coyotes, marmots, red squirrels, pikas, and ground squirrels—in all, 30 mammal species, 140 birds, 8 reptiles, 2,000 insects, and 300 plants. Hardly a barren place after all.

For those interested in adventure, the **Great Rift National Natural Landmark**❖ covers the huge, practically roadless area between Craters of the Moon and the Snake River. Among other volcanic features, kipukas (from the Hawaiian for "oasis in lava") are noteworthy. These are islands of vegetation (from lichens to juniper trees) on remnants of older lava that were not overwhelmed by more recent flows. To a biologist, these islands provide examples of how vegetation might develop in other areas if left undisturbed. Access is from the south, on unpaved roads off Route 39 northwest of American Falls. Although not for the family sedan, this challenging country offers its own rewards.

In this discussion of geologic oddities, it seems appropriate to include two collections of hoodoos, **Gooding City of Rocks**❖ and **Little City of Rocks** (not to be confused with City of Rocks National Reserve, a National Park Service site south of Burley). These two sites, several miles apart, consist of volcanic tuff eroded to form eccentric shapes—columns, mushrooms, spires, windows, and arches—suggesting to some observers an ancient, melted city. Of the two, Little City, located along Route 46 north of Gooding, is the more accessible; the other requires a nine-mile drive on rough roads but is worth the effort for those in an exploring mood.

ABOVE: *Rattlesnakes "smell" by flicking their tongues to pick up scent particles and "see" with heat sensors that help compile an infrared profile of objects.*

LEFT: *Well-adapted to ferocious winds and scorching sunlight, a buckwheat shrub blossoms amid tufts of grass on the parched cinder floor of Craters of the Moon.*

OVERLEAF: *Sunset delineates the crest of the Bruneau Dunes, great mounds of windborne sand that collected in an abandoned channel of the Snake River.*

THE LOWER SNAKE RIVER VALLEY: FROM BRUNEAU TO NAMPA

South of Mountain Home, the Snake River Valley seems blessed with abundant water, although the surrounding land receives less than 10 inches of precipitation per year. In at least one place, **Bruneau Dunes State Park❖,** the water is a happy accident. The dunes, near the town of Bruneau, are located in Eagle Cove, an abandoned meander of the Snake River that traps wind-blown sand. Compared to others in the Northern Rockies, the 600-acre dune field is relatively small, but the dunes are unusually big. Here the largest single dune in America, 470 feet high, contains an unusually deep crater between its two summits. Stranger still are several small lakes and wetlands at the foot of the dunes.

The water arrived after construction of a dam across the Snake River, which created a reservoir and the **C. J. Strike Wildlife Management Area❖**—a major wintering site for waterfowl and a popular fishing lake. The dam also raised the area water table, enabling water to seep into low areas at the base of the nearby dunes. Of all places where water might suddenly appear in the desert, this is surely one of the most scenic. The result resembles a Sahara Desert oasis complete with bass anglers and a swimming beach—an Arabian Nights fantasy, American-style.

Camels would not seem out of place; and in fact, the ancestors of modern camels did live in the area, as shown by fossils in the park visitor center. In addition to camel bones, the display includes the remains of mammoths (a huge femur and part of a pelvis), giant ground sloths, and a six-foot-long minnow, as well as turtle shells, pinecones, pine nuts, fossil wood, trilobites, a sabertooth skull, and more. All but the mammoth pelvis were found in lakebed sediments within 50 miles of the park.

Beyond the park's wetlands, modern species are those consistent with the high desert environment of sagebrush and grassland. Birds include American kestrels, red-tailed hawks, sage grouse, turkey vultures, and ravens; barn, long-eared, short-eared, burrowing, screech, and great horned owls; and bald and golden eagles, northern harriers, and other raptors. Black-tailed jackrabbits are practically a symbol of the desert, prized by badgers and coyotes along with the larger birds of prey. In keeping with the prickly environment, there are scorpions and spadefoot toads and numerous reptiles, including Great Basin gopher snakes, blue racers, western long-nosed snakes, striped whip snakes, western rattlers, and various lizards.

Downstream along the Snake are several more opportunities for recreation and wildlife viewing. **Deer Flat National Wildlife Refuge**❖ contains two units. One, Lake Lowell, is important for migratory birds, especially in the fall, when up to 100,000 ducks and 10,000 geese gather here. Practically a suburb of Nampa (access from Route 55), it is one of the region's most accessible birding locations. The second unit, encompassing 107 islands in the lower Snake River, is accessible only by boat.

Southeast of Nampa off Route 69 via Kuna is the **Snake River Birds of Prey National Conservation Area**❖, dedicated to protecting one of the world's densest concentrations of nesting birds of prey. Fourteen species nest here, including prairie falcons, golden eagles, ospreys, and red-tailed hawks. Others migrate through the area, attracted by ideal topography: High cliffs, rising above approximately 80 miles of the Snake River, provide nesting and perching sites and create the updrafts favored by soaring birds. As for prey, the ground cover includes winterfat, a low shrub similar to sage and a favorite food of Townsend's ground squirrels, which are a favorite food of prairie falcons. There are more prairie falcons (five percent of the world's known nesting population) here than anywhere else on earth—as many as 200 nesting pairs. Black-tailed jackrabbits live in and eat sagebrush, and they in turn feed golden eagles.

Signs on I-84 near Nampa direct visitors to an overlook where a short trail leads to Dedication Point on the canyon rim. The view of the canyon and river is a pleasant surprise in these dry, flat surroundings. The canyon bottom can be reached via the Swan Falls Dam road just upstream; it can also be used as a boat launching point. The best time to visit is spring, when courting and nesting activities are at their peak. Most of the birds leave after nesting. Seeing the birds can be problematic because they do not form herds like elk or gather in predictable places like waterbirds.

THE WILD SOUTHWEST

The southwestern corner of Idaho is the state's mystery spot, a land of high desert and long tracts with no trees or mountains in sight. There are miles of sagebrush as open as Tibet, punctuated by basalt outcrops like the rubble of old fortresses. Water, what little there is, runs off the

Owyhee Range and down through canyons cut deeply into layers of rhyolite interspersed with lakebed sediments. These canyons provide relief from dry and forbidding terrain, but they are rugged and difficult of access. The main ones—Jarbidge and Bruneau—are tough white-water runs in the spring and become unrunnable in summer as water levels fall to trickles. No roads parallel the streams, and some of the canyons are dry in summer.

This is exploring country, requiring good maps, four-wheel-drive trucks, tolerance for rough roads, and a good dose of local information from someone who has been out there. Asked about a canyon reported to be a lovely hiking spot, Bureau of Land Management personnel around Bruneau claimed ignorance. The one resident who had been there described the canyon bottom as an unpleasant tangle of poison oak and rattlers, adding that he'd rather walk cattle trails along the rim, "but only if you put a gun to my head."

A good starting point is the **Owyhee Uplands National Backcountry Byway❖**, a series of primitive roads usually passable for ordinary cars that traverses more than a hundred miles of varied terrain from Grand View to Jordan Valley, just over the Oregon border. Southeast of Grand View is **Bruneau Canyon❖**, an 800-foot-deep gorge known mostly among river runners, who find its white water challenging and its scenery wonderful. Few others are familiar with this natural gem, partly because access is so difficult. The canyon walls are nearly vertical and in places only 10 yards apart. There is a

ABOVE: *A prairie falcon prepares a meal of ground squirrel along the rim of the Snake River Gorge. Rodents are a favorite, but prairie falcons also eat lizards and insects and even bag small birds in mid-flight.*

LEFT: *Remote cliffs of the Snake River Birds of Prey Area provide secluded nesting sites for falcons, eagles, ospreys, and hawks, and the surrounding desert surface of the Snake River Plain offers them an abundant menu of rodents.*

39

rough road leading to an overlook south of Bruneau, but otherwise this is a place for those seeking rugged, self-powered adventure. More local advice: The best way to explore this area is in someone else's truck.

A Thousand Springs and the Gate of Death: East Along the Snake to Massacre Rocks

Smoother roads lead to the east, most notably Route 30, which between Tuttle and Twin Falls is called the Thousand Springs Scenic Route. In the Snake River Valley near the town of Hagerman is another geologic site, **Malad Gorge State Park**❖ (access from I-84). At its center is a spectacular narrow gorge filled with gorgeous (what else?) springwater. Clear and almost painfully beautiful, the water is part of a large complex of springs that burst to life in this section of the Snake River Canyon. This is the terminus of the Snake River aquifer, which derives its water from as far away as Yellowstone and the headwaters of the Henrys Fork River, where this driving route began.

The geologic story of Malad Gorge is one of shifting rivers and varying flows. At one time, the Snake River ran north of its current course, until a lava flow deflected the Snake and the Big Wood River southward, where they formed this channel at Malad Gorge. Later, more volcanic activity pushed the Snake even farther south; the Big Wood River (having joined the Little Wood River to form the Malad River) still flows in this channel when there is sufficient water.

The gorge was cut by retreating rapids that followed lines of weakness in the rock. It was formed during the Pleistocene epoch, when big glaciers in mountains to the north produced large quantities of silt-laden water. These days the Malad is not strong enough to carve rock; in summer, irrigation demands upstream can suck it dry. Yet even in the driest years, the gorge echoes with sounds of generous water from the springs.

The park's scenic drive leads out to a point for viewing the diversion dam that channels this springwater to thirsty fields. The best vantage spot, however, is a footbridge that spans the gulf above the dizzying drop into the Devil's Washbowl. From here, trails lead to the north branch gorge and other points of interest.

Considering the dryness of this country, and the magic of springwater bursting from volcanic cliffs, the **Thousand Springs** area is surprisingly little-known. During the summer, irrigation reduces the entire

ABOVE: *Purple camas flowers sweep across a mountain basin along the Oregon Trail southeast of Boise. Explorer William Clark wrote that a similar field of pale blue camas resembled "a lake of fine clear water."*

Snake River, that ebullient mountain stream flowing with such spirit out of the Rocky Mountains, to a mere trickle. One of this region's major points of interest, the 212-foot-high Shoshone Falls, has been destroyed by the twin insults of a power-generating station and a seasonal lack of water. Yet despite its apparent death, the river comes to life again here, resurrected by the springs to flow as pure and clear as in its headwaters. Few rivers get this sort of second chance.

Some of the springs in the area of **Niagara Springs❖** retain their natural beauty. Like Malad Gorge, Niagara Springs is reached from I-84 (Exit 157). The region includes not only Niagara Springs but several others that support a state steelhead hatchery, called the "world's largest trout ranch," and a fishing pond aptly named **Crystal Springs Lake.** These waters pour into a sparkling stretch of the reborn Snake River loaded with American white pelicans, double-crested cormorants, Canada geese, mallards, great blue herons, and other waterbirds. When

OVERLEAF: *Palisades of rhyolite cliffs rise above the East Fork of the Owyhee River in Idaho's isolated southwestern corner—an unforgiving region of sagebrush, rattlesnakes, gravel dust, and haunting beauty.*

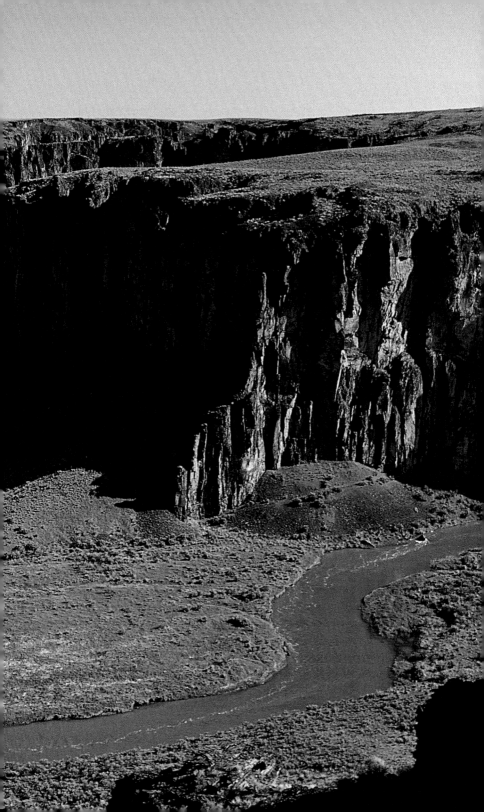

the Snake contributes significant water from upstream, a boulder-bed white-water rapid develops at this point.

From Twin Falls it is about 75 miles east on I-86 to **Massacre Rocks State Park❖,** which has been known by other lurid names: Gate of Death and Devil's Gate. The names refer to a narrow place in the rocks that might have made a good ambush site for Shoshone Indians during the days of the Oregon Trail. There is no evidence that such an ambush ever occurred, although in 1862 ten immigrants died in a fight four miles to the east. Nowadays the interstate punches a broad path through the rocks, making it hard to imagine the natural constriction that so worried those traveling in covered wagons.

Massacre Rocks are the remains of a dense lava plug from the throat of an old volcano that has long since eroded away. Also visible here are signs of the Bonneville flood, which more than filled the river valley and tore loose big chunks of basalt from the canyon walls. A nature trail behind the visitor center winds through some of these boulders, which lie where the floodwaters left them.

For a narrow strip of land squeezed between the interstate and the river, the park offers an unusual diversity of habitats for birds and small animals. Above the river grow sagebrush and juniper. Near the river and on adjacent Goat Island, riparian vegetation thrives. The result is a place where white- and black-tailed jackrabbits live within sight of beavers and muskrats. More than 200 species of birds have been identified, in greatest variety during spring and fall.

MOUNTAINS AND MARSHES: IDAHO'S SOUTHEASTERN CORNER

Although adjacent to the Snake River Plain, the mountains and broad valleys of southeastern Idaho seem a world apart. Unaffected by the hot spot, this region shows how the plain might look had that great series of volcanic events never occurred (although geologists say the basin-and-range faulting that built these mountains might be a result of the same forces that created the hot spot).

RIGHT: *Knobs of ancient weathered granite rise over an autumn blaze of aspen at City of Rocks National Reserve. Granite often erodes into fantastical shapes but rarely so intricately as it has done here.*

ABOVE: *A banded whooping crane joins a large flock of sandhill cranes. Whooping cranes live on the verge of extinction, but fertilized eggs placed in sandhill nests have increased their population in the Rockies.*

One set of rocks has outlasted all these events. Some 45 miles south of Burley via Route 77 near Almo, they are currently visible in spectacular form at **City of Rocks National Reserve❖,** which is managed under an unusual partnership between the National Park Service and the Idaho Department of Parks and Recreation. The "city" is an erosional spectacle of 2.5-billion-year-old granite, some of the oldest and most beautiful exposed rock on the continent. Individual crystals protrude from the deeply weathered rock, and the lines from cracks make shadows in oblique light angles. These are the bones of the continent, carved and smoothed by the elements, bleached white, protruding from a gentle, sparsely forested mountain slope.

At about 6,000 feet, the air is cool. Pinyon and juniper trees dominate, and at higher elevations are groves of aspen, Douglas fir, and lodgepole pine. Trails and roads wind on white quartz sand among the rocks, which seem to change shape when seen from different angles. The place feels like a garden, and many visitors wonder why City of Rocks is not more celebrated. It is famous among technical rock climbers, who find in the spires and smooth faces some of the most aesthetically pleasing routes anywhere and are not eager to promote tourism. For that matter, visitors who have experienced the commercially primitive peace and beauty of the area—no souvenir stands for many miles—are also inclined to remain mum about its attractions.

From here, small ranges march eastward to the Wyoming border.

None of them stand out like the Tetons or the Sawtooths, but most offer the basic pleasures of forest and meadow. Of several national forests, **Caribou National Forest❖,** bordering Wyoming north of Montpelier, manages the lion's share of these mountainous public lands. The Caribou is a fragmented assortment of forest units with little cohesiveness but much variety. Access is easy because there are no large wilderness units. Whereas forestland occupies the heights, the valleys are set with ranches, farms, and small towns. Although no particular site focuses attention, many miles of forest roads wind to campgrounds and scenic areas. Popular among locals are **St. Charles Canyon** and **Minnetonka Cave,** both off Route 89 near Bear Lake.

This area is at the southern end of the state-designated Bear Lake–Caribou Scenic Route (Routes 89, 30, and 34), which climbs the Bear River drainage to the high marshes of Grays Lake, ending at the town of Freedom, Wyoming. The north-south drive is anchored by two important national wildlife refuges. The one at the southern end, **Bear Lake National Wildlife Refuge❖,** is a nesting site for Great Basin Canada geese, along with other waterfowl, including large numbers of white-faced ibis. A road along the north side of the refuge provides good birding in spring and fall.

Grays Lake National Wildlife Refuge❖, at the northern end of the drive off Route 34, is best known for cranes. The lake is actually a large marsh mostly covered with cattails and bulrushes. It provides habitat for a diversity of waterbirds, including the largest breeding population of sandhill cranes in the world. It has also played an important role in the recovery of endangered whooping cranes. During autumn migration, as many as 3,000 sandhills gather here. A gravel road circles the marsh and offers some good bird-watching; the interior of the refuge is closed to visitors throughout the important summer months. Although the refuge is essential, the sandhills teach us a lesson each spring. During April and May, in hayfields and marshes to the south (Cokeville, Wyoming, is notable), these spectacular birds, the most ancient bird species on earth, can be seen pausing on their way north to feed and congregate and practice their mating dances. They do so along highways in places that are in no way protected or specially designated for their use. Their world, like ours, is a seamless whole. And like us, they need all of it, not just a few refuges, if they are to survive.

CHAPTER TWO

CENTRAL IDAHO
AND THE PANHANDLE

T
hough largely unknown among casual visitors to the Rocky
Mountains, central Idaho and the Panhandle take in a sprawling territory of exceptionally diverse wild lands. Between the
brown hills of Boise and the lush cedar groves of the
Panhandle, roads dip in and out of deserts, curve through forested river
valleys, skirt high mountain ranges, and plunge to the arid floors of the
deepest canyons in North America. The region offers a fine mix of habitat and terrain that seems to blend a smooth version of Montana's high
country with the rain forests of Oregon and the deserts of Arizona.

An immense core of public land anchors the region and constitutes
probably the wildest tract of backcountry in the contiguous United
States. Roughly a rectangle measuring 100 miles wide by 150 long, the
tract includes three wilderness areas surrounded by portions of eight
national forests. The nucleus of the area combines nearly four million
acres of virtually continuous wilderness in the Frank Church–River of
No Return, Selway-Bitterroot, and Gospel Hump wilderness areas.
Satellite lands include the Sawtooth and Hells Canyon national recreation areas, each containing its own small wilderness area. Highways
coast along the perimeter of the wild land, but only a handful of

LEFT: *Carved by glaciers from a mass of pink and white granite, the Sawtooth Range towers above the headwaters of the Salmon River, which
trickles gently over cobbles in the Sawtooth National Recreational Area.*

rugged forest roads lead into the heart of it.

Some of the wildest rivers in the West rip through central Idaho. The most important of these is the Salmon River, which rises in the Sawtooth Valley, makes a broad curve to the north, and then charges almost due west across the state. Along the way, it cuts through the Salmon River Canyon, the second-deepest gorge in North America. Its turbulent waters are no less forbidding today than they were to the early explorers and prospectors who named it River of No Return because it is not navigable upstream. The Salmon drains much of central Idaho, gathering in its various forks and the waters of other rivers before rushing into the Snake River Canyon (Hells Canyon), North America's deepest gorge. Other important streams include the Selway, Lochsa, Clearwater, Payette, Coeur d'Alene, St. Joe, and Priest rivers.

With few exceptions—such as the Sawtooth Range—the mountains of central Idaho and the Panhandle roll gently over the land. Often deeply forested, the ranges are not all that high or spectacular. Compared with Montana's Beartooths or Wyoming's Tetons, they seem tranquil, soft, benign. But their smooth contours belie a violent and fascinating geology that includes the possible impact of a giant meteorite, torrents of lava, and the greatest floods in recorded geologic history.

Our route starts in Boise and draws a ragged circle around Central Idaho's core of wild land. It leads northeast through the Sawtooth Mountains and follows the Salmon River north as far as roads allow, then skips into Montana's Bitterroot Valley—the only northbound course available. After continuing north to Lolo Pass, the route descends west through the beautiful Lochsa River Valley and then south into the canyon country of the Snake and Salmon rivers before returning to Boise. A major side trip beginning at Kooskia (some 50 miles south of Lewiston), runs up the Panhandle, and visits the three major lakes of northern Idaho.

FROM BOISE TO THE SAWTOOTHS

From Boise, Route 21 climbs off the Snake River Plain and follows a series of twisting, rimrocked chasms into the swollen brown hills that rise north of the city. Although the high plains desert landscape may seem monotonous at first, it supports a wide variety of plants and animals specially adapted to the very harsh environment. Sagebrush,

grasses and flowers, pygmy rabbits, spadefoot toads, sagebrush voles, and many others all cope ingeniously with a severe lack of moisture, tremendous temperature variations, and strong winds. For example, to keep from drying out, spadefoot toads bury themselves in moist soils during the day and disinter themselves at night. And to beat the literal deadline of the evaporating pools where they are conceived, spadefoot tadpoles develop at twice the rate of most frogs.

As the road climbs into the hills, views of the **Snake River Plain** open up behind. Extending from Oregon to Yellowstone, the plain is the track left by a hot spot in the earth's mantle that began melting the overlying sheet of continental crust 17 million years ago. As the North American continent moves southwest, the hot spot, though stationary, appears to migrate to the northeast. It leaves its mark on the surface of the earth in much the same way that a blowtorch scars a sheet of plastic drawn across its flame.

Between Boise and Banner Summit roughly 4,000 feet of elevation are gained by driving over the crest of a huge granite blister that rose through the earth's crust 70 to 90 million years ago. Called the Idaho Batholith, it stretches northeast from Boise to the town of Stanley and north from Mountain Home past Riggins, in the Hells Canyon area. As it rose during the Sevier orogeny, it formed some of the mountains of eastern Idaho.

With the change in elevation comes an increase in moisture, which is reflected in plants along the road. Grass thickens on bare hillsides, and drought-resistant ponderosa pines appear in scattered groups. Soon, the ponderosas collect themselves into proper forests, and other species of conifers join them.

Near Idaho City the terrain flattens, and piles of white cobbles appear among the trees. These are the leavings of miners who found gold along the **South Fork of the Payette River** in the 1860s. By using water cannons to wash soil from the surrounding hills and later methodically employing dredging equipment, they utterly changed the landscape. Mining here and near Pierce (to the north, about 50 miles east of Lewiston) also fueled the tragic Nez Percé War of 1877.

LEFT: *The Harris Creek Toll Road between Idaho City and Horseshoe Bend winds through the arid, snow-dusted foothills north of Boise. The road passes a few broken-down mining towns founded in the 1860s.*

Beyond Idaho City, Route 21 leads into the heart of **Boise National Forest❖,** which embraces nearly three million acres of thickly forested mountain terrain. Its huge area is only one hunk of a much larger expanse of national forest and wilderness lands that sprawl throughout central Idaho.

Several miles shy of Lowman, the road curves out of the deep forest into the sunlight. Dead trees and stumps stand on a rounded knob. This is the edge of a large area burned by fires during the summer of 1989. Dozens of lightning strikes at the end of July ignited a series of intense fires that burned for nearly a month, quickly overwhelmed human attempts to control the flames, and scorched 72 square miles. A blaze of this magnitude clears the forest about once every century. Fire strengthens the ecosystem by fertilizing the soil, making way for a wider diversity of tree species, and opening the forest floor to broadleaved plants that provide valuable forage for deer, elk, and moose, as well as smaller mammals and birds. A mile or so beyond Lowman, **Kirkham Hot Springs** streams over a set of cliffs and pools and empties into the South Fork.

SAWTOOTH NATIONAL RECREATION AREA

For most travelers, the **Sawtooth Range** comes as a pleasant shock. After miles of navigating huge humpbacked hills and driving through corridors of dense forest, one emerges from the woods and glides across a broad meadow toward Stanley. Suddenly, over the treetops, the splintered peaks of the Sawtooths thrust into view, a turbulent cluster of pinnacles, crags, and jagged rock towers. These form a mountain range unlike any other visible from the roads of central Idaho. Its serrated crest extends roughly 30 miles south and forms the centerpiece of the **Sawtooth National Recreation Area❖.**

This large and splendid territory of more than 1,100 square miles encompasses four mountain ranges and includes dozens of peaks that exceed 10,000 feet. In the high country, tiny alpine lakes nestle into basins, cirques, and potholes where mountain goats or bighorn sheep graze in lush wildflower meadows. On the lower slopes, dense evergreen forests provide daylight cover for deer and elk that wander out onto the grassy bottomlands in the evening. Hot springs trickle into pools beside the streams, and several large mountain lakes hug the base of the Sawtooths.

ABOVE: *Picnickers from Pearl, once a busy gold-mining center north of Boise, pause in 1902 for a snapshot on Williams Road. The boom town that sustained this happy group faded slowly into the dust after 1945.*

Route 75 leads south from Stanley and follows two beautiful but very different valleys through the heart of the recreation area. The first is the spacious **Sawtooth Valley,** a broad prairie trough that runs about 25 miles between the Sawtooths and the foothills of the **White Cloud Peaks.** The uppermost waters of the **Salmon River** flow down from the walls of the valley, collect on the grassy plain, and stream north past Stanley. The White Clouds are as high as the Sawtooths—some of them exceed 11,000 feet—but the foothills obscure a view of them from the road.

On the other hand, it's hard to miss the Sawtooths. Their fractured granite ramparts and steep talus fields sweep high over the forest. Most of the Sawtooths consist of Paleozoic and Mesozoic sedimentary rocks laid down in a series of overlapping (imbricate) thrust sheets. Then, during various ice ages, glaciers gouged out the peaks and plowed down onto the valley floor, leaving big moraines as foothills

OVERLEAF: *A popular trailhead for hiking and horseback trips into the Sawtooth Wilderness, Pettit Lake is one of several large alpine lakes dammed by glacial moraines along the base of the Sawtooth Range.*

and large basins, which formed lakes.

The peaks visible from the road are part of the **Sawtooth Wilderness Area,** which composes a little less than a third of the national recreation area. The intricate landscape is a tight maze of knife-edged ridges and crumbling precipices that divide the myriad watercourses into chains of small lakes, streams, and meadows. Hiking distances are short and quite rewarding. Foot traffic is heavy. The Stanley Ranger Station publishes a list of popular hikes for the wilderness and the White Cloud Peaks.

Several large lakes lie among the moraines at the base of the mountains. The biggest is **Redfish Lake,** named for the thousands of sockeye salmon that once clogged its spawning grounds every autumn. Today the sockeye is nearly gone. The lake is a stunner—a broad sheet of blue-green water surrounded by lodgepole pines and nearly overwhelmed by the gnarly facades of two spectacular peaks. A visitor center offers interpretative services, and an excursion boat from Redfish Lake Lodge cruises to a trailhead at the far end of the lake.

Just down the road, the **Sawtooth Fish Hatchery❖** struggles to maintain the annual spawning runs of sockeye and chinook salmon. The Idaho sockeye, which travels 900 miles between the Pacific and the Sawtooth Valley, is on the endangered species list. The outlook for the chinook, though alarming, is not quite so grim. Years ago, thousands made the long upstream trip. However, the construction of hydroelectric dams on the Snake and Columbia rivers devastated both the sockeye and chinook populations. From 1989 to 1992, fewer than five sockeye returned each season, and the number of returning chinook dropped to just a few hundred.

Although the hatchery rears and releases more than two million chinook smolts (fish about two years old) every year, a series of eight dams kills 77 to 96 percent of the young fish before they can reach the sea. Most die in the spinning turbines, despite the installation of screens by the power company. Many others are eaten by squawfish and other predators that would not pose a threat without the large, still pools behind the dams. Biologists say that more smolts would survive if stream flows through the reservoirs were dramatically increased during the spring and early summer. The political problem is that neither agriculture nor the power industry benefits from boosting flows during that season.

The sockeye population is so fragile that fisheries biologists have been trapping the few returning adults and the meager stream of ocean-bound smolts for use in a captive-breeding program. They hope eventually to rear enough young fish to begin releasing smolts from the Sawtooth Valley again. The American Fisheries Society regards the Columbia River Basin sockeye population as "functionally extinct."

Beyond the fish hatchery, Route 75 continues for miles over the wide valley floor. Hawks by day and owls by night glide over the grass, flowers, and sagebrush, picking off voles, ground squirrels, chipmunks, and mice. At the head of the valley, the road climbs to the Galena Overlook, which provides a fine view of the Sawtooth Range cutting across the skyline to the northwest. To the south the Sawtooths merge with the brawny **Smoky Mountains.** From the overlook the headwaters of the Salmon are just a squiggle of willows far below on the broad prairie floor. Barely wide enough at that point to merit creek status, the Salmon eventually gathers most of the water that falls in central Idaho and roars through one of the deepest gorges in North America—deeper than the Grand Canyon.

The road tops out at Galena Summit, elevation 11,170 feet, then plunges down into the forests of the Big Wood River Valley. The high peaks of bare rock to the north are the **Boulder Mountains,** spectacular not only for their height and rugged shape, but also for their unusually coarse texture and the various colors that appear in the cliffs— pink, red, tan, and grayish green.

The Big Wood Valley is narrower and more densely forested than the Sawtooth area. Farther south, the valley opens up a bit. Rolling hills and benchlands sprawl at the base of the mountains. Fine meadows of prairie grass interrupt the lodgepole-pine and Douglas-fir forest. Through it all, the **Big Wood River** runs like a heartache, threading its way through the hills to Ketchum and passing through the **Sawtooth National Forest❖** as it makes its way to the Snake River Plain.

Our route now doubles back from Ketchum to Stanley. From there, Route 75 follows the Salmon River east through a tight gorge. Clean, cold, and fast-moving, the Salmon charges past large boulders and cliffs that protrude from the steep walls and forests of the chasm. This rough stretch of river drops 15 feet to the mile, producing class IV rapids that challenge kayakers and white-water rafters.

Too often, water in the West seems like forbidden fruit. It's so beautiful, so clean, and so clear that the urge to swim may be overwhelming. But the water is so cold that without a wetsuit visitors can do little more than stand at the edge and admire it. That's why the natural hot springs along this stretch of the Salmon are such a treat. Several small pools are tucked into the bends and curves of the river, and one large series of pools, **Sunbeam Hot Springs,** is just shy of the crossroads village of Sunbeam.

ABOVE: *Bold, gregarious, and smart, Clark's nutcracker is a notorious camp robber first noted by Lewis and Clark in 1806. It sports a long, pointed bill to break open pine seeds and clings to tree trunks like a woodpecker to hunt grubs.*

RIGHT: *Running across the crest of the Lost River Range, layers of limestone are uplifted and tilted almost to vertical. The flat basalt surface of the Snake River Plain beyond surrounds Big Southern Butte, a massive dome of rhyolite that erupted 300,000 years ago.*

FROM THE SAWTOOTHS TO LOST TRAIL PASS

Route 75 follows the Salmon through small canyons that grow progressively wider and drier. Beyond Clayton, both river and road turn northeast and head into an expansive valley surrounded by desert hills, enormous heaps that extend for miles; with their rubble-smothered cliffs, they sometimes resemble the colorful drip-castle formations common to badlands. The hills are a vast pile of eroded debris that spewed from enormous volcanoes northwest of the present-day town of Challis about 50 million years ago. The complex mass of lava and compressed ash reaches depths of several thousand feet and covers much of central Idaho. Our route runs north through it nearly to the town of Salmon.

Approaching Challis, Route 75 picks up Route 93. The gravelly, multicolored ramparts to the southeast are the **Lost River Range,** which extends for roughly 75 miles to the edge of the Snake River Plain and includes Idaho's highest peak, Mount

Borah, elevation 12,662 feet. The range runs through **Challis National Forest❖,** 2.5 million acres of desert, forest, and mountain that form the southeastern front of central Idaho's sprawling core of public lands. The peaks to the northwest are the southern edge of the **Salmon River Mountains,** which sprawl along the edge of the Frank Church–River of No Return Wilderness.

Route 93 continues along the Salmon River, passing beautiful hollows where 20- to 30-foot cliffs rise from the water and gravel bars stretch lazily beneath the shade of cottonwoods, aspens, and sometimes junipers. Before long, the road crosses the **Pahsimeroi River** and edges along the northwestern lobe of the **Lemhi Range,** part of the 1.7 million acres of **Salmon National Forest❖,** which runs along the state's eastern border.

Just south of Salmon, travelers round a bend and emerge onto the broad floor of the Lemhi Valley. The high, forested range of peaks across the valley to the east are the **Beaverhead Mountains,** which are composed of a block of sedimentary rock more than a billion years old that slid eastward tens of miles during the general uplift of the Rocky Mountains roughly 60 to 70 million years ago.

North of town, the valley narrows and Route 93 passes into a lovely gorge where the powerful Salmon River carves deep troughs against bluffs 50 to 100 feet high. A lavish bottomland, rich with prairie grass, shrubs, and spreading cottonwoods, rolls along the riverbanks. On this placid stretch of the Salmon live great blue herons, cliff swallows, mule deer, pronghorn, and sometimes river otters. It's a fine canoe run. At one particularly beautiful bend, the Salmon gathers in its North Fork and makes a sharp turn west. Our itinerary does the same, turning off Route 93 and following Forest Road 030 west from North Fork to Shoup.

This is the start of the **Salmon River Canyon,** an enormous gash in the ground that cuts across central Idaho. It is the second-deepest gorge in North America, and it joins the deepest—the **Snake River Canyon** or Hells Canyon—on Idaho's western border. As it runs across the state, the canyon passes through the largest tract of wild land in the Lower 48.

At the core of these lands sprawls the **Frank Church–River of**

LEFT: *A smooth sumac bush drops its scarlet autumn foliage on the rocky banks of the Salmon River. Native Americans ate the shrub's young sprouts as a salad and chewed its sour fruit to quench thirst.*

No Return Wilderness❖, 2.3 million acres of steep mountains, deep canyons, extensive forests, and long stretches of fierce white water. By itself, it comprises the largest wilderness area outside Alaska. But to the north and just across a primitive road lie another 1.3 million acres of wilderness called the **Selway-Bitterroot Wilderness❖.** Surrounding these two large areas are eight national forests, two small wilderness areas, and two national recreation areas. Roughly speaking, these lands represent practically the whole of central Idaho—from Route 12 south to the Sawtooths, and from Riggins near the Oregon border east to Montana.

The Salmon River is the most dominant feature in the region. It drains 14,000 square miles, flows 425 miles, and drops more than 7,000 vertical feet between its headwaters in the Sawtooth Valley and its confluence with the Snake River. It carves a canyon 180 miles long and in some places a mile deep. White-water float trips run the river west from North Fork to Riggins—an excellent way to get a taste of the wilderness.

These wilderness areas include an incredible variety of habitats. There are high mountain lakes, marshes, prairies, and deep forests. Expansive stands of Douglas fir and lodgepole pine cover most of the Frank Church–River of No Return Wilderness; ponderosa pines grow at lower, drier elevations, and Engelmann spruce and subalpine fir live in the high country. To these forest communities, the Selway-Bitterroot Wilderness adds stands of old-growth western red cedar and hemlock. The area supports a diverse population of animals—240 species of birds, 9 amphibians, 21 reptiles, and most of the major mammals usually associated with wild country. There are deer, elk, bighorn sheep, mountain goats, black bears, moose, and mountain lions. There are some indications that wolves roam the backcountry (and more are to be reintroduced there by the U.S. Fish and Wildlife Service), but, alas, grizzly bears do not.

From Shoup, a forest road continues downstream for about 20 miles to Corn Creek Campground, where it dead-ends. Our route returns to North Fork, runs north to Lost Trail Pass on Route 93, and then continues north to the town of Lolo, on the way dropping into Montana's Bitterroot Valley (described in Chapter 3, pages 103–8).

From Lolo Pass to Syringa

From Lolo, turn west on Route 12, which passes through gentle

ABOVE: *Generally timid around humans, black bears amble throughout the mountains and forests of Idaho, grazing on new grass and sedges, plucking berries, digging roots, and busting apart stumps for grubs.*

foothills on the way to Lolo Pass. The tree cover here is fairly typical of the dry, cold Northern Rockies—lots of Douglas fir and lodgepole pine, with Engelmann spruce in the high country. The forest changes dramatically after the pass. On the west side of the Continental Divide, warm Pacific air drops most of its moisture before crossing the Bitterroot Range into Montana. The result is a forest that would look more at home in the Pacific Northwest—or perhaps Eden. Moisture-loving trees such as western red cedar, Douglas fir, and Engelmann spruce thrive here. So do ferns. Thick layers of moss cover the forest floor with a spongy carpet of iridescent green that smothers fallen tree trunks and dampens all noise.

Old-growth cedars have thick, silvery trunks covered with spiraling strips of bark. If not logged, they can grow to tremendous size. The **Devoto Memorial Grove❖,** just a mile or two before the town of Powell, preserves a speck of the old-growth forest. There are large cedars and a nature trail of sorts, all dedicated to Bernard De Voto (1897–1955), a noted historian of the West. But the huge clear-cut just a few hundred yards above the oldest trees and the logging trucks that

ABOVE: *Deciduous conifers that drop their needles annually, golden larches show their autumnal colors among stands of dark fir near Lolo Pass.*
RIGHT: *The Lochsa River, a famous kayak run during high water, sweeps gently through a forest of cedar and hemlock in central Idaho.*

roar through the grove on Route 12 destroy the atmosphere of the place.

About 10 miles farther along, at the Warm Springs trailhead, a foot-bridge spans the Lochsa River and a mile-long path leads back through the rain forest to **Jerry Johnson Hot Springs❖.** Beyond the veil of cedar, larch, and Douglas fir, the sounds of the road fall away. Shafts of sunlight cut between the trunks, illuminating mist rising off the forest floor. Aerial-feeding lichens drape from the trees like fairy-tale beards. Big owls coast through the branches, and water ouzels pump their legs by the stream. The hot springs is idyllic—a ribbon of hot water that runs over a mossy cliff and collects in deep, rocky pools.

The **Lochsa River❖** brawls through the valley at high water. Its deep holes, big drop-offs, and endless rapids make for solid class IV white water and earn forbidding names for certain sections of the river—Killer Fang, Bloody Mary, Termination, Grim Reaper. All along the south side of the river, trails lead from the valley into the back-

country of the Selway-Bitterroot Wilderness.

At Lowell, the **Selway River** pours into the Lochsa to form the Middle Fork of the Clearwater. A 20-mile road turns southeast at the town and parallels the Selway to **Selway Falls,** a thundering mass of foam and green water divided by a boulder the size of a two-story house. The Selway, a magnificent white-water river, is considered one of the most challenging in the West. Early in the season, in the spring, some of its rapids are fatally dangerous and are portaged by even the most experienced boaters.

Even after stream volumes drop in late summer, the Selway is unmistakably a serious piece of water. Near the banks, water runs in familiar shades of pale green and emerald. But as the riverbed drops off, these amiable riffles and pools slip from sight beneath silent sheets of clear, black water. And despite its depth, the river channel moves quickly, even when the surface appears glassy and serene. This depth is unusual in the Rockies, where travelers get used to rivers they can wade across. There is an unexpected, even foreboding, element in the depth and velocity of the Selway.

ABOVE: *The mountain lady's slipper was first noted by Lewis and Clark. While some still grow in Idaho, this nearly extinct species of orchid has been decimated by people who have tried to transplant it to residential gardens, where it invariably dies.*

The river corridor supports a rich variety of wildlife, including black bears, elk, moose, white-tailed deer, river otters, and ospreys. Several miles up the river road, at the O'Hara Campground, is a 1.5-mile interpretative trail leading to a cedar forest with an understory of rich green ferns. The road dead-ends about 1.5 miles from the wilderness boundary, and a fine trail leads upriver.

From Lowell, the Middle Fork of the Clearwater runs west over a wide bed of rounded stones and boulders. Beyond the town of Syringa, the hills begin to lose their tree cover, and meadows come into view on the floodplain. Soon, some very strange rock formations appear beside the river and in the hills. Rendered even weirder by moss clinging to their wrinkled surfaces, these lava flows are part of a staggering volume of molten basalt that poured across the Northwest about 16 or 17 million years ago. In a matter of days, the lava overran thousands of square miles of territory and began to form the Columbia Plateau. (Some geologists hold that an enormous meteorite smashed into the area and caused the cracks and lava flows.)

IDAHO'S PANHANDLE

This route bounds north from Kooskia (a town about 50 miles southeast of Lewiston) into the Panhandle through landscape typical of most of Idaho's mountainous areas—gentle, forested, not spectacularly high, but sweet, benign, and friendly. It visits the three major lakes of northern Idaho—Coeur d'Alene, Pend Oreille, and Priest—and ends at the latter.

ABOVE: *Named for the explorer Meriwether Lewis, the Lewis woodpecker catches insects on the wing in open country with large trees, such as ponderosa pines. Louis Agassiz Fuertes did this watercolor portrait in 1911.*

At Kooskia, the South and Middle forks of the Clearwater join to form the main branch of the **Clearwater River,** a wide sheet of water that sails along the northern boundary of the Nez Percé Indian Reservation. Take Route 12 northwest to Orofino, where the long, winding Forest Road 4769 leads northeast to Dworshak Reservoir, an impounded section of the North Fork. Those who make the drive will find a few interesting spots near the town of Elk River—Elk Creek Falls, the Morris Cedar Grove, and the largest western red cedar in Idaho.

Orofino lies along the old margin of the North American continent.

Intensely sheared masses of gray diorite just below Dworshak Dam mark the collision of tropical volcanic islands with the old west coast about 100 million years ago. From Orofino to Lewiston, Route 12 follows the Clearwater through a deep canyon that cuts through the Columbia Plateau. On the approach to Lewiston, be advised that the fetid smell has nothing to do with your traveling partner. The odor is produced when the Potlatch pulp mill recycles chemicals used to break down cellulose fibers for paper.

Follow Route 95 north from Lewiston. An overlook at the rim of the canyon opens a vista to the confluence of the Clearwater and Snake rivers and imparts a fine sense of the landscape that has thus far been hidden by the high walls of the canyon.

Several miles north of Viola, Route 6 heads northeast into the **Idaho Panhandle National Forests**❖ along the Palouse River. Like much of the Panhandle, the forests here were heavily logged at the turn of the century for the old-growth western white pines that once grew in profusion throughout the Northwest. In **Clearwater National Forest**❖ one of these magnificent trees stands at the **Giant White Pine Campground**❖. White pine trunks—tall, straight, massive, and relatively unblemished by knots—were sought for ships' masts and trim for houses. But most of the forests were cleared to make wooden matches, which Americans used at

ABOVE: *More than 50 pairs of osprey nest along Coeur d'Alene Lake. Males feed females from courtship through egg-laying, then haul in six pounds of fish daily for a brood of three.*

LEFT: *The St. Joe River crosses the southern end of Coeur d'Alene Lake. Curving natural levees created over thousands of years protect the river from lake waters that rose behind a 1906 dam.*

OVERLEAF: *The sun sets over Lake Pend Oreille, which is so deep (1,200 feet) that World War II submariners trained here. The lake is now a haven for waterfowl, shorebirds, and eagles.*

71

the rate of 100 million a day until paper matches, cigarette lighters, and electric stoves and lights were invented.

Beyond Emida, take Route 3 north through a meadow and forest land-scape to **Heyburn State Park❖,** which lies at the marshy end of **Coeur d'Alene Lake.** With its series of looping trails, this park is an area for peo-ple who crave the serenity of a deep forest. Cedars, grand firs, and some old-growth ponderosa pines grow on the slopes surrounding the lake, and the forest floor is thick with ferns, shrubs, mosses, and grasses. The views are short and intimate, and wildlife includes numerous birds, some animals, and various types of amphibians, including red-legged frogs and a species of salamander unique to the Coeur d'Alene area.

Next to the lake are acres and acres of marshland—great boggy flats dotted with ponds, sloughs, and meandering streams—a habitat of inti-mate scenery best visited by canoe. Bulrushes sweep the gunwales, frogs jerk across the shallow water, and families of ducks paddle by, the fuzzy little ones crowding behind their mothers.

Out on the lake, ospreys soar overhead. Coeur d'Alene Lake and the three flooded lakes that now form its southern tip claim the largest nesting population of the birds in North America. Wood ducks and great blue herons also nest here.

From the park, take Route 97 north along the crooked shoreline, passing the **Coeur d'Alene River** and a chain of small lakes renowned for waterfowl viewing, especially during the spring and autumn migra-tory seasons. Unfortunately, lead and other heavy metals contaminate the lower Coeur d'Alene River and the lakes—part of the price for min-ing more than 500,000 ounces of gold and more than a billion of silver from the surrounding mountains. Health warnings urge visitors not to breathe the dust, touch the soil or mud, or eat much fish and waterfowl.

Route 97 rounds some high bluffs at the north end of the lake and then joins Interstate 90. Follow the interstate to the city of Coeur d'Alene, pick up Route 95, and head north. **Farragut State Park❖** lies along the southern shore of **Lake Pend Oreille,** which reaches an as-tounding depth of more than 1,200 feet. The lake (pronounced POND-er-ay) was formed by a stranded block of glacial ice that left a spacious basin after it melted. The lake is very long, roughly 70 miles, but it often seems smaller because its maximum width is just 6 miles. At the park, the lake is narrower yet, enabling visitors to sit at the **Willow**

Picnic Area and watch mountain goats on the cliffs across the water. The cliffs are part of the **Coeur d'Alene Mountains,** which run southeast from the north end of the lake far into Montana.

To get a sense of the lake's true dimensions, continue north to Sandpoint on Route 95. Seen from the long bridge, the waters of the lake open up to the east, and the spectacular **Cabinet Mountains** burst into view. Route 200 going east after the bridge offers grand vistas of the lake and leads through wetland areas populated by moose and many types of waterfowl.

During the great ice ages, an ice dam formed at the lake, backing up the Clarks Fork River drainage and forming a vast lake. Eventually, the dam burst and the impounded water drained thunderously in a matter of days. This process repeated itself many times, creating the most ferocious floods in recorded geologic history (see page 108).

To reach **Priest Lake❖** in the very northern portion of the Panhandle, return to Sandpoint and take Route 2 west, then Route 57 north. Priest is another large, beautiful lake, surrounded by dense forest and ringed by a narrow ribbon of sand. A mile-long loop trail leads from the Stagger Inn Campground through the **Roosevelt Grove of Ancient Cedars❖,** a fine stand of old-growth forest with a bonus: **Granite Falls,** which drops about 40 feet and roars around a high forehead of white granite. Priest Lake itself offers a bonus for visitors with boats: five national-forest campgrounds on Kalispell Island. A shoestring population of woodland caribou live north of **Upper Priest Lake,** but they are rarely seen.

To return to central Idaho and rejoin the main route head back on Route 2, Route 57, and south on Route 95 to Lewiston. A side trip east on Route 12 leads to Kooskia. Or, continue south on Route 95 and rejoin the route at Grangeville.

HELLS CANYON NATIONAL RECREATION AREA

About 15 miles west at Syringa, our circuit of central Idaho travels north, following Route 13 south from Kooskia up the **South Fork of the Clearwater.** As it enters the hills, the river begins to rush through a series of chasms. Turning east, Route 14 follows the most spectacular and longest of these between rock-plated walls rising hundreds of feet over the river. From Elk City, forest roads extend east and south to

Above: *Snow brightens the mountainous and wooded terrain of the Gospel Hump Wilderness, one of several large tracts of wild land that sprawl across central Idaho from the borders of Montana to Oregon.*

trailheads for the Selway-Bitterroot, Frank Church–River of No Return, and Gospel Hump wildernesses. A primitive road stretches east clear to Montana's Bitterroot Valley.

Route 13 runs over billowing hills onto a broad plateau of rich prairie. At Grangeville, turn south on Route 95 to **White Bird Summit,** elevation 4,245 feet. There, high above the Salmon River Canyon, a vast and broken abyss of rumpled hills, tilted prairies, bare mounds, heaps, and ridges piles off across the landscape to the horizon.

In the distance, to the southwest, a ring of crags called the Seven Devils sits atop a high, forested ridge in the **Hells Canyon Wilderness.** The ridge divides the Salmon River Canyon and the Snake River Canyon, also known as Hells Canyon, and marks the eastern boundary of **Hells Canyon National Recreation Area❖.** Roughly 7,500 vertical feet separate the Seven Devils peaks from the floor of Salmon River Canyon. The corresponding drop on the other side of the divide measures about 8,000 feet. The Salmon River flows into this region from the east, bangs into the divide beneath the Seven Devils, and then turns

ABOVE: *Mountain lion cubs need to remain with their mother for two years to master complex hunting techniques. To survive they must kill deer quickly—without being kicked, gored, or slammed into trees.*

north. It passes roughly 3,000 vertical feet beneath White Bird Summit, then curls around the north end of the divide and joins the Snake.

On the way to the bottom of the gorge, a roadside exhibit overlooks **White Bird Canyon Battlefield,** site of the first battle in the 1877 Nez Percé War. It is part of the **Nez Percé National Historic Park❖,** unique among American national parks in consisting of 24 separate sites, scattered throughout what was once Nez Percé land.

Hells Canyon, at approximately 8,000 feet the deepest gorge in North America, cuts through the middle of this 650,000-acre tract of desert chasms, forested ridgetops, and high, jagged peaks that straddle the border of Idaho and Oregon. Although difficult for the casual traveler to visit, Hells Canyon is worth the effort. Few places combine outstanding beauty with such fascinating geology and such a wide diversity of plants, animals, and terrain.

At any of a number of high overlooks in the Hells Canyon region, it's interesting to note that for roughly 700 million years this was the west coast of North America: Open ocean lay beyond. Then, about 150 million

77

years ago, the continent began to move west. Year by year, inch by inch, the floor of what was by then the Pacific Ocean collided with the North American continental plate and dived sluggishly under Idaho, melting back into the earth's mantle. Everything attached to the oceanic plate moved with it—islands, scraps of continental crust, even whole micro-continents. Tropical volcanic islands that once stood hundreds of miles offshore eventually appeared on the horizon, slowly moved toward the coast, and were finally mashed against western Idaho. Today's visitors can climb down into the gorge beneath the Seven Devils and watch the Snake River rush over the remains of those island's coral reefs.

About 16 or 17 million years ago—well after this same tectonic-plate collision helped build the Rocky Mountains—something caused the conti-nental crust to crack. Basalt lava welled up from the earth's mantle and then spilled over much of Oregon, Washington, and western Idaho. Lava flowed many times over millions of years and built up the Columbia Plateau—a sprawling, irregular pile of basalt extending between the Rocky and Cascade mountains. Both the Snake and Salmon river canyons cut through it. Some geologists hypothesize that a giant meteorite arced out of the sky and slammed into southeastern Oregon, forming a huge crater and cracking the crust, thereby causing the massive lava flows.

Thanks to extreme differences in elevation, Hells Canyon compress-es an amazing variety of habitats into a relatively small area. During a typical summer day, the arid canyon floor bakes in 100-degree temper-atures. Meanwhile, up in the Seven Devils area, forests of grand fir and lush wildflower meadows soak up water melting from snowfields. Between these two extremes sprawls a vast area of ridges and hills, benches, bluffs, plateaus, and side canyons. Bunchgrass and other prairie plants cover most of the intermediate zone, but a smattering of forests, mainly Douglas fir or ponderosa pine, also grow there.

Wildlife is diverse and abundant—cougars (mountain lions), black bears, bighorn sheep, mountain goats, and lynx all live here. The canyon area also supports one of the largest elk herds in North

RIGHT: *Vivid Indian paintbrush blooms in a lush wildflower meadow in the rugged Seven Devils peaks of Hells Canyon National Recreation Area.*
OVERLEAF: *The Snake River rolls through Hells Canyon, North America's deepest gorge; 8,000 feet separate the river from the rim's highest point.*

America, and many raptors find the hunting good among the grass-lands and quieter pools along the river.

The Snake crashes through the gorge for 100 free-flowing miles. The 32-mile run from Hells Canyon Dam to Pittsburg Landing is famous among white-water boaters for its challenging rapids and wild setting. Nearly 70 miles of the Snake are protected by the Wild and Scenic Rivers Act. When combined with tributary streams that run through surrounding protected lands, this portion of the Snake appears to be the largest water-course in the lower 48 states still in a predominantly wilderness condition.

Despite the unique and wild character of Hells Canyon, plans to de-velop it keep cropping up. Loggers want to cut its stands of old-growth ponderosa pine. Others have suggested building a big recreational ve-hicle park at the remote and archaeologically significant Pittsburg Landing. The power industry has asked to build two more dams on the Snake, just downstream of the wild and scenic boundary—even though most experts agree that existing dams are largely responsible for the collapse of sockeye salmon spawning runs in Idaho.

Visitors wanting to take advantage of opportunities to see the Hells Canyon country from Idaho can pick up maps and advice at a U.S. Forest Service ranger station in Riggins or at Hells Gate State Park in Lewiston. The first chance presents itself at the base of White Bird Summit. There, Forest Road 493 climbs over the divide between the two big rivers and dead-ends at **Pittsburg Landing** in the heart of the gorge. For thousands of years, Native Americans camped in the prairie grasslands near the landing and tapped petroglyphs into the cliffs above the river. Today the area is popular with white-water boaters. A backpacking trail leads 31 miles upriver.

Just south of Riggins, Forest Road 517 climbs roughly 6,500 feet to **Heaven's Gate Lookout** and the **Seven Devils** area, the highest point in the recreation area. The road runs from the desert bottomland of the Salmon River Canyon through rolling prairie meadows and groves of aspens and cottonwoods into a dense evergreen forest. At the top, it traverses a wide meadow, and the gnarly peaks of the Seven Devils creep over the crest of the ridge. From the Heaven's Gate parking area, visitors can walk up to the lookout on the **Heaven's Gate Scenic Trail,** where the lines of the two canyons are visible as they curl 50 miles northwest and converge.

Although not part of Hells Canyon National Recreation Area, another road leads west from Riggins up the Salmon River Canyon for about 20 miles. The clear, green water of the Salmon coasts along, occasionally breaking into rapids and running past fine swimming holes—tongues of sand studded with boulders and shaded by ponderosa pines.

Farther off our main route (south from Riggins via Route 95 to Cambridge, then Route 71 to Copperfield and Forest Road 454), **Hells Canyon Dam** offers one of the most spectacular views of the canyon. There, the gorge appears as a narrow corridor of volcanic rock cliffs rising thousands of feet above the Snake. White-water boaters put in here for one of the roughest rides in the West. It is also where the road ends. In summer, a jet-boat concession runs excursions to the first serious set of rapids. To get there by automobile, visitors must drive far around to the southwest—through the towns of New Meadows, Council, Cambridge, and Copperfield.

FROM RIGGINS TO BOISE

Running south from Riggins, Route 95 follows the banks of the **Little Snake River** and soon climbs out of the arid, humpbacked hills into the forest. At the town of New Meadows, take Route 55 south to McCall. Both McCall and **Payette Lake** lie at the upper end of a valley formed when a portion of the earth's crust dropped along faults. The basin filled with glacial outwash from the mountains to the east, and the outwash impounded Payette Lake. **Ponderosa State Park❖**—with its impressive stands of old-growth ponderosa pines, cliffs, and beaches—lies on a narrow spit of land extending into the lake.

Route 55 runs across a broad valley floor south of McCall and skirts the Cascade Reservoir. The mountains to the east are part of the Idaho Batholith, the same rock formation our route ascended from Boise toward the Sawtooths. The road follows the **North Fork of the Payette** down a long, forested chasm of granite interrupted occasionally by a wide meadow. Between Smiths Ferry and Banks, the North Fork is a spectator sport—an unbelievably difficult stretch of white water that attracts expert kayakers from around the world. During the summer, kayak-watching is exciting and sometimes downright scary.

Near Banks, the tree cover falls away and familiar, rounded brown hills rise on the outskirts of Boise.

MONTANA

CHAPTER THREE

WESTERN MONTANA

High, rugged, and still mostly wild, the mountains of western Montana unite and define a region of tremendous beauty. From Canada to Yellowstone and from the Great Plains to Idaho, range after range of magnificent peaks tower over broad valleys cloaked in thick prairie grass and sagebrush. Gnarly cottonwoods and thickets of willow bushes trace the meandering paths of rivers with dazzlingly clear water. Pronghorn roam the flats. Elk and deer graze along the fringe of dense evergreen forests. Bears, both black and grizzly, amble the high country, sometimes spooking bighorn sheep and mountain goats.

Each of the dozens of mountain ranges that make up western Montana has its own unique creation story. But in broad outline, most of them trace their origins to a collision between the Pacific oceanic plate and the continental plate of North America. Like a fender bender in slow motion, the collision compressed the western edge of North America between 90 and 70 million years ago and created a wide, meandering welt of highlands.

About the same time, vast masses of magma rose through the crust and crystallized into huge bulges of granite. The continuing collision, as well as heat from the magma, forced the layers of rock to unstable

PRECEDING PAGES: *In Glacier National Park, ancient sedimentary rocks cut by glaciers support a fascinating array of lichens and alpine wildflowers.*
LEFT: Cow parsnip—*a favorite food of elk, black bears, and grizzlies—blossoms beneath a glacial cirque at Glacier's Avalanche Lake.*

heights. In some places, great sheets of sedimentary rock that had been forming for more than a billion years were thrust eastward for dozens of miles. In other places, slabs of the crust itself shifted eastward. Millions of years of erosion, volcanic activity, earthquakes, and glacial ice shaped the ancestral Rockies into the mountains we see today. Although the mountain ranges have much in common, there are differences. Some seem little more than vast heaps of gravel with a sparse covering of prairie grass thrown on to hold the dirt in place. Others support dense forests from base to summit. Many were carved by glaciers into dramatic formations. Others were smoothed over by the ice and seem rather dull in comparison. The southern valleys are broader, flatter, lazier somehow, and convey a sense of the plains and high desert. In the north, large mountain lakes abound.

The peaks claw a tremendous amount of rain and snow from passing clouds, then divide the water and send it rushing back to the Atlantic and Pacific oceans. In southwestern Montana, the mountain slopes weave the currents of the Gallatin, Madison, and Jefferson rivers into the Missouri, which makes a broad northeastward arc across the plains, gaining strength from dozens of tributary rivers that run off the eastern slopes of the Rockies. On the west side of the Continental Divide, the important rivers are the Bitterroot, the Blackfoot, the Flathead and its various forks, the Kootenai, and the Clark Fork.

Glacier National Park is the major point of interest in the region. Home to grizzly bears, wolves, mountain goats, and bighorn sheep, Glacier and the protected lands that surround it preserve an amazing variety of habitats in a landscape ranging from prairie to alpine tundra.

The park forms the northern boundary of our circular journey through western Montana. Beginning at the headwaters of the Missouri River, northwest of Bozeman, the route moves south through the mountain ranges of the southwest, turning north to the Bitterroot Valley and Missoula. It continues north through buffalo country to Kalispell and Glacier National Park and then returns along the Rocky Mountain Front and through mining country to the starting point south

---

OVERLEAF: *With the Mission Range as a backdrop, bison graze on the rumpled prairie grasslands of the National Bison Range south of Flathead Lake. The preserve is also home to deer, elk, and even mountain goats.*

ABOVE: *An unknown artist added this charming drawing to Patrick Gass's 1806 journal from the Lewis and Clark expedition. The treed hunter had to wait three hours until the doglike grizzly finally wandered away.*

of Helena. At Kalispell, a side trip loops through the rugged expanse of the Kootenai National Forest.

In the past 150 years, colossal changes have occurred in western Montana. The buffalo are gone. The grizzlies have disappeared from the plains and are hiding out in the high country. Pickup trucks kill more moose and elk than wolves ever will. Strip mines chew into the mountainsides and dams back up the rivers. Nevertheless, the people who live here consider western Montana the last best place in the Lower 48. And they've got cause.

MISSOURI HEADWATERS: SOUTH TO THE YELLOWSTONE BOUNDARY

When they headed up the Missouri River from St. Louis in the spring of 1804, explorers Meriwether Lewis and William Clark hoped the river would be a dependable water route to the Pacific Coast. Instead, it brought them to southwestern Montana, where the great arcing course of the Missouri splinters into a confusing network of tributary rivers, creeks, and icy brooks that fan out into the surrounding mountains like cracks in a broken windshield. The start of the Missouri, and the point where its

ABOVE: *At Missouri River Headwaters State Park, the Jefferson, Gallatin, and Madison rivers join to form the Missouri. When Lewis and Clark camped here in 1805, the men kept busy hunting and making "mockersons."*

clear route through the West begins to fracture, can be found at **Missouri River Headwaters State Park❖**, roughly 30 miles northwest of Bozeman (access from I-90 to Route 205 to Route 286). There, the U.S. Geological Survey places the river's source at the confluence of the Madison and Jefferson rivers. A third tributary, the Gallatin, kicks in about a quarter of a mile downstream. All these important currents bend lazily across a broad, rolling plain and join in full view of the mountain ranges they drain: the Bridger and Gallatin ranges to the east, the Madison Range to the south, and the Tobacco Root Mountains to the southwest.

At the park, a wide block of stone and gravel called Fort Rock rises some 20 feet off the prairie and offers an excellent view of the surroundings. Exhibits on Fort Rock identify the mountains, the rivers and their confluences, and sites mentioned in the Lewis and Clark journals.

Return to Three Forks and drive 19 miles west on Route 2 to visit **Lewis and Clark Caverns** in **Lewis and Clark Canyons State Park❖**, one of the largest limestone cave systems in the Northwest. Take Route 2 west of Three Forks and follow the Jefferson River through hay fields and sagebrush prairies to a narrow valley that runs between steep, scrubby hillsides. Loads of white-tailed and mule deer feed in this tight

93

valley in the evenings. Open for two-hour guided tours from May 1 to September 30, the caverns are a string of large underground rooms connected by narrow passageways. Beautiful dripstone formations hang from the ceilings and cavern walls, as does a colony of western big-eared bats. A campground is available at the park as well.

Heading south from the caverns area, Route 287 (which intersects Route 2 near Three Forks) bounds over grassy hills rolling from the densely forested eastern slopes of the Tobacco Root Mountains. At Norris, there is a fine hot-springs pool, a favorite among locals. From the town, a 10-mile drive east on Route 84 leads to **Bear Trap Canyon❖,** a spectacular gorge some 1,500 feet deep, where the Madison River pours through in a series of rapids dear to white-water boaters. Those who wish to remain dry can follow a trail along the riverbank. Bear Trap Road is very rough, but the walk beside the Madison River is worth every jolt, bounce, and pothole.

The canyon, like most of the protected natural areas of the region (although it is managed by the Bureau of Land Management), is part of the **Beaverhead National Forest❖,** an immense patchwork of lands that sprawls throughout southwestern Montana. The forest encompasses several mountain ranges, some of the finest rivers in the West, and more than 250 small lakes—many lying at the base of high mountain cirques. It also includes the **Lee Metcalf Wilderness Area❖,** which takes in part of the Madison Range and embraces Bear Trap Canyon.

From Norris south for some 55 miles, Route 287 follows the Madison River Valley, a classic western Montana landscape. The broad valley floor unfolds peacefully between two high mountain ranges: the Tobacco Root Mountains to the west, the Madison Range to the east.

Near the town of Ennis, the Tobacco Roots dissolve into the gentler features of the Gravelly Range as the Madison Range grows more impressive, adding bulk, height, and naked rock to its formidable topography. Around Cameron, some of its peaks exceed 10,000 feet. Geologists report that the range consists mainly of a vast block of 2.7-billion-year-old rock, which has risen from the basement of the earth's crust, gaining at least 5,000 feet in the last 2 million years. Ancient history? Not so. Slipping on faults along its base, the Madison Range continues to rise today. Usually the seismic activity remains imperceptible, but sometimes it triggers a major earthquake. One of those, the Madison Canyon

Earthquake, struck in 1959 about 40 miles southeast of Cameron.

In that area Route 287 takes a sharp bend to the east and climbs straight toward the mouth of the **Madison River Canyon Earthquake Area❖.** As the hills and rock walls close in on the road, a vast, semicircular scar appears high on the slope across the river. The rock that once occupied the scar peeled away on August 17, 1959, during an earthquake measuring 7.1 on the Richter scale. Some 40 million cubic yards of rubble—enough to fill the Houston Astrodome up to the cheap seats—crashed down from the heights with such force that its leading edge was carried 420 feet up the opposite wall of the canyon. The slide buried a campground, killing at least 28 people. It also dammed the Madison River, creating **Earthquake Lake❖,** which swings into view as the road tops the massive heap of slide debris. A visitor center built on the slide provides excellent exhibits about the earthquake. Route 287 wraps around the northern shore of the lake, passing the silver-gray trunks of trees that died as the lake level rose. Today, bald eagles and ospreys make nests in the snags.

The earthquake also marked the landscape at **Cabin Creek Campground.** There, the forest floor split apart as the Madison Range rose and the valley bottom dropped, increasing the vertical distance between them by some 15 feet and creating a gravelly embankment called a fault scarp. An interpretative trail follows the meandering path of the scarp through the woods and across Cabin Creek.

Just up the road, a dam holding back **Hebgen Lake❖** looms over the valley floor. Built in 1915, the dam was an object of great concern during and shortly after the quake. As the earth shook, the south shore rose and the north shore dropped. The water lurched north, flooding the highway and shoreline buildings. Then the water rolled back and forth in huge standing waves, some sloshing over the dam, which cracked, but held.

West to Red Rock Lakes

From the eastern shore of Hebgen Lake to the town of West Yellowstone, Route 287 runs along the edge of the flat, volcanic plateau that makes up much of Yellowstone National Park to the east. It leads through a lodgepole-pine forest and soon picks up the Madison River, which flows quietly through a grassy bottomland, rainbow and brown trout dimpling its placid surface. Some stretches of the river seem to at-

ABOVE: *A trumpeter swan moves through the reeds at Red Rock Lakes. These magnificent birds were nearly extinct by the 1930s, but thanks to conservation and wildlife refuges, the swans are making a comeback.*

tract trumpeter swans, but the most reliable place to see them is **Red Rock Lakes National Wildlife Refuge❖**, which is 40 miles west of West Yellowstone. To get to the refuge, follow Route 20 south from West Yellowstone. On clear days, just beyond the road to Henrys Lake State Park, the highest peaks of the **Teton Range** rise in the distant southeast. Shortly afterward, a well-marked gravel road turns west from the highway and heads directly for the high peaks of the Centennials. After 25 miles of western bluebirds and pronghorn, the road descends to the refuge.

The refuge sprawls over a broad, open valley at the base of the **Centennial Mountains.** Lush with grasses and wildflowers and dotted with a series of shallow lakes and crystalline ponds, it is a sanctuary for many types of birds, especially the trumpeter swan, once threatened by extinction. Today the trumpeter is making a recovery—thanks in large part to this 44,100-acre refuge, where the birds come to nest, raise their young, and sometimes spend the winter.

The lakes, ponds, and marshes of the refuge get most of their water from snow melting in the mountains. The abundance of moisture supports moose, which thrive on aquatic vegetation. Muskrats, beavers, shorebirds, and waterfowl find their particular niches among the bulrushes, reeds, willows, and aspens that grow along the water's edge.

The trumpeter swans are the main attraction. Weighing 20 to 30 pounds and boasting wingspans up to eight feet, they are North America's largest wildfowl. These enormous white birds glide across the glassy surface of the lake with their heads held high, their black bills dipping occasionally into the water for a bite to eat, and their plumage often glowing orange at sunset. When they lift off the water after a long acceleration, their wide wings bat the surface of the lake with a percussive *ka-chunk, ka-chunk, ka-chunk* until they finally clear the runway, retract the landing gear, and make a broad, ascending pass in the face of the Centennials.

By 1935, when the refuge was established, fewer than 100 of these magnificent birds remained in the greater Yellowstone ecosystem. Since that time, the regional swan population has grown to 600, and some 1,750 Canadian trumpeters join them every year at wintering areas throughout this portion of the Rockies.

Typically, some three dozen families of trumpeters spend the spring and summer in and around Red Rock Lakes. Although young swans pair off for life at age 2–3, they do not lay their first eggs until age 4–6. The pen, or female, lays in early May. Cygnets hatch in mid-June. Within a day or two, they waddle from the nest and take to the water. At first they stick close to their parents, feasting on a protein-rich diet of insects, crustaceans, and aquatic beetles that the adults stir up from the muck of the lakebed with their feet. After a month they adopt the diet of their elders: mainly aquatic plants and an occasional snail, worm, or other invertebrate. Flight school begins in October, when the young birds flap and run awkwardly across the water at the urging of their parents. After the youngsters have perfected their aerial skills, the families take off for their wintering areas, here and elsewhere along the juncture of Montana, Idaho, and Wyoming.

THE SOUTHWEST

From Red Rock Lakes west, the road continues along sagebrush flats as the Centennials fade into the dry, rounded foothills surrounding Monida

Pass. Heading north on I-15, travelers pass a range of low peaks west of the road called the **Tendoy Mountains.** A fault line runs across the base of the range from the town of Lima north nearly to the Clark Canyon Reservoir. Slips along the fault account for the series of triangular, or pyramidal, faces that appear on the flanks of the mountains.

Off to the east, a meandering line of willow thickets and cottonwood groves marks the course of the Red Rock River, which empties into Clark Canyon Reservoir. The water emerging under the dam is the **Beaverhead River,** one of Montana's better trout-fishing streams.

During the 1860s, prospectors found gold in the hills west of Dillon. Their discovery on Grasshopper Creek in 1862 kicked off a gold rush that soon spread over much of southwestern Montana and inaugurated one of the state's most important industries. Through the years, different eras of mining and mining technology have left their marks all over the state's landscape. West of Dillon, near Route 278, stand the remains of Bannack, Montana's first territorial capital and now a ghost town turned state park. Its double row of weathered buildings is being restored. East of Dillon, several large open-pit talc mines operate in the Ruby and Gravelly ranges. Together they form one of the largest talc-producing districts in the world.

Beyond Dillon, I-15 pulls away from the Beaverhead River, picking up another blue-ribbon trout stream, the Big Hole River, also home to a rare population of Arctic grayling. It bends around the northern perimeter of the **Pioneer Mountains,** the range of high peaks visible to the northwest. A few miles north of Melrose, take the Moose Creek Road exit from I-15 and follow the gravel road east toward that cleft in the forested hills. Unroll the windows for a bracing whiff of sagebrush. A few miles up the ever-narrowing road, the first massive column of nearly white granite appears straight ahead announcing the **Humbug Spires Primitive Area❖,** where pinnacles of granite 70 million years old tower above the treetops. This quiet pocket of shade and running water offers a pleasant contrast to the speed and heat of the interstate. Hawks wheel overhead and nest among the spires. Tree trunks sway and creak in the wind. Tiny brook trout rise for bugs in the pools behind beaver dams.

RIGHT: *Abundant on the high desert basins of the Northern Rockies, prickly pear cacti, like these blooming beside the Beaverhead River, conserve water with a dense wax coating that slows evaporation.*

About ten miles north, at the town of Divide, Route 43 plunges west into the Big Hole River Canyon, a winding chasm that squirms through the narrow space between the Pioneer Mountains to the south and the **Fleecer Range.** Bluffs of sedimentary rock overhang the rushing water and sometimes the road. Here and there, slopes of tumbled boulders form the banks of the Big Hole. Elsewhere, groves of cottonwoods and small prairie flats border the current. In late summer, the flats buzz with grasshoppers, which sometimes misjudge the trajectory of their flight paths and plop into the river, where they make fine meals for trout. Several miles beyond the town of Wise River, Route 274 leads north to the **Mount Haggin Wildlife Management Area❖,** an especially promising spot for seeing elk, moose, and nesting sandhill cranes.

Return to Route 43, where the walls of the Big Hole Canyon recede, and soon high, rugged peaks appear in the distance. They form the northern end of the **Anaconda Range,** a spectacular array of mountains carved by glaciers into a serrated ridge that includes cirques, snowfields, waterfalls, and lovely alpine lakes. Several of the summits reach 10,000 feet. The Anacondas extend 40 miles to the southwest and form the western rim of the Big Hole

ABOVE: *Adaptable, highly intelligent, and not in the least bit finicky, coyotes eat almost anything: insects, berries, road kill, rabbits, and rodents. They even bob streams for crayfish.*

LEFT: *Typical of western Montana's broad, rolling landscape, these grassland meadows swell beneath the peaks of the Anaconda-Pintler Wilderness Area.*

Valley. They are also a significant part of the **Anaconda–Pintler Wilderness Area❖**—158,000 acres of nearly pristine alpine landscape, where shaggy white mountain goats hop among the crags. Those who are less nimble can enjoy the same rarified air by hiking a 45-mile trail that traverses the crest of the peaks along the Continental Divide.

Emerging from the northern edge of the Pioneers, Route 43 turns south and climbs onto the wide, flat plain of the **Big Hole Valley❖,**

101

which is hemmed in by the Pintlers, the Bitterroot Range (to the south), and the Pioneers (to the east).

The Big Hole Valley is, incredibly, a huge gap that opened 70 million years ago when an immense block of the earth's crust slid eastward and came to rest as the Pioneer Mountains. In the millions of years following that event, gravel and sediments washed out of the surrounding mountains and filled the valley to a depth of some 14,000 feet. Today, the Big Hole River is doing its best to strip away the debris.

Our route follows the river and Route 43 to the town of Wisdom, then heads west to the junction of the Anaconda and Bitterroot ranges. There, a visitor center overlooks a grassy hollow tucked against the foot of densely forested mountains. A crystalline stream, the North Fork of the Big Hole, twists through the lush bottomland. With firewood nearby, water at hand, plenty of grass for horses, and a soul-expanding view of three mountain ranges, the site made a splendid campsite for generations of Native Americans. Today it is remembered as a lousy place to die.

The **Big Hole National Battlefield❖,** as this bittersweet tract of ground is known, preserves the site where some 100 people died in August 1877 during a desperate battle involving the U.S. Army, civilian volunteers, and a portion of the Nez Percé tribe. The roots of the conflict echo the same sad song that haunted many of the violent clashes between Anglo and Indian civilizations. Gold and a white demand that the Nez Percé give up most of their reservation set the stage for the 1877 Nez Percé War and the tribe's epic and unsuccessful odyssey toward freedom in Canada.

Though outgunned and outmanned, the 800 Nez Percé repelled army attacks during three major engagements as they retreated across Idaho. Here they rested. But at dawn on August 9, a group of 162 troops and civilian volunteers charged out of the lodgepole-pine forest across the hollow from today's visitor center and attacked the sleeping village. There were, roughly, 125 warriors among the Nez Percé. After an initial phase of bloody confusion among the tepees, the warriors rallied and drove the troops back across the river and onto a wooded knoll. There, the Nez Percé pinned them down for 24 hours while the rest of the tribe made its escape. Some 60 to 90 Nez Percé—braves, women, children, and old people—were killed. So were 29 of the U.S. Army's force.

The visitor center offers a spotting scope, binoculars, an exhibit of the weapons used in the battle, and a short video explaining the conflict. Two excellent interpretative trails lead through the battlefield. One climbs the hill where the troops attacked and later retreated. The other parallels the river through willow thickets and across the grassy bottomland to the Nez Percé camp, where the conical frames of tepees, weathered to a silvery gray, stand like sun-bleached bones.

THE BITTERROOT VALLEY

From the battlefield, Route 43 runs into the steep, forested slopes of the Bitterroot Range, an important group of mountains that stretch from the extreme southwest corner of Montana to Canada. Turn north on Route 93, which tops the mountains at **Lost Trail Pass** (elevation 7,014 feet) and then drops into the **Bitterroot River Valley.** It also crosses the Continental Divide and leaves the Beaverhead National Forest behind. From here north to Missoula, Route 93 passes through the **Bitterroot National Forest❖,** 1.6 million acres of deep forest, glaciated peaks, valleys, and beautiful mountain lakes. Logging trucks commonly stop for a brake check at the head of the pass, and travelers will notice areas that have been clear cut throughout the Bitterroot. The valley is a logging center, and the towns reflect their economic dependence on cutting trees. Hand-painted signs supporting the logging industry appear in many of the houses and businesses. A popular bumper sticker in the town of Darby during the early 1990s read Wilderness, Land of No Use.

As the road bends and curves toward Sula, a different species of tree can be seen growing on open, sunny slopes. Very tall and straight, with plates of rough, reddish bark, long needles, and relatively few branches below its upper reaches, the tree is the ponderosa pine. Resistant to drought, ponderosas claim dry and sandy territory shunned by other trees. They grow all over the semiarid Bitterroot Valley. Close up, the trees exude a rich aroma that reminds most people of vanilla extract or cream soda.

The Bitterroot Valley, like the Big Hole, is a gap that formed when a large block of the earth's crust moved eastward some 70 to 75 million years ago. In this case, the block came to rest as the **Sapphire Range❖**—the mild, round-topped hills on the right side of the valley as one heads north. One theory holds that both the Sapphire and the

103

Pioneer blocks may have slipped eastward on a sole of magma, riding as if on a thick smear of grease. As the Sapphire block moved, it exposed the underlying granite—rock destined to become a large part of the Bitterroot Range, which rises some 5,000 feet above the valley floor.

At the southern end of the valley, Route 473 follows the West Fork of the Bitterroot River back into the mountains to **Painted Rocks State Park❖**. On a map the site looks promising, but the 20-some-mile drive is worthwhile only during spring and early summer. The park borders a large reservoir that gradually drains every summer, revealing broad mud flats peppered with the stumps of trees and crisscrossed with tire tracks. By autumn, Painted Rocks has about as much aesthetic appeal as a freshly opened strip mine.

ABOVE: *Bitterroot, Montana's pink state flower, is officially known as* **Lewisia rediviva** *in honor of the early western explorer Meriwether Lewis.*

RIGHT: *As dawn breaks over Trapper Peak in Montana's Bitterroot Range, an inversion of cold air artistically traps a valley full of clouds.*

In the southern Bitterroot Valley, slopes by the road are so steep and the foothills of both mountain ranges so high that one catches only fleeting glimpses of the spectacular Bitterroots. North of Hamilton, however, the valley widens, and the highway runs far enough east to offer some fine panoramas of the rugged peaks. The range owes its jagged skyline to glaciers that gnawed, gouged, and plowed their way through the granite during several ice ages.

The Bitterroots form the eastern boundary of the **Selway-Bitterroot Wilderness Area❖,** 1.3 million acres of high peaks, steep canyons, wild rivers, and jewel-like alpine lakes. Most of the big-game animals associated with wild country live there—black bears, mountain goats, bighorn sheep, mountain lions, elk, and deer. The bulk of the wilderness lies in Idaho, but it also embraces the entire crest of the Bitterroots and much of their eastern slopes.

Lake Como, a few miles west of Darby, stretches for three miles from the feet of the impressive Como Peaks, elevation 9,530 feet. Trails from the two national-forest campgrounds lead around the lake, into Rock Creek Canyon, and then into the high country. The loop trail around the lake makes a pleasant half-day jaunt.

A side trip to **Lost Horse Observation Point,** several miles northwest of Darby, gives a good taste of the Bitterroot backcountry. North of town, take Lost Horse Road west from Route 93 and follow the signs. In dry weather, the trip takes 40 minutes of prudent driving over very narrow, rugged roads. The road ends on a point of rocks thrust out hundreds of feet over Lost Horse Creek. Two troughlike valleys diverge and run off to the west, wrapping around opposite sides of an enormous ridge littered with talus slopes, patches of forest, and broad bands of cliffs. To the south there are sweeping, close-up views of some of the highest peaks in the Bitterroot Range. Turn to the east for a fine panorama of the Bitterroot Valley and the Sapphire Range.

Northeast of Stevensville, the **Lee Metcalf National Wildlife Refuge❖** protects nesting and migratory habitat for roughly 225 species of waterfowl, raptors, upland birds, and songbirds. The large, rather showy yellow-headed blackbird is abundant here, and in nesting season visitors may well hear its cacaphonous song, which sounds as if the bird were being strangled. The refuge also supports a large population of white-tailed deer, easily spotted in the evening from the county road that runs through the refuge. The road passes a series of ponds where nesting Canada geese, blackbirds, and ducks can be seen. Great horned owls and hawks nest in the cottonwood snags and hunt rodents in the brush and grasslands. Ospreys nest in the snags or on platforms constructed just for them, and fish the ponds.

The refuge is one of just a handful of sites in the West where ospreys reluctantly share their nests with Canada geese. Although geese do not nest in trees, they happily usurp osprey nests if they get the chance. Here they get the chance every spring because they return to the refuge earlier than the ospreys, which like to reuse their nests year

---

LEFT: *Fierce in demeanor, but in fact rather timid carrion-feeders, bald eagles mate for life and raise two offspring each season. They share nurturing duties in an enormous nest that they refurbish each year.*

after year. Usually the geese lay their eggs, launch their young, and vacate the nest before the ospreys appear in early April; but sometimes the paths of the two birds cross, and battles erupt. The ospreys dive-bomb the nest. The geese hang tough, bobbing their heads and trying their best to look dangerous. Usually the geese succeed. The ospreys either build a new nest or wait for the squatters to leave.

THE MISSOULA AREA

As Route 93 approaches Missoula, the valley widens and the mountains soften into rounded foothills. Coming up is the expansive valley of the **Clark Fork River,** which flows northwest for about 150 miles from Missoula to Pend Oreille Lake in Idaho. While gazing down that immense furrow, consider this: Water once filled it to a depth of some 2,000 feet, backing up far into the Bitterroot Valley and extending southeast along the Clark Fork toward today's city of Deer Lodge, about 60 miles southeast of Missoula. Then imagine this incredible volume of water suddenly flushing away to the northwest—a body of water half the size of Lake Michigan, gone in a few days. Geologists tell us that this phenomenon, called the Bretz-Missoula floods, happened in the Clark Fork Valley not once, but at least 41 times, starting about 15,000 years ago at the height of the last ice age.

Here's how it happened. As the big regional glaciers moved south, one lobe of the Cordilleran ice sheet dammed the Clark Fork River at the east end of Pend Oreille Lake. Behind that ice dam, 500 cubic miles of water collected over the next 58 years, forming Glacial Lake Missoula. Then the dam floatéd and broke apart. A wall of water 2,000 feet high crashed through the opening and roared all the way to the Pacific Ocean, scouring out river valleys, ripping boulders out of the bedrock, and building up enormous ripple marks. The water careened through the narrower valleys at speeds of at least 45 miles per hour. It blasted through Clark Fork Valley at a volume of 8 to 10 cubic miles per hour—10 times the combined stream flow of all the rivers in the world today.

Beyond Missoula, Route 93 climbs through a notch in the **Rattlesnake Mountains** and emerges on a higher valley floor. Twenty miles ahead is the massive, spreading front of the Mission Mountains. The back slopes of the Rattlesnakes are on the right. Glaciers carved the high country of the Rattlesnakes into a lovely alpine display of narrow, steep-sided canyons, cirque basins, and hanging valleys (not visible from this point). About 61,000 acres of the range have been set aside as the **Rattlesnake National Recreation Area and Wilderness❖.**

NORTH TO BUFFALO COUNTRY

North of Arlee, Route 93 picks up the **Jocko River** and follows it through a grassy valley enclosed by gentle hills. Years ago, valleys like this one all over the Rocky Mountain West supported herds of bison, the primary source of food and shelter for the native tribes that roamed the mountains, plains, and river valleys. For thousands of years, the bison and those who lived off their meat, hides, bones, and tendons struck a harmonious balance. Both thrived. Then, in the early nineteenth century, Anglo civilization spread westward. Within 75 years, the bison teetered on the brink of extinction, as did the Native American way of life.

The **National Bison Range❖** preserves, at least for the buff, a small shred of the way things used to be. (Follow the signs west from the town of Ravalli to the preserve.) There, in the Flathead Indian Reservation, a herd of 300 to 400 bison graze on 19,000 acres set aside in 1908. The setting is spectacular. Palouse prairie grasslands roll off the flanks of a steep ridge and stretch across the valley to the base of the awesome Mission Mountains. Through the mounds of dry prairie flows Mission Creek, a heartbreakingly beautiful ribbon of swift water shaded by junipers, cottonwoods, aspens, and birches. White-tailed deer find cover there among the tangles of alders, thornapples, and willows. Red-winged blackbirds natter from the bottlebrush ends of cattails that grow along the creek's lazier bends. And bison amble down to the current from time to time.

Years ago, some 30 million bison clipped the grasses of North America, inhabiting roughly two thirds of the continent—from the Atlantic across the Rockies and from the Gulf of Mexico far into the southwestern provinces of Canada. As white settlement along the eastern seaboard moved southward and westward, suitable habitat for bison shrank, and the species' population gradually diminished. The great slaughter came in the 1870s and 1880s, when thousands of white buffalo hunters decimated the herds. On a good day, a hunter could kill as many as a hundred animals. The hunters left most of the buffalo to rot and drove the species to extinction with the tacit approval of a federal government eager to break the native tribes. By 1900, less than 100 wild bison were known to exist.

The National Bison Range started with 41 animals bought from small, domesticated herds. Although the population has fluctuated through the years, managers try to keep the base wintering herd to 350 by holding an annual roundup and sale of surplus animals.

A 19-mile loop road climbs 2,000 feet over Red Sleep Mountain, offering tremendous views of the Mission Valley and many opportunities to see not only bison but elk, deer, pronghorn (also called antelope), bighorn sheep, coyotes, and a broad variety of birds and wildflowers.

Often, bison appear at a distance: brown dots on an olive hillside, maybe a dozen at a time. Occasionally, a lone bull plugs along beside the road, enormous head wagging from side to side, muscles rippling beneath the short hair of its lean hindquarters. It may pause to graze close enough for you to see the way its dark tongue curls around each bundle of grass. Shutting off the engine, you can hear the bull tearing stalks from the ground (sounds a bit like parting Velcro). You might also hear it breathe—a low, curdling whoosh, like the sound of a match tossed on charcoal soaked in gasoline.

Game managers at the bison range also supervise two wildlife refuges on the floor of the Mission Valley, **Ninepipe** and **Pablo National Wildlife Refuges.** (Take Route 212 east from the bison range and follow the signs. Contact the National Bison Range staff for information.) Some 80,000 southbound birds, including colonial nesters, double-crested cormorants, and great blue herons, descend on the refuges every autumn, and about half that many every spring. Glacial potholes, which abound on the valley floor, provide excellent habitat for nesting ducks, green-winged teal, Canada geese, northern harrier hawks, pheasants, violet-green swallows, the yellow-headed blackbird, and songbirds. With a view of the magnificent **Mission Range** bursting from the prairie a scant ten miles to the east, these are two of the most spectacular wildlife refuges in the West. Heavily glaciated, the sharp crest of the Missions forms the **Mission Mountain Wilderness❖,** a 74,000-acre tract of cirque, stream, and subalpine forest. It lies between the **Flathead Indian Reservation,** which occupies much of the Flathead River Valley, and the **Flathead National Forest❖,** which sprawls to the east and north of the Missions. Best access to this steep and un-

ABOVE: *Displaced almost everywhere by cattle, bison are North America's largest land mammals. Ironically, bison fight off predators, endure harsh winters, and thrive on natural vegetation better than cattle do.*

forgiving wilderness area is from the east, in the Swan River Valley, but the best views are from the ponds at Ninepipe and Pablo.

THE FLATHEAD DRAINAGE

Our journey continues north on Route 93, over a prairie-pothole landscape left by glaciers during the ice ages. Just south of Polson, the road tops the crest of a large moraine, and suddenly the shimmering surface of **Flathead Lake** stretches beyond. Forested hills bulge along its shores, and a series of islands divide it like a row of stepping-stones.

The largest natural freshwater lake in the West, Flathead lies in a basin formed during the last ice age by a huge block of stranded ice. Sediments were pushed ahead of the block of ice; when it finally melted, it left the depression now occupied by the lake's waters.

Flathead is a beautiful lake—clean, warm enough to swim for most of the summer, and home to many bald eagles and ospreys, which nest in the high trees or on man-made platforms and glide out over the water to fish. The lake surrounds **Wild Horse Island❖,** a state park accessible only by boat (tour vessels cruise there daily). A few wild horses still live on the island, but bighorn sheep, mule deer, and coyotes are more numerous. The island's knobby uplands offer fine views of the lake and the surrounding hills in all directions.

During the 1980s, Montana's department of fish and wildlife set out to improve upon nature by trying to boost the size of kokanee salmon in the Flathead drainage. Instead, their efforts caused the collapse of the population. The fisheries managers took their cue from Canadian biologists who had introduced a half-inch crustacean called the opossum shrimp as a food source for kokanee in British Columbia's Kootenay Lakes. Soon, the lakes' kokanee salmon swelled from an average size of less than a pound to as large as 7–8 pounds. Hoping for similar results, Montanans introduced the shrimp into Whitefish Lake, which drains into Flathead Lake. Disaster followed. The salmon population plummeted throughout the Flathead drainage because the shrimp compete directly for the kokanee's main food source, zooplankton. And, unlike the fish in Canada, the salmon did not eat many shrimp because the shrimp fed during the day and settled to the lake bottoms at night, when the kokanee rose to feed. (The strategy worked in the Cana-

ABOVE: *Sweetvetch and yellow paintbrush intermingle in the medium-dry soils of the plains, foothills, and forested areas of the Northern Rockies. Roots of the sweetvetch taste like licorice; rodents feast on its pods.*
RIGHT: *The heavily glaciated Mission Range looms over the extensive wetlands of Ninepipe National Wildlife Refuge. More than 180 bird species flit, dive, paddle, stalk, and soar amid the refuge's 800 glacial potholes.*
OVERLEAF: *Notorious gluttons that travel en masse, Bohemian and cedar waxwings raid a mountain ash for its ripe, nutritious fruit. Perhaps for fun, flocks perched on wires will often pass a single berry up and down the line.*

112

dian lakes because springs there circulate the water, forcing shrimp near the surface for night-feeding salmon.) In the 1980s, a spectacular run of some 150,000 kokanee drew hundreds of bald eagles to Glacier National Park's McDonald Creek every autumn. No more.

Flathead, along with other deep, cold Montana lakes, is home to the bull trout, a voracious feeder that can grow to a weight of 20 pounds or more, although most fish caught these days are smaller, to anglers' dismay. A landlocked variety of Dolly Varden, bull trout run into small lake tributaries to spawn. Their numbers are declining as well, as adequate spawning habitat is diminishing, as is the quality of water, to which they are extremely sensitive.

Continue on Route 93 up the west side of the lake to Kalispell. From there, Route 93 runs north to Whitefish, where a trip through the Kootenai National Forest begins. To complete the longer circular trip, follow Route 2 to Glacier National Park and the immense Flathead National Forest. A description of the Kootenai trip begins below; the Flathead and Glacier Lakes sections follow.

THE KOOTENAI NATIONAL FOREST

The **Kootenai National Forest**❖ covers virtually all of the extreme northwestern corner of Montana and embraces several mountain ranges including the Cabinet, Purcell, and Salish. Except for the crags of the Cabinets, the mountains in this region offer little in the way of rugged alpine vistas. Instead, they bowl along as fulsome, rounded hills or broad-shouldered ridges covered with forests from bottom to top. Thus, the roads on this 225-mile loop run mainly through the trees, picking up a river or a lake here and there and only occasionally commanding a view that drops visitors' jaws.

The itinerary follows Route 93 northwest of Kalispell and makes its way along the bottom of the **Rocky Mountain Trench,** an immense trough, some 900 miles long, that extends along the western slopes of the Rockies from St. Ignatius, Montana (about 30 miles north of Missoula), to the Yukon. The stretch in Montana probably represents a gap that opened behind a series of great slabs in the earth's upper crust that slid eastward about 70 million years ago. The slabs came to rest as Glacier National Park and the Rocky Mountain Front. Later, glaciers filled the trench as far south as the Mission and Swan valleys.

ABOVE: *North of Flathead Lake, the West's largest natural body of freshwater, the Flathead River makes a graceful oxbow bend as it winds through an agricultural valley in the shadow of the Swan Range.*

Close to the Canadian border, the Cordilleran ice sheet was deep enough to cover and smooth off most of the mountains, which explains their gentle topography.

The mountains to the east of Route 93 from Whitefish to Eureka are the **Whitefish Range,** which extends through both the Kootenai and Flathead national forests. North of Fortine, a 28-mile road runs northeast to the Therriault Lakes and a trailhead for the **Ten Lakes Scenic Area.** The road runs through stands of cottonwoods, larches, and western red cedars before dead-ending at Therriault Lakes, two deep mountain lakes ringed by dense forest and set against the foot of some high but not spectacular mountain peaks. Several trails climb to the scenic area, where handfuls of tiny lakes nestle into glacially carved basins.

North of Eureka, double back to the southwest on Route 37 and drop down to the shores of **Lake Koocanusa,** a 90-mile reservoir created on the Kootenai River by the Libby Dam. Spectacular even after the dam, the canyon must have been a truly amazing stretch of river when the current surged through unchecked. Today, the water laps quietly beneath bluffs of gray rock that step back ledge by ledge to the rim of the canyon.

117

The operation of the Libby Dam affected more than the surging current. White sturgeon, a spectacular species that can reach 1,800 pounds, making it one of the largest freshwater fish in North America, have almost entirely failed to reproduce in the Kootenai River since 1974, when the dam began disrupting the natural water flow. In 1990, Idaho's fish and game department concluded that unless dam operation were changed, the sturgeon would become extinct. In 1994, the U.S. Fish and Wildlife Service placed the western Montana population, among others, on the endangered species list.

ABOVE: *The lynx boosts its hunting efficiency each winter because its wide, furry paws act as snowshoes and its ear tufts amplify any sound in snow-muted forests. Here it runs down a snowshoe hare, its favorite prey.*

RIGHT: *The massive trunk of an ancient western red cedar soars more than 150 feet above the forest floor in the Ross Creek Scenic Area of Giant Cedars, west of the Cabinet Mountains.*

Follow Route 37 south to Libby and turn west on Route 2, where the river thunders over **Kootenai Falls,** the largest undammed falls in the Northern Rockies. A wide sheet of deep-blue water shatters at the head of a series of gray cliffs, then drops some 200 feet over stair-stepping ledges where the turquoise- and emerald-colored water plummets and pools, pauses, then rushes onward through the gorge.

The area just west of the Cabinet Mountains is the wettest spot in the Rockies, supporting mossy forests of western red cedars, hemlocks, larches, and white pines. At the **Ross Creek Scenic Area of Giant Cedars** (about a dozen miles south of Route 2 off Route 56), a mile-long trail winds beneath cedars 175 feet high and 8 feet in diameter. On the way back to the highway from the cedar grove, an opening in the trees offers a fine view across the Bull River Valley to the highest peaks in the **Cabinet Mountain Wilderness.**

The Cabinets form a jagged crest of glacially sharpened points that stab into the sky. They are made of the same sedimentary rock that com-

poses the gentle slopes of the Purcells, north of the Kootenai River. The difference is that the Cabinets were high enough to avoid being completely enveloped by ice age glaciers. Instead, small mountain glaciers scooped out the high country, leaving steep-sided cirques and spiny ridges. The wilderness area protects a narrow corridor of 94,000 acres that straddles the Continental Divide for about 35 miles. Many short trails, excellent for day hikes, extend into the mountains from east and west. To complete the side trip, return north to Route 2 and follow it south along the base of the Cabinets and back through the forest to Kalispell.

FLATHEAD NATIONAL FOREST

Starting at the Canadian border, the **Flathead National Forest❖** extends southeast most of the way to Helena and embraces some 2.6 million acres of wild, mountainous terrain. It includes several heavily forested mountain ranges with peaks approaching 10,000 feet, portions of four wilderness areas, and more than 200 miles of river protected by wild and scenic status.

Part of the Flathead rises abruptly from the plain east of Kalispell as a prominent ridge of high, black mountains—the Swan Range. There, the forest service has set aside a 15,000-acre parcel exclusively for foot travelers. Called the **Jewel Basin Hiking Area❖,** it attracts mostly day-hikers to a series of relatively short trails that loop past alpine lakes, streams, snowfields, and wildflower meadows. (Take Route 35 south from Kalispell, go east on Route 83, then north on Forest Road 5392 toward Echo Lake.)

East of Columbia Falls, Route 2 passes through Badrock Canyon, a narrow, glacially carved corridor that separates the northern tip of the Swan Range from the southern tip of the Whitefish Range. The **Flathead River** flows through the canyon as a broad sheet of clear, turquoise water sweeping over a bed of smooth, multicolored pebbles. Three forks of the Flathead River drain the wild country surrounding Glacier Park— the North Fork, Middle Fork, and South Fork. Although the river seems tame enough here, rapids up to class V exist on the Middle and South forks, and up to class III on the North Fork. Portions of the forks form the 220-mile **Flathead Wild and Scenic River** system.

GLACIER NATIONAL PARK

Famous for its tremendous alpine panoramas and its fine network of hiking trails, **Glacier National Park❖** ranks easily among the most dazzling, and accessible, natural areas in North America. It encompasses 1,583 square miles of magnificent peaks that burst from the surrounding evergreen forests and tower over large mountain lakes. Glaciers and snowfields cling to the summits, and their meltwater forms hundreds of waterfalls and creeks that slip over the rims of hanging valleys, collect into pools, dodge around boulders, and charge through the trees into the lakes far below. All that moisture sustains an abundance of radiant wildflowers and a marvelous variety of trees— from impressive groves of old-growth cedar and hemlock to the scraggly dwarfs of subalpine fir that eke out a living at timberline.

Throughout this landscape wander some of the most impressive animals on the continent. Shaggy white mountain goats pick their way among the cliffs. Bighorn sheep pause to chew their cuds on the steep boulder fields. Mountain lions drop from branches onto the backs of white-tailed and mule deer. Grizzly bears turn over big rocks with a casual flip of the paw and then lap up the bugs underneath before they can scurry off. Here too live black bears, elk, moose, golden eagles, hawks, and many other species that roam not only within Glacier's official boundaries, but beyond, into the millions of acres of wild lands to the south, west, and north.

To hikers, Glacier is a footloose joy. Vistas are so broad that sometimes the whole world seems visible, yet getting there never seems to take very long. Elevation gain and loss are sufficient to convey the sense of a grand landscape without overwhelming most quadriceps and hamstrings. Also, the trails lead through a wonderful variety of terrain. Some ring lakes. Others wind through deep forest to thundering waterfalls and dazzling gorges. Several trails climb the spine of the Continental Divide, and one stretches off along the crest of the divide for dozens of miles—as though it were built for the goats.

Glacier's scenery is the result of a geologic process that began more than 1.5 billion years ago, when western Montana was flat. Layers of sand, silt, and limey mud washed down onto it and settled into layers

OVERLEAF: *Glacier lilies (or dogtooth violets) carpet a subalpine meadow beneath Bishop's Cap and Mount Gould in Glacier National Park. Bears eat the lilies' bulbs; elk, deer, and bighorns are partial to the pods.*

of sediment that piled up to depths of three to five miles. This immense slab rose along with the rest of the ancestral Rockies about 70 million years ago, when the earth's crustal plates collided along the western edge of North America. Then it broke away and was forced eastward in a form of faulting, perhaps across a lubricating layer of clay and silt, until it finally came to rest in what is now Glacier National Park. The

cliffs that rise suddenly from the plains on the east side of the park represent the leading edge of that great slab, called the Lewis Overthrust Block. Although its bottom layer is about 1.5 billion years old, it rests on rock just 60 to 70 million years old.

For tens of millions of years, erosion chipped away and carried off the upper layers of the overthrust block. Eventually, the rocks we see today were exposed, awaiting only the onset of the great ice ages to carve the peaks and ridges into their present forms. Today about 50 new glaciers, relative dwarfs, chisel away at some of the peaks. They began forming some 3,000 years ago and are not remnants of the giants that shaped the landscape as we know it.

Seen from the prairie east of Glacier, the mountains are much more than an impressive assembly of rock and snow. From the grass to the tops of the mountains, the land covers a wide spectrum of communities, or life zones, each characterized by certain species of plants and animals. In mountain re-

Above: *A food for deer and elk in early spring when other forage is scarce, the colorful shooting star blooms throughout the Northern Rockies from April to July, depending on elevation. It prefers moist to wet soil in open places on the plains, hills, and mountain slopes.*

Left: *Colorful stones and pebbles lie along the forested shoreline of Lake McDonald in Glacier National Park. Broken up and transported by glaciers and streams, the stones originated in different layers of sedimentary rock high in the park's peaks.*

ABOVE: *Mainly vegetarians, grizzly bears visit mountain meadows in the spring to snack on grasses, sedges, and wildflowers such as the glacier lily.*

RIGHT: *With her kid, a mountain goat losing her winter fur ascends into a patch of bear grass in Glacier's upper reaches.*

gions, elevation compresses the spectrum of habitats. The higher the land, the shorter the growing season and the greater the amount of precipitation. The climate differences are similar to those encountered while traveling from south to north. However, at sea level, one would have to travel roughly 3,100 miles to experience the range of habitats encountered while driving over Logan Pass in an afternoon.

Wetlands teem with plants, insects, fish, amphibians, waterfowl, and semi-aquatic mammals such as beavers, muskrats, and mink. They also attract large mammals, including moose. Tongues of prairie grass extend into most of the eastern valleys and appear in some of Glacier's western lands. The fescue, oat grass, and wildflowers in these meadows support elk and deer as well as a bountiful variety of small rodents, which in turn provide carry-out meals for such predators as hawks, owls, coyotes, and badgers.

Groves of aspens, cottonwoods, and other deciduous trees grow along the edge of meadows, lakes, and streams. At higher elevations, the shorter growing season favors evergreen trees, which need not produce a new crop of leaves each year. The middle slopes of the parks' mountains consist mainly of lodgepole pines, spruces, and firs. On Glacier's west side, though, the moderating influ-

ence of moist Pacific air supports a deep forest of cedars, western larches, and hemlocks. This habitat, with its rich understory of shrubs and small plants, is home to black bears, deer, woodpeckers, and such unusual animals as northern flying squirrels and northern pygmy owls.

Between the deep forests and timberline lies the subalpine zone, where Engelmann spruces, whitebark pines, and subalpine firs compete for a foothold with thickets of berry bushes and meadows of wildflowers, sedges, and grasses. This is the domain of grizzly bears, bighorn sheep, wolverines, marmots, golden-mantled ground squirrels, and, in the highest reaches, mountain goats.

Finally, the alpine tundra zone rises above timberline on the tops of the parks' highest mountains and resembles the vast, treeless areas of the Arctic. The few trees that survive the harsh climate hug the ground, twisting and bending around rocks that protect them from the wind. It's a tough place to live, and few animals other than the mountain goat and pika (a tiny hare) spend much time here.

Our route through Glacier begins along the shore of **Lake McDonald,** the largest body of water in the park. **Going-to-the-Sun Road** (Park Road 1) skirts its shoreline and heads for the mountains.

Much of the park's moist west side supports a cedar and hemlock

forest and other vegetation more typical of the Pacific Northwest than the Northern Rockies. In fact, the McDonald Valley, with its moss-laden stands of old-growth cedar, represents the easternmost extension of the Pacific Northwest rain forest. Near the Avalanche Creek Campground, a mile-long loop called **Trail of the Cedars** meanders among colossal trunks of western red cedars, hemlocks, and black cottonwoods. Here, the turquoise waters of Avalanche Creek swirl through a narrow gorge of red mudstone.

Park Road 1 continues along the floor of the valley, now crowded on both sides by the high cliffs of mountains that rise 5,000 to 6,000 feet above the pavement. At **Red Rock Point,** McDonald Creek zig-zags and pools between tilted blocks of red mudstone in perhaps the most beautiful watercourse along the park's roads.

As it climbs toward Logan Pass, the road traverses the flanks of the **Garden Wall,** a knife-edged ridge, or arête, created by glaciers that gnawed away on opposite sides of the ridge. At the highest elevation, vistas improve and other examples of glacial activity abound. Back down in the McDonald Valley, the U-shaped profile of the glacier that created it is visible. There are also cirques and amphitheaters shaped like broken bowls, hanging valleys, horns, and moraines.

Logan Pass, elevation 6,680 feet, was formed where two glaciers finally chewed through the upper ramparts of the Garden Wall. The spot opens up an amazing panorama of mountain ranges, plunging valley walls, high cliffs, wildflower meadows, and brushy avalanche chutes. A visitor center stocks books, posters, and videos. Park ranger-naturalists also lead two popular daily walks. One climbs across a broad wildflower meadow to the **Hidden Lake Overlook,** where visitors can stand at the rim of a spectacular cirque and look down at the lake. The other hike follows the **Highline Trail** for a few miles along the Garden Wall. The chances of seeing mountain goats and marmots on either hike are very good.

From Logan Pass, Park Road 1 winds down into the St. Mary Valley, another broad, steep-sided trough carved by an enormous glacier. The

---

LEFT: *Goat Mountain looms over a field of prairie wildflowers along Glacier's St. Mary Lake. These meadows, which lie along the forest fringe, teem with life: rodents, coyotes, deer, elk, hawks, and owls.*

129

RIGHT: *Divide Mountain (left) and Curly Bear Mountain rise more than 3,600 feet over the shore of St. Mary Lake on Glacier's east side.*

peaks that line the rim of this valley are, believe it or not, even more spectacular than those on the other side of the pass. Partway down, an exhibit identifies **Jackson Glacier,** one of the few active glaciers visible from the park's roads. Here, the forest is a dense blend of mainly Engelmann spruce and subalpine fir. Black bears thrive in such forests, but visitors are more likely to see red squirrels, aggressive little menaces who give every passing hiker an earful and eat not only seeds, nuts, and fungi, but also baby birds.

The road descends to **St. Mary Lake,** higher, colder, and windier than its counterpart in the McDonald Valley. Trails at the head end of the lake lead to three lovely cascades: **Baring Falls, St. Mary Falls,** and **Virginia Falls.** In the bright-red mudstone at the St. Mary Falls trail- head, look for ripple marks and cracks formed hundreds of millions of years ago as the sedimentary layers were deposited.

Just a mile or so farther along the road, **Going-to-the-Sun Point** offers a tremendous view of the valley's major peaks, as well as the spectacular effects of glaciation. The road breaks out of the trees ap- proaching Rising Sun Campground and crosses a mixed landscape of broad, grassy meadows bordered by aspens and evergreens. These lovely fields of wildflowers and prairie grasses seem peaceful and tame to us humans, but mayhem, butchery, and slaughter regulate the lives of the animals that live here. Coyotes, owls, hawks, and snakes ambush deer mice, yellow pine chipmunks, and meadow voles, which must knock out several litters a year to keep ahead of the predators.

Our route leaves Glacier at St. Mary. Another rewarding stop in the park's east side is the **Many Glacier** area (turn north on Route 89 and west into the park at the town of Babb), a glacially carved basin sur- rounded by peaks, dotted by chains of lakes, and dripping with water- falls. There, the **Many Glacier Hotel,** one of the grand old lodges from the park's early days, does a brisk business on the shore of

Swiftcurrent Lake. It's a good place to spot both grizzlies and black bears, bighorn sheep, and mountain goats. Return to Babb and drive south on Route 89 to reach **Two Medicine Valley,** west of Kiowa, a quieter pocket of the park set in yet another glacial basin only a shade less dramatic than Many Glacier.

THE ROCKY MOUNTAIN FRONT

The first part of the trip to Helena follows Route 89 south, paralleling the leading edge of the Rocky Mountains from a distance of roughly 25 miles. Grand vistas open up of a wrinkled prairie landscape, devoid of trees, that breaks against the base of a spectacular range of mountains. The peaks run south to the horizon, forming a high wall of cliffs, ridges, and glacially carved valleys known as the **Rocky Mountain Front.** This seemingly endless barricade of rock was pushed out onto the prairie about 70 million years ago as great overthrust slabs. What can be seen from the road is merely the first slab. Piled tightly behind it, crest after crest of equally impressive slabs extend for roughly 80 miles to the Mission Mountains.

The peaks visible from the road form a protective wall around a vast tract of land set aside as three contiguous wilderness areas. Taken together, the **Bob Marshall❖, Great Bear❖,** and **Scapegoat❖** wildernesses constitute roughly 1.5 million acres of precipitous canyons, thick forests,

ABOVE: *In the Bob Marshall Wilderness, a spectacular field of creamy white bear grass stretches beneath the 1,000-foot Chinese Wall. Bear grass stalks rise 3 feet and bloom as infrequently as once in seven years.*

unbridled rivers, and prairie meadows. They sprawl southeast from Glacier for almost 125 miles, taking in much of the Continental Divide along the way. Add to them the roughly one million acres of surrounding national forest, and they form an ecosystem larger than Delaware and Rhode Island combined. Not a bad place to get out and stretch the legs.

Bob Marshall (1901–39) would have thought so. A potent force in the preservation of wild lands as a senior forest-service official and influential writer, Marshall often rambled more than 30 miles on day hikes and once clocked 70 miles in a single day. The roughly one million acres of wilderness that now bears his name would no doubt please him. "The Bob," as most locals call it, extends 60 miles along the Continental Divide and offers plenty of room to roam. Perhaps its best-known landform is the Chinese Wall, a remarkable line of 1,000-foot limestone cliffs that run down the center of the wilderness. The Great

Bear Wilderness wraps around the northern edge of the Bob, the Scapegoat around the southern.

This broad expanse of wild land is famous for its wildlife. Grizzlies amble through high and low country. Black bears roam the forests. Moose wade the wetlands. Elk and deer split their time between meadow and forest fringe. One of the largest herds of bighorn sheep in the nation lives here. So do mountain goats, wolverines, cougars, coyotes, and even a small population of wolves. The abundance and variety of animals large and small confirm the health of the ecosystem and invigorate the land with a sense of wildness that has evaporated from most of the United States south of Montana.

The only way into the heart of this impressive country is on foot or on horseback. However, our route passes several areas at the edge of the wilderness where, without much trouble, visitors can catch a glimpse of what lies beyond.

At Bynum, some 50 miles south of Glacier on Route 89, a drive of about a half hour west on Blackleaf Road leads to the **Blackleaf Wildlife Management Area❖,** a lovely mix of rolling prairie grasslands, marsh, forest, and dizzying cliffs. From the prominent sandstone formation called Antelope Butte, look for mule deer, elk, and sometimes bears. Grizzlies frequent Blackleaf during the spring. The road dead-ends at Blackleaf Canyon, where a trail passes through a narrow gap formed by a set of cliffs that rise some 2,000 feet. Raptors nest in the rocks, and a herd of 75 mountain goats live among the crags.

South of Choteau, with the Rocky Mountain Front as a distant backdrop, Route 89 passes the **Freezeout Lake Wildlife Management Area❖,** which provides important nesting habitat for many types of birds and attracts thick flocks of waterfowl during spring and autumn migration. As a major stopover on the Pacific Flyway, Freezeout is at its glory in March and early November, when raucous flocks of snow geese and tundra swans (formerly called whistling swans) fill the skies like fistfuls of white confetti thrown before the wind. As many as 10,000 tundra swans gather on the preserve. Snow geese often congregate in numbers of roughly 30,000 to 40,000 and have been known to sweep through in one massive wave of some 300,000 birds. With the arrival of hundreds of thousands of other, more common species, Freezeout often boasts the highest concentrations of waterfowl in Montana.

133

Return to Choteau and turn south on Route 287. Northwest of Augusta, Sun River Road threads its way through a sheer limestone wall and leads into **Sun River Canyon❖**, home to one of the largest herds of bighorn sheep in North America. In this area, row upon row of high, steep-sided mountain ridges converge on the Sun River from north and south. Rock lies close to the surface, and broad fields of grass dodge around the edges of cliffs, evergreen forests, and groves of aspens and cottonwoods. The mix of running water, grass, and forest provides excellent habitat for elk and deer, and the cliffs offer the high, protected country favored by bighorn sheep. Some 700 to 900 sheep wander the grassy hillsides and talus fields of the canyon in scattered groups of rams, ewes, and kids.

BACK TO THE MISSOURI

Our trip follows Route 287 south from Augusta, slowly pulling away from the Rocky Mountain Front and beginning a long descent from the high plains into the gullies, ravines, and small valleys that surround the Missouri River. After Route 287 joins I-15, go south, take the next exit, Route 434 to Wolf Creek, and pick up the Holter Lake Recreation Road.

This is the start of the **Missouri River Road,** a 35-mile stretch of relaxation. The road follows the river through the Adel Mountains, where the Missouri bends around towering formations of volcanic rock—great bulbous outcroppings that protrude from the hillsides or rise sheer from the water's edge. Rich with aquatic vegetation, the Missouri River flows clean and clear, taking on a shade of emerald green in the deep pools and kicking up riffles over the gravel bars.

At the Hardy Creek exit, get back on I-15 and head south. About 18 miles beyond Wolf Creek, a side road runs back to the **Gates of the Mountains,** where the impounded waters of the Missouri lap at the walls of an impressive canyon of white limestone. The rock formation is supposed to be the set of cliffs that Lewis and Clark named while exploring the Missouri in 1804 in hopes that the passage would lead them through the Rockies. But geologists point out that the explorers wrote

---

LEFT: *Bighorn sheep generally frequent mountain slopes with sparse tree growth. In winter, because they cannot paw through deep snow to feed, bighorns need dry terrain with less than 60 inches of snowfall.*

about a set of black cliffs, not white, and suggest that the true Gates of the Mountains lies farther downriver in the Adel Mountains. In any case, the canyon winds past **Gates of the Mountains Wilderness❖,** where boaters and hikers often spot golden and bald eagles, ospreys, bighorn sheep, mountain goats, mule deer, and elk. A charter boat runs tours through the canyon twice daily from June through September.

The interstate descends onto a wide, grassy basin surrounding Helena. The mountains to the southeast are the **Big Belts.** The large body of water is **Canyon Ferry Lake❖,** one of a series of reservoirs that pool behind dams extending beyond Great Falls. Our route follows I-15 into the **Boulder Mountains❖,** a beautiful series of rounded hills covered by deep forests that open now and then around broad meadows of prairie grass. The bulk of the Boulder range formed when a mass of granitic magma formed miles beneath the earth's surface 70 to 80 million years ago and crystallized in an enormous mound called a batholith. Faulting raised the batholith; erosion exposed it.

The highway passes the sites of several mining camps and towns that flickered briefly to life during one boom or another and then faded. Mining has left its mark throughout the state in the form of ghost towns, shafts in the hillsides, heaps of tailings (residue from ore), dredging debris, headframes, cableways, and open pits. It has also formed generations of Montanans who have made and continue to make a living from the mines. Nowhere in Montana is the legacy of mining more apparent than in **Butte,** where copper was king for more than a century.

As the highway descends from Elk Park Pass toward the flats surrounding Butte, the terraced walls of the Berkely Pit swing into view on the right. The strip mine opened in 1955 and miners bored into the mountainside for 28 years, creating a hole 1,800 feet deep and more

than a mile across. By 1983, the price of copper had fallen so far behind production costs that the mine was shut down, ending more
than a hundred years of productive mining in the Butte area.
Underground mining boomed around the turn of the century, continued into the mid-1970s, and left a series of shafts that run under the
present city like an ant colony.

At Butte, take I-90 east over Homestake Pass and return to the headwaters area of the Missouri River. Passing the town of Cardwell, look to
the north for proof that open pit mining is alive and well in the mountains of Montana. The large serpentine scar on the east flanks of the
Bull Mountains is the **Golden Sunlight Mine❖.** Underground miners
began working the claim in the 1890s. The pit was opened in 1982.

CHAPTER FOUR

EASTERN MONTANA

O ut in the middle of its great open spaces, eastern Montana feels bigger than the imagination—landscape as phenomenon. Here begin (or end, depending on which way one is looking) the Great Plains. From the foothills of the Rockies to east North Dakota, and stretching onward south through the midsection of the country, this region of sky has long challenged and amazed travelers.

Driving across eastern Montana is more than a trip, it's a career, or so goes the joke, but the saying is true only for those who equate open space with an absence of feature. The spectacle of the plains is found not in landforms but in skyforms—the big sky, the tides of wind, the movements of great weather, and the thoughts that these expanses engender. Some people find the exposure intimidating. Others revel in the clean lines and far horizons. Like gardeners and blue-water sailors, each is drawn to a different form of paradise.

True to its name (a Spanish word meaning "mountain country"), even Montana's flat sections aren't really flat, not with the tabletop smoothness found on the plains farther east, partly because the big continental glaciers bulldozed only the northeastern corner of the state. The rest of eastern Montana swells and dips and pokes occasional rocky vertebrae into

LEFT: *On an autumn day, cottonwoods shimmer with golden foliage along the Yellowstone River in Montana's Paradise Valley. Deeply glaciated summits of the Absaroka Range tower over the eastern foothills.*

the wind. Near major drainages, the terrain breaks into badlands that in turn melt toward cottonwood-lined river bottoms. Far from passive and prostrate, as they are sometimes characterized, the plains seem to beat against the foothills of the Rockies like a vast, slow-moving sea whose grass-covered surface shimmers in gusts of oceanic air.

Once there was almost no plant cover but grass—or more accurately, the mix of grasses, herbs, low shrubs, and other plants that make up the natural prairie. Most of that native cover is long gone, turned under the blades of plows and replaced by wheat, sugar beets, milo, flax, alfalfa, and other crops. What remains of natural vegetation is found scattered across the most arid and broken parts of the country, which coincidentally are among the most visually interesting, and in the tree-filled bottomlands along rivers and streams. These are ancient landscapes. Visitors don't have to wonder how they looked 5,000 years ago, and they can easily guess where people back then would have walked and camped.

Many of the natural areas of eastern Montana are wildlife refuges centered on wetlands—usually prairie potholes and river bottoms. Contrasting with those, and balancing their lushness, are the dusty badlands that occur throughout the region. For the most part, the region is dry, short-grass prairie lying west of the hundredth longitudinal meridian, a line defined by surveyors, vegetation, farm crops, and precipitation. The meridian cuts the Dakotas down the middle. East of the meridian, rainfall averages more than 20 inches per year. West of it, rainfall is less—sometimes much less—and evaporation rates are high. Subsoil moisture is insufficient to support forests, causing the first white visitors to declare the land unfit for agriculture. They were wrong: Thanks to irrigation and dry-farming techniques, Montana raises large quantities of wheat and other crops. Although winters can be hard, summer is poignant and sweet beyond expectation.

Structurally, this region is bounded by the Rocky Mountains in the west and North Dakota in the east. It includes several minor mountain ranges in the western section. Two great rivers drain the area, the

---

OVERLEAF: *South of Livingston, a drift boat glides with the current of the Yellowstone River, which is famous for its trout fishing. Emigrant Peak, freshly dusted by autumn snow showers, presides above.*

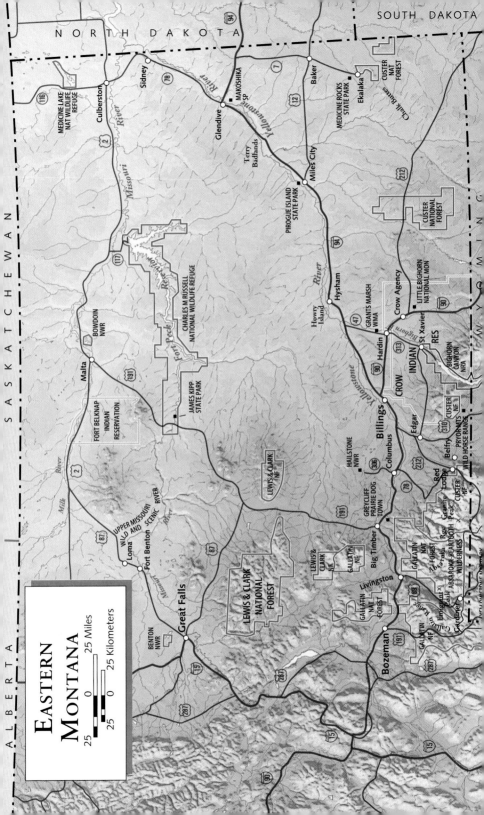

Missouri and the Yellowstone. Rising near each other in the southwestern part of the state, they follow roughly parallel courses before mingling their flows almost precisely on the North Dakota border. These rivers, and their valleys, serve as anchors for our driving route.

It begins on the Yellowstone River at the north boundary of Yellowstone National Park and generally follows the river to North Dakota. Heading back west and traveling upstream, it follows the Missouri to Great Falls, finally wandering south through small mountain ranges standing as outliers of the Rocky Mountains and ending the loop at the town of Livingston.

This is no Sunday drive. Montana, even just half of it, is a big place, and the best natural areas are widely scattered. Getting from one to another can take the better part of a day. Nonetheless, for those attracted to what Montana justifiably calls Big Sky Country, one of the pleasures of visiting these sites is the territory. Certain sections of highway stand out: the drive from Red Lodge, just above the Wyoming border, across the reservation to Crow Agency; from Miles City east to Baker, near the North Dakota line; from Malta on the Milk River south to the Missouri River. In these places, the natural shape of the land is still evident, large chunks of geography remain unfenced, and the vegetation resembles what grew here 150 years ago, before there was a single city or farm in what we now call Montana. Add enormous herds of buffalo to the scene, imagine the freedom one had on horseback, and it's possible to understand why some people loved this place so passionately and others came away appalled. If nothing else, consider parts of this route as alternatives to a high-speed auto transit on an interstate. The byways aren't much longer, and time spent in some of these places won't be wasted.

THE SHADOW OF PARADISE:
FROM YELLOWSTONE TO COLUMBUS

Beginning at Gardiner, Route 89 crosses the Yellowstone River and follows it into Paradise Valley, a name that in summer seems only a slight overstatement. The Yellowstone sparkles between banks covered with

---

LEFT: *Wildflowers cloak a moist alpine meadow high in the Absaroka-Beartooth Wilderness. Yellow composites grow among red monkeyflowers, which are often pollinated by hummingbirds and sphinx moths.*

cottonwood trees. Irrigated alfalfa fields paint the valley floor a lush green. To the west rises the Gallatin Range, while to the east the craggy, snow-topped Absarokas present an impressive rampart. Among the summits, Emigrant Peak is noteworthy, its green, thickly forested slopes scored by avalanche paths.

In addition to state-owned fishing access sites along the river, public lands in this area are contained largely by the **Gallatin National Forest❖**, which includes the Absaroka and, along with **Custer National Forest❖**, the Beartooth mountains. These are the ranges that brace Yellowstone on its northeastern corner. The Absarokas march well into Wyoming, but the Beartooths are limited for the most part to the Montana side of things. Although adjacent, they are quite different in character. The Absarokas are veneered with volcanic rubble from eruptions that occurred 50 million years ago. Well-drained, they contain relatively few lakes.

The Beartooths, however, harbor more than 300 lakes because they

ABOVE: *Ever alert for danger, black-tailed prairie dogs live in extended "towns" of underground burrows. With distinctive barks sentries warn of approaching predators.*

LEFT: *A crumbling summit is reflected in the still waters of Horseshoe Lake, one of hundreds of small lakes scattered throughout the Absaroka-Beartooth Wilderness.*

are composed of impermeable 2.7-billion-year-old granite—the same rock that lies mostly invisible beneath the volcanic debris of the Absarokas. That this ancient core stands exposed in the Beartooths is explained by an astonishing event. A thick layer of sedimentary rock once lay atop the granite; the plateau was pushed up from the north, like a trapdoor opening. As the angle increased, the overlying sediments slid off toward the southeast in one of those massive earth movements that defy our sense of time and scale—we seldom think of such sizable entities of rock moving across country, nor do we think such movements swift, though they may be so geologically speaking. Having shucked its burden, the current summit of the plateau is a smooth incline tilted down toward Wyoming, streaming with water and dotted with shallow lakes. The northern flank, in contrast, presents a near-vertical rampart some 6,000 feet high with sheer granite cliffs reminiscent of California's Yosemite Valley.

The 945,000-acre **Absaroka-Beartooth Wilderness**❖ (part of which is within the Gallatin National Forest) protects the high country of both ranges, and while the Absaroka section has much to offer hikers and backpackers, the Beartooths are exceptional. Among the summits is **Granite Peak** (12,799 feet), the highest point in Montana, along with a small constellation of other peaks hardly less impressive. Because they climb the north-facing escarpment, trails from the Montana side are strenuous; from the Wyoming side, ascents are more gradual. Various access points are worth visiting, notably East Rosebud Lake and Emerald Lake in the Beartooths, and the Boulder River drainage in the Absarokas.

At Livingston, the river turns east (follow I-90) and the country opens out beneath an expansive sky. For centuries, perhaps millennia, the Yellowstone has provided a natural travel route. William Clark went down it on his return from the Pacific in 1806. The first fur traders followed it into the mountains, and gradually, through persistence and with the help of smallpox and the U.S. Army, white settlers took the land from the Blackfoot tribe, who once fiercely defended the area around what is now Bozeman. The Absaroka, or Crow, tribe, who live farther downstream, can tell similar stories.

Since then, ranching has altered the landscape. Herefords and Black Angus have replaced buffalo. Wolves are gone, along with grizzlies and black-footed ferrets and other animals that once lived in abundance on the plains. Ranchers voice little nostalgia for the native fauna, perhaps least of all for prairie dogs, whose burrows create a hazard for livestock. Extirpated from most of the West, they survive only in isolated reserves, including **Greycliff Prairie Dog Town,** off I-90 about seven miles east of Big Timber.

Black-tailed prairie dogs are related not to dogs but to ground squirrels. Prairie dogs are found only in North America on short-grass prairies. Plump, engaging little characters, they are always on alert, barking in warning when

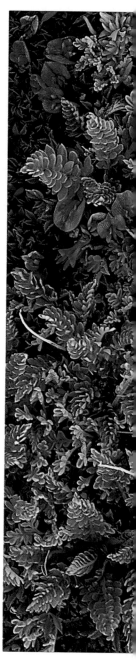

RIGHT: *Tiny wildflowers carpet the alpine tundra of the Beartooth Plateau. Harsh winds, brief summers, and high rates of evaporation force tundra plants to sink deep tap roots, grow small, bloom quickly, and conserve moisture in cushionlike mats.*

disturbed and diving for cover below ground. Their burrows are as deep as 14 feet, with two or more entrances. Visitors who sit quietly will eventually see them resurface and put on a small-scale but highly entertaining wildlife show. The alarm bark, delivered on all fours with a twitching tail, is a warning to other dogs in the community. When danger has passed, they stand on hind legs and shout "Wee-ooo!" throwing their heads back in a quick motion that looks like they are about to flip over backward. The call is repeated through the town until dozens of dogs are calling as if in unrestrainable pleasure over the absence of danger.

North of Columbus about 30 miles on Route 306 is **Hailstone National Wildlife Refuge❖,** one of several satellite refuges (including Halfbreed, Lake Mason, and War Horse) that are managed as units of the Charles M. Russell National Wildlife Refuge. All four refuges are seasonally rich in birdlife, including white pelicans, great blue herons, black rails, long-billed curlews, numerous dabbling ducks, shorebirds, upland game birds, and birds of prey.

On the way to the refuge, Route 306 climbs up from the river bottom over broken sandstone terraces before topping out on the rolling plains, where the only trees grow in rectangular windbreaks planted around farm homes. This country is deceptive. It looks plain. Some say dull. But like the ocean, its depths await discovery. Along back roads, northern harrier hawks glide low, acrobatic barnstormers in search of careless rodents. Badger holes appear as mysterious dark places in the road banks. Looking as big as a pterodactyl, a golden eagle launches itself from a fence post and flaps ponderously away. And over a low rise, where visitors might least expect to find one, lies a big shallow lake.

Hailstone is an alkaline lake, a natural depression augmented by a low earthen dam. Surrounded by dry country complete with yuccas and prickly pear cacti, the water appears precious—as it truly is for migrating waterfowl, which make their way from one such oasis to the next in their long journeys. Worsening an already bad situation, 1992 marked the eighth year of drought in this region. Over the years, many prairie

---

LEFT: *Bigborn Lake snakes between arid limestone cliffs at Bigborn Canyon National Recreation Area. Now impounded for 71 miles behind Yellowtail Dam, the powerful Bigborn River carved the canyon.*

water sources have dried up or been plowed under. Much important habitat has disappeared beneath reservoirs, which, although wet, provide little cover, nesting sites, or food for shorebirds and waterfowl. Such occurrences make designated refuges like Hailstone all the more important. A county road leaves Route 306 at Rapelje; four miles east, the Hailstone Basin Road goes north to good viewing sites of the lake. In spring, American avocets, which have bright russet heads and upturned sterns with strong black and white stripes, sail past looking like schooners dressed for a parade. Male meadowlarks call from high points in the short grass. A good whistler can fool them into thinking they have a rival in the neighborhood.

HIGH PLAINS DRIFTING: THE CROW INDIAN RESERVATION

North of the Yellowstone River, the Beartooth Plateau more than 50 miles south commands the southern horizon. It looms ever larger on the road to the old coal-mining town of Red Lodge (take Routes 306 and 78 south). Here the Beartooth Highway (Route 212), an outstanding scenic byway, takes vehicles into the rarified world of the alpine zone of miniature tundra plants and mountain goats that live above the trees. The drive heads south from Red Lodge, scrambles up the escarpment in a series of switchbacks, and tops out at 10,947-foot-high Beartooth Pass. Few highways in America provide such an expansive view of a world usually reserved for mountaineers and hikers.

Red Lodge occupies a small valley at the base of the mountains. In some parts of the Rockies, such a location would make one feel at the bottom of things. A Montana peculiarity, however, is that although the mountains look very high indeed, the plains at their feet never feel low. Nowhere is this phenomenon truer than on the splendid drive from Red Lodge across the Crow Indian Reservation to St. Xavier (take Route 308 east to Belfry, turn north on Route 72, and at Edgar turn east). The road through the reservation rides the swells of a sea of rolling hills. The coulees are protected, but on the hilltops, there are mighty views of sky and distant snow-covered mountains. Although some of the land is cultivated, over large areas the sod lies unbroken, and visitors can imagine how people with horses, in a land as yet unfenced and filled with buffalo, would fight to keep it.

Above: *Wild mustangs dash across a prairie at the foot of the Pryor Mountains. Brought to America by Spaniards, horses profoundly altered how Native American tribes hunted, fought, and lived on the Great Plains.*

At St. Xavier, follow Route 313 south to Bighorn Canyon. Flowing through the heart of the Crow Reservation, the Bighorn River backs up behind the Yellowtail Dam to form a 71-mile-long reservoir, the focus of the **Bighorn Canyon National Recreation Area❖.** In the grip of high limestone cliffs, the lake affords good fishing and sightseeing for those with boats—powerboats above the dam; rafts, canoes, and dories (motors prohibited) in the 13 miles of river below it. The clear water pouring out beneath the dam at a constant cool temperature creates ideal conditions for rainbow and brown trout, making this one of the best trout streams in the Rockies. Also, the river remains unfrozen all winter and for some miles downstream provides wintering habitat for waterbirds, especially in the two-mile impoundment created just below the main dam by the much smaller Afterbay Dam. This shallow lake serves as a surge tank, smoothing out the fluctuations in river

Overleaf: *The snow-clad Pryor Mountains soar over the high plains desert near the Wyoming-Montana border. Fossils of ostrichlike dinosaurs were discovered along the Pryors' western slopes in the 1960s.*

flows caused by rapidly changing electrical demands. Thousands of birds congregate here in winter. Species include Canada geese, mallards, canvasbacks, redheads, hooded mergansers, grebes, greenwinged teal, and double-crested cormorants. The cliffs overlooking the canyon provide good nesting and roosting sites for bald eagles and various raptors, notably (but not often seen) peregrine falcons. That peregrines are here at all is the result of good fortune and hard work. Nearly exterminated by the effects of DDT and loss of habitat, they are making a slow recovery through scientific reintroduction efforts.

Although almost all of Bighorn Lake is in Montana, access to the south end is through Wyoming, via Route 37 from the town of Lovell. Those without boats will find that end more rewarding, not only for the rugged scenery but also for the **Pryor Mountain Wild Horse Range❖,** home of what some regard as descendants of the first horses brought to America by the Spanish (see description in Chapter 5).

From Bighorn Canyon, our itinerary follows the clear waters of the Bighorn northward to its junction with the Yellowstone via Routes 313 and 47 through the town of Hardin. For a short, worthwhile detour take I-90 south at Hardin about 30 miles to Garryowen and **Little Bighorn Battlefield National Monument❖.** Formerly called Custer Battlefield, it was renamed to acknowledge both sides that fought at this most historic and famous of western battlefields. Although it is a historical monument and not a nature preserve, the battlefield warrants mention in this book because understanding the natural scene in the West depends on one's ability to see things the way they were before the land was settled by non-Indians. This bloodied patch of ground evokes strong images and feelings in all who stand among its grass-covered hills and ponder the watersheds of history. That portentous day on the Little Bighorn represented the apex of power for the native combatants, but also their last hurrah. Their cause was hopeless, their way of life doomed—and their defeat of Custer only hastened the end. Having felt the sadness that haunts these hills, one's sense of the surrounding landscape is forever changed.

EAST ALONG THE YELLOWSTONE TO GLENDIVE

About eight miles north of Hardin, on Route 47, **Grant Marsh Wildlife Management Area❖** is a far happier patch of ground, thick with cotton-

ABOVE: *Accompanying the Maximilian expedition in 1833, Swiss artist Karl Bodmer documented an elk antler shrine built by the Blackfeet near the Yellowstone River. Adding an antler brought a hunter good luck.*

wood trees and birdlife. An improved gravel road leads past a cattail marsh and parallels the riverbank for a short distance. In winter, the water from Bighorn Reservoir rarely freezes. The open river attracts a variety of waterfowl and a significant number of bald eagles. By late April the eagles have dispersed, and wild asparagus is beginning to sprout.

Twenty miles farther north, at Custer, we rejoin the **Yellowstone River** (follow I-94). The longest undammed river in the United States outside Alaska, it flows 671 miles from Wyoming's Teton Wilderness—south of Yellowstone National Park—to the North Dakota border. Through Montana it is largely bordered by private land, making it of interest mostly to boaters. However, public access sites are frequent, and nonboaters will appreciate these riverine natural areas for wildlife watching, picnicking, or simply resting in the shade of cottonwood trees.

The river once provided a magnificent wildlife display. On their return from the Pacific Coast in 1806, Lewis and Clark explored different

157

parts of Montana. Lewis went north while Clark followed the Yellowstone, first on horseback and then, having found large enough cottonwood trunks, by dugout canoe. Clark's journals are filled with notes on animals: July 28: "The elk on the bank of the river were so abundant that we have not been out of sight of them today"; August 1: They encountered a herd of bison crossing the river "as thick as they could swim." The herd of animals was a quarter of a mile wide and took more than an hour to make the crossing. Elk, buffalo, grizzly bears, and wolves are no longer present along the river or on the surrounding plains. Mule and white-tailed deer are the biggest of the wild animals remaining, and our attention is drawn to the birds that still live here in large numbers.

Among the birds, wood ducks seem as unlikely as parrots. With their brilliant plumage and inclination to perch in trees, they look more like natives of Costa Rica. Instead, they live in many places along the Yellowstone, including **Howry Island❖,** about eight miles west of the town of Hysham. On the island, dense undergrowth makes walking a bit like burrowing through a brier patch; but the sight of six or eight wood ducks sitting in a cottonwood tree is worth considerable effort. Also resident on the island are songbirds (including yellow warblers), red-headed woodpeckers, wild turkeys, bald eagles, red-tailed hawks, great horned owls, white-tailed deer, red foxes, beavers, and fox squirrels.

About 70 miles farther downstream, across the river from Miles City, is another river-bottom site called **Pirogue Island State Park❖.** The setting is similar, but dirt roads provide trails for bird-watchers and hikers, and grassy meadows break up the wooded areas. Species are similar to those on Howry Island.

Just beyond Miles City, a long but interesting tangent away from the river valley and I-94 leads east on Route 12 to Baker, then south on Route 7 to **Medicine Rocks State Park❖.** Getting there, as the ad used to say, is half the fun. Anyone who envisions eastern Montana as a flat place is in for a surprise. It's a rough old hide, upon which colorful badlands alternate with eccentric juniper-covered hills. Muddy creeks mean-

---

LEFT: *At Medicine Rocks State Park, bizarre sandstone monuments dot the prairie. Columns, turrets, even a natural arch stand in the center of small depressions, their surfaces pockmarked by wind erosion.*

der through cottonwood bottoms, and thin stands of ponderosa pines occupy the high points.

This area is drained by the Powder River, which flows north out of Wyoming. The Powder is one of those improbable western rivers that early settlers liked to describe jokingly as "an inch deep, a mile wide, and flowing uphill" and as "too thick to drink, too thin to plow." Actually, argued the pragmatists, it makes a pretty good drink if you dump it out and fill the cup with whiskey.

For Plains Indians, the Powder River was prime buffalo country. With the shaggy herds exterminated and the Indians corralled on reservations, the endless grasslands became the domain of cattle kings from as far away as Europe who maintained corporate offices in European capitals. They ran enormous herds that roamed the hills like buffalo. Cows aren't as hardy as bison, however, and when the inevitable bad winter hit in 1886, losses were terrible. Cattle drifted with the wind until they died. Some herds were never found, and the giant ranches never recovered. Most of the ranches in this country are now family-size, although here that still means thousands of acres. The most recent boom is based on coal. Under these dun-colored hills lies a vast amount of coal—billions of tons, along with significant quantities of oil and natural gas.

ABOVE: *Western grebes scurry across Medicine Lake; in the spring, they engage in elaborate courtship rituals.*
LEFT: *Remote and rarely visited, Medicine Lake is a fine spot to watch birds: herons, cormorants, cranes, ducks, geese, grebes, and pelicans.*

About 30 miles south of Baker, Medicine Rocks State Park stands as an island of moisture, shade, and timber in the sea of prairie. On warm summer days, along with other hills and buttes in the area, it provides an oasis of shade and a fine vantage point for looking out across the big open. Breezes sigh through ponderosa pines and hold soaring raptors aloft, but the most unusual features of the park are the sandstone outcrops rising like hoodoos—wind-polished and perforated like so many petrified chunks of Swiss cheese. To Plains Indians, this was a sacred place, a place of medicine. More recently, visitors express their relationship with the land by carving their names in the soft rock.

Farther south is a small unit of the **Custer National Forest❖.** Worthwhile sites include **Chalk Buttes**, south of Ekalaka. The buttes rise hundreds of feet over a strange landscape of smooth rocky swells interspersed with patches of vegetation.

Back in the Yellowstone River valley on I-94, we come to **Terry Badlands❖.** The theme of badlands echoes throughout the nonmountainous sections of this book. More than mere curiosities, badlands are a western phenomenon resulting from a combination of overall aridity and thick deposits of soft sediments such as clay, shale, and poorly cemented, easily eroded sandstone. Travelers are frequently reminded that although

161

grass grows well here, and agriculture is possible with irrigation, the western plains can be as dry as old bones. Dryness keeps the vegetation thin, allowing occasional rainstorms to melt away the soft ground, in this case the Fort Union Formation, which covers much of eastern Montana.

Of the state's badlands, the one near Terry ranks high. Gentle grass-covered meadows drop off into erosional fantasies covering an area of 43,000 acres. Visible from the interstate across the river, the site is undeveloped (rough dirt roads provide access), which is all the better for its sense of isolated beauty. The roads, like so many in this part of the country, are impassable when wet—four-wheel drive and chains notwithstanding.

Other extensive badlands are found just outside Glendive, about 35 miles farther east, in **Makoshika State Park❖**. Here, erosion has cut into the Hell Creek Formation, a deposit dating from the age of dinosaurs. These hills are full of bones, including skeletons of *Tyrannosaurus rex*, everyone's favorite fossil (but what a terror it must have been in the flesh!) Now its remains lie mixed with those of hadrosaurs, ankylosaurs, triceratops, ornithomimus, and others. Recently, a complete juvenile triceratops skeleton was found when a worker practically sat on the tip of a brow tine protruding from the clay. The skull is on display at the new visitor center. The park offers several scenic drives, a self-guided auto tour, and an interesting interpretative trail.

North of Glendive, the Yellowstone River approaches the end of its long journey across the state. Its confluence with the Missouri lies ahead. Before reaching it, there is one more notable river-bottom site, **Elk Island❖**. The road winds through a cottonwood forest for about a mile before emerging at a grassy glade beside the river. The area is known for its high-density population of white-tailed deer and—unusual in Montana—fireflies.

WEST WITH THE MISSOURI

Leaving I-94 at Glendive and traveling northwest at Sidney on Route 16 affords our first glimpse of the Missouri, which pioneers called the Big Muddy. Flowing for most of its course over soft sediments, it always carried a load, not only of mud but forests of cottonwood trees that it tore from banks in the continual process of remaking its channel. In a matter of hours during spring floods, the river could bulldoze entire bottomlands measuring hundreds of acres. Sweeping downstream or hung up on the ever-shifting riverbed, the resulting debris was a terror to boatmen. Worst of all were "sawyers." Massive cottonwood trunks with their branches stripped off and their roots still clinging to the bank, sawyers oscillated in the current. Submerged one minute, exploding to the surface the next, they could destroy or capsize boats without warning. Before 1805, as witnessed from the settlements of the Mississippi Valley, spring floods were like messengers sweeping down from the Rockies, bringing news from the wild interior of an unmapped, unfenced, unbroken country.

Lewis and Clark, the first whites to travel the length of the Missouri, found it highly impressive. Near the confluence of the Yellowstone, Lewis wrote this description on April 24, 1805: "I asscended to the top of the cutt bluff this morning, from whence I had a most delightfull view of the country, the whole of which except the vally formed by the Missouri is void of timber or underbrush, exposing to the first glance of the spectator immence herds of Buffaloe, Elk, deer & Antelopes feeding in one common and boundless pasture."

Members of the exploring party were continually agape over the numbers of large animals encountered. "It is now only amusement for Capt. C. and myself to kill as much meat as the party can consum," noted Lewis on May 6. Along with buffalo, elk, deer, antelope, and Audubon bighorn sheep (a now-extinct species that Clark called ibi) appeared the whole range of prairie predators—grizzlies, prairie wolves, coyotes, and cougars are all mentioned. Geese and ducks and swans flew overhead in vast numbers, scattering away from the river upon the expedition's approach. So much has disappeared since then. The Missouri is thoroughly dammed, its floods controlled, its wildlife diminished. Today we seek the remnants of that grand scene.

One such place is **Medicine Lake National Wildlife Refuge❖**, covering a total of 31,457 acres off Route 16 north of Culbertson. In addition to Medicine Lake and a cluster of surrounding wetlands, the refuge also administers the **Northeast Montana Wildlife Management District,** consisting of numerous small wetlands across three counties. This part of Montana shows the mark of the great continental glaciers, which left behind a landscape of smoothed hills and

ABOVE: *American white pelicans nest on islands to avoid predators and, not built for diving, paddle the surface, swinging and filling their bills*

prairie potholes that support hundreds of lakes and marshes. Covering large areas of the northern plains in both Canada and the United States, this glaciated region is said to produce 50 percent of the waterfowl originating in the 48 states.

And not just waterbirds. The refuge contains habitat for upland species like sharp-tailed grouse, ring-necked pheasants, lark buntings, burrowing owls, meadowlarks, and others. The little birds that erupt

with up to three pounds of fish daily. Pelicans generally hatch two chicks, but the second usually starves due to harassment by its older sibling.

from the margin of the refuge's self-guided loop road upon the approach of a car are probably chestnut-collared longspurs. And the flying creatures that enter in large numbers through open windows and cause hikers to perform a strange flapping dance reminiscent of mating cranes are probably what Meriwether Lewis called "musquetoes."

The refuge contains one of the country's largest remaining American white pelican rookeries. Islands provide safe nesting sites for these

165

magnificent fliers (and substandard walkers). Also nesting at Medicine Lake are double-crested cormorants, California and ring-billed gulls, great blue herons, Canada geese, various species of ducks, and a small population of endangered piping plovers. A sad note: Eight years of drought and diminishing habitat continue to erode waterfowl populations. Of the 250,000 birds that used to pass through here in the spring and fall, the number is now closer to 100,000. In 1993, water levels were five feet below management targets, low enough to allow shallow lakes to freeze solid. The resulting fish die-off attracted more than a hundred bald eagles in late winter, an interesting sight but poor compensation for the larger environmental damage.

Another sort of loss occurred along the Missouri after construction of the Fort Peck Dam in the 1930s (return to Culbertson on Route 16, turn west on Route 2, and follow Route 117 south from Nashua). The dam created a huge, dendritic reservoir about 100 air-line miles long with a 1,600-mile shoreline and a surface area of 245,000 acres. Although it helped control seasonal flooding downstream, the dam drowned a vast and productive river bottom. Bounded by steep shale and clay banks, and subject to large fluctuations in water level, the reservoir lacks the wetlands needed to nurture populations of waterfowl and shorebirds and to provide spawning grounds for fish. Instead, the 1.1-million-acre **Charles M. Russell National Wildlife Refuge❖,** which surrounds and includes the reservoir, is dedicated primarily to upland species—mule deer, pronghorn, sharp-tailed and sage grouse, prairie dogs, mountain plovers, and others. Elk have been successfully reintroduced from Yellowstone National Park, and Rocky Mountain bighorns have been substituted for the extinct Audubon sheep.

Numerous roads penetrate the refuge, leading across the high breaks to points along the shoreline. While some roads are graveled and passable in all weather, many are clay tracks, which when wet will stop even the most formidably equipped off-road vehicle. In general, those interested in boating and fishing (most refuge visitors) head for the downstream end of the lake. Those looking for wildlife should visit the western, upstream end (follow Route 191 from Malta), where a surviving stretch of free-flowing river winds through broad, densely wooded bottoms. Approaching the western end from Fort Peck, Route 2 white-lines it across some of the flattest country in Montana—truly, the land of the Big Sky. Summer cumulus clouds form white ranks like ghosts of the mighty bison herds that once pounded across these open plains. In a landscape with few landmarks, dark cloud shadows provide depth and texture. Francis Parkman, an American historian who traveled west in 1846, likened a buffalo herd moving over the plains to "the black shadow of a cloud." Now we reverse the image: We look at the clouds and see bison.

Seven miles east of Malta on old U.S. Highway 2, 15,500-acre **Bowdoin National Wildlife Refuge❖** provides habitat similar to that of Medicine Lake. Located on the Central Flyway, the refuge is important to migratory waterfowl, and the best time to see large populations of these birds is spring or fall. Breeding species include American white pelicans, double-crested cormorants, white-faced ibis, great blue and black-crowned night herons, sora rails, American bitterns, five species of grebes (western, pied-billed, red-necked, horned, and eared), and those delightfully named shorebirds—willets, curlews, godwits, and phalaropes. Upland species are also common, including sharp-tailed grouse, also called "prairie dancers" for the males' elaborate, prancing mating display. A self-guided tour road circles Lake Bowdoin, allowing access for birders and a good chance to see a band of white-tailed deer waving their amazing tails like flags at an Olympic ceremony as they bound through the brush.

Bowdoin reveals an interesting glacial history. The Missouri River used to flow through here on its way to Hudson Bay. That route ended in the Pleistocene, when the continental ice sheet forced the river south to its current channel. When the ice melted, the old valley reappeared; it now provides a broad path for a much smaller stream, the Milk River.

From Malta, turn south on Route 191 to arrive back at the Charles Russell National Wildlife Refuge, where a 20-mile self-guided auto tour offers a good introduction to the Missouri Breaks landscape. Starting just north of the Route 191 bridge over the Missouri, Route 101, an all-weather gravel road, leads east along the river for a few miles before climbing the bluffs and rolling across open prairie. Seeing the river valley from here helps visitors understand how the term "Missouri Breaks" originated. There is no distinct edge to the river valley. The prairie simply breaks up into hundreds of little ravines, or coulees, that become bigger ones, and bigger ones yet, until they open onto the

ABOVE: *In his watercolor* **View of the Stone Walls** *(1833), Karl Bodmer accurately recorded the fantastical outcroppings along the Missouri that Meriwether Lewis had described as "scenes of visionary enchantment."*

river. The coulees support ribbons of ponderosa pine and juniper, while the ridges are clear of forest.

The breaks are spectacular any time of year, while the high plains, often raked by sharp winds, are sweetest in summer, when the air is still and the rounded contours are covered with fresh grass and water flows in the coulees. Meadowlarks sing from fence posts, making one wonder where they sat before there were fences, and northern harriers dip low, barnstorming after rodents. Float trips can be made from **James Kipp Recreation Area❖,** a park and boat ramp at the Route 191 bridge, to several points downstream. Most of those traveling the river seem to be fishing—for pallid or shovel-nosed sturgeon, paddlefish, ling (also called burbot), channel catfish, and others—but bird-watching is also good.

The natural beauty of this section of the Missouri is so appealing that one is soon tempted to run the entire 149-mile **Upper Missouri Wild and Scenic River✧**, which stretches from Fort Benton to Fort Peck Lake. Wild, isolated, and fine for boating, this is the river pretty much as Lewis and Clark saw it in 1805–6. Access is entirely by boat, and the whole trip can take a week or more. Nonetheless, because a few roads come to or cross the river, shorter trips are possible, including the 21 miles from Fort Benton to Loma Ferry, or the slightly longer Loma Ferry to Virgelle Ferry.

From the Charles Russell National Wildlife Refuge, return north to Route 2 on Route 66, which crosses the Fort Belknap Indian Reservation. The mountains on the east are called the Little Rockies, which appear to be part of a regional naming convention. In the area to the west are also the Little Snowy Range, the Big Snowy Range, the Little Belts, the Big Belts, and of course the (big) Rockies, still out of sight to the west. The Little Rockies provide some recreational opportunities in the area around Zortman, although an enormous open-pit gold mine recently developed there does nothing to improve the scenery.

Back on Route 2, head west and at Havre take Route 87 southwest to Great Falls and the 12,383-acre **Benton Lake National Wildlife Refuge✧** (access from Route 225). Like other refuges in the system, this one has established a self-guided driving tour. For much of its length it follows dikes between marsh and open water, making it a real treat for bird-watchers. The layout is no accident. Good nesting habitat is often made, not born naturally. The very presence of reliable water is the result of a pipeline from Muddy Creek, some distance away. The dikes, along with a system of artificial islands and water-control structures, are specifically designed to enhance conditions for ground-nesting waterbirds. That the same structures make it easy for visitors to see the inhabitants is a pleasant coincidence. Birds (both migrants and nesters) include up to 5,000 whistling swans (now called tundra swans) and 40,000 snow geese, along with Canada geese, various ducks, American avocets, white-faced ibis, black-necked stilts, willets, grebes, golden eagles, and peregrine falcons.

At Great Falls, Lewis and Clark made one of their few exploration mistakes. Rather than leaving the river and striking off cross-country on an existing Indian trail, they spent 25 days portaging their boats around the cascades and continued up the Missouri, in effect taking a long detour on the way to the coast. Rather than follow either path, we turn south on Route 89 toward Livingston and wander through the Little Belt Mountains, which are part of the **Lewis and Clark National Forest❖.** The range is a faulted crustal arch caused by hard Precambrian rocks that were lifted beneath softer limestone and other sediments, which then eroded off the core. Because streams flowing from the high, hard center have cut narrow canyons through the limestone on the periphery of the range, its foothills offer more dramatic scenery than its summits, which tend to be rounded and timbered. Although less spectacular than their more famous neighbors, the Little Belts offer the same piney forests, river canyons, and pleasant U.S. Forest Service campgrounds.

This country, while pleasant simply to drive through, requires curiosity, slow travel, and a U.S. Forest Service map to find the unexpected, little-known pleasures. Among them are the Middle Fork of the Judith River, a roadless area marked by a deep river canyon, few visitors, good fishing, and fine scenery—truly a local's spot, reached from the town of Utica; get there by following gravel Forest Road 274 from Route 12 east of White Sulphur Springs. Another local favorite is the Smith River, a popular three-day float-fishing trip. The launch is located northwest of White Sulphur Springs on Route 360. Flowing through land of mixed ownership, the river is regarded as one of Montana's floating gems and is very popular with anglers in June.

RIGHT: *The Missouri River Breaks—amazing pillars, pipes, and mushroom caps of eroded sandstone—stand in the shallow canyon that the river has cut across central Montana. Paddlefish along this stretch reach 140 pounds.*

WYOMING

CHAPTER FIVE

WESTERN WYOMING

Thoughts of western Wyoming begin with Yellowstone. The world's first national park dominates the landscape and provides a natural focus of attention. So much originates here. So many things are explained by the natural conditions of this high plateau.

Mountain ranges gather around Yellowstone as if attending a convention. Clockwise from the north are the Gallatins, the Absarokas, the Beartooths, the Bighorns, the Wind River Range, the Gros Ventres, the Salt River Range, the Tetons, the Madison Range, and others.

The summit of Wyoming, Gannett Peak, rises 13,804 feet in the Wind River Mountains. Just across the border in the Beartooth Mountains, Granite Peak (12,799 feet) is the highest point in Montana. The Continental Divide wanders through from northwest to southeast, shedding water toward the Pacific and the Atlantic. Rivers that begin here include the Snake, the Madison, the Gallatin, the Green, the Wind, and of course the Yellowstone. All of them rise from snowmelt. They tumble icy and clear from the high summits and alpine lakes, through deep forest and deeper canyons, eventually joining the Missouri, the Colorado, and the Columbia rivers on their long journey to the sea.

PRECEDING PAGES: *The Snake River's Oxbow Bend offers a classic view of the Teton Range, dominated here by 12,605-foot Mount Moran (right).*

LEFT: *Arguably the best-known site in any national park, Yellowstone's Old Faithful regularly spews a plume of steaming water 100 to 180 feet high.*

This region is not all mountains. It includes the broad desert of the Bighorn Basin, the lowest and warmest part of Wyoming, where yucca and prickly pear cacti grow on the rims of deep canyons. The basin is a geologic wonderland of anticlines (arches of stratified rock) and fault zones, a place of open sky, oil wells, and dinosaur bones among the badlands. Likewise, down in the southwestern corner of the state is another landscape of canyons and colored rock loaded with fossils. Travelers are sometimes dismayed by the lonesome bigness of such places, but to natives, this is classic Wyoming—wind-raked basins with snowy mountains rising on far horizons.

Picture this journey by horseback: The rider has spent the winter in Powder River country, in the northeastern part of the state. It's spring, time to move on, and there are friends waiting at Fort Bridger, in the southwestern corner. To get there as soon as possible, the rider heads south, skirts the end of the Bighorn Mountains, and rides long days over the open desert hills to South Pass, where the Continental Divide climbs down off the crest of the Wind River Range. It's cold up there in the spring (which here means June), and down below in the Green River basin, it's not much warmer. Wyoming, the saying goes, is filled with sagebrush and wind—in equal amounts—but what a fine, wild, free, and open feeling it gives one. Like being out on the ocean within sight of islands, one is cut loose on a sea of sagebrush, where every swell is high enough to mark the journey's progress by the directional beacons of those shining peaks. By the time the rider reaches Fort Bridger, the route defines the edge of this region. It includes everything on the sunset side of the horse, everything to the west and north of that long trail across Wyoming.

Our route includes a few more turns than our rider's. It begins by exploring Yellowstone National Park and the Bighorn Basin, heads toward South Pass, and then turns north through the Green Valley to the majestic Grand Tetons and Jackson Hole. We conclude our journey with a swing through Wyoming's sparsely populated southwestern corner.

YELLOWSTONE NATIONAL PARK

Almost anywhere in the world, the name Yellowstone is recognized. It was the world's first national park—created, ironically, in a wild, remote corner of a country that was busily settling and subduing that

M O N T A N A

89

Yellowstone

212

Tower
Junction

Canyon

YELLOWSTONE
NATIONAL
PARK

West
Thumb

OLD
FAITHFUL
GEYSER

Yellowstone
Lake

191

J D ROCKEFELLER
MEM PKWY

TETON

GRAND
TETON
NAT PARK

26

NAT

JEDIDAH SMITH
WILDERNESS

NATELK
REFUGE

GROS
VENTRE
WILDERNESS

Jackson

Teton Range

Jackson
Hole

Gros Ventre Rd.

FOREST

BRIDGER

Green River Lakes

BRIDGER
WILDERNESS
AREA

Wind River Range

Salt River Range

BRIDGER
NAT
FOREST

Pinedale

89

30

191

FOSSIL BUTTE
NAT MONUMENT

Kemmerer

30

372

SEEDSKADEE
NATIONAL
WILDLIFE
REFUGE

Green River

80

NORTH

SHOSHONE
NAT
FOREST

ABSAROKA WILDERNESS

120

14A

Lovell

Cody

14

16

20

Absaroka

WASHAKIE

SHOSHONE

NAT

WILDERNESS

Range

FOREST

Wind River

WIND RIVER

287

FITZPATRICK
WILDERNESS

Gannett
Peak
13804

INDIAN

134

RESERVATION

Wind River Range

NAT

FOREST

SINKS CANYON
SP

POPO AGIE
WILDERNESS

SHOSHONE
NF

South
Pass

28

Farson

Eden

80

BIGHORN CANYON
NRA

BIGHORN

YELLOWTAIL
WILDLIFE HABITAT
MANAGEMENT UNIT

14

Greybull

Shell

MEDICINE
WHEEL
NAT HIST LM

RED GULCH
NAT BACKCOUNTRY
BYWAY

Manderson

Gooseberry
Formations

431

120

Shell Cyn.

NAT

FOREST

Cloud
Peak
13175

CLOUD
PEAK
WILDERNESS

MEDICINE LODGE
STATE
ARCHAELOGICAL
SITE

87

14

25

Bighorn Basin

Bighorn R.

Thermopolis

Hyattville

Worland

OCEAN LAKE
WMA

20

26

Riverton

Lander

287

220

Bighorn Range

789

Rock Springs

FLAMING
GORGE
NAT REC
AREA

Flaming
Gorge
Res

191

80

U T A H

C O L O R A D O

WESTERN
WYOMING

25   0   25 Miles

25   0   25 Kilometers

ABOVE: *Purple lupine, red paintbrush, and white bistort brighten this early summer view of Buffalo Flats in Yellowstone National Park. Beyond their*

very wildness. To set aside a piece of it with the idea that people in the future might find it interesting was an important new idea.

As such, the historic value of **Yellowstone National Park❖** has grown since its establishment in 1872. At the same time, its significance as a natural area has, if anything, increased. Although the first visitors were most impressed by the park's geysers and hot springs, they had no way of knowing how much Yellowstone would eventually contribute to our geologic understanding of the earth. Nor could they have foreseen the biologic role Yellowstone would play. After all, in the 1870s the park's wildlife was pleasant but unremarkable. One didn't have to travel to Yellowstone to see bison. Out on the plains, great herds of the animals stopped trains, and people shot at them with revolvers.

More than a century later, we still view Yellowstone's thermal activity with a sense of wonder. But the real treasure of the park—what sets it apart from so many other scenic landscapes—is its wildlife. Virtually all the mammals that were present 150 years ago still survive here, including elk, deer, bison, pronghorn, moose, bighorn sheep,

delicate beauty, the plants also nurture wildlife. Grizzly and black bears, for instance, eat the tasty roots of the bistort, and elk graze on its leaves.

grizzly bears, black bears, mountain lions, coyotes, badgers, pine martens, weasels, and many others. Perhaps, if recent sightings prove true, even the wolf has returned after having been exterminated more than 50 years ago. Certainly, it will return. In 1994 the U.S. Fish and Wildlife Service received formal approval for its plan to release gray wolves in Yellowstone and central Idaho. The goal is to develop about ten breeding pairs in these areas by 2002.

Birdlife is also abundant. American white pelicans nest at the south end of Yellowstone Lake. Trumpeter swans, once on the brink of extinction, float regally on the park's rivers. Sandhill cranes are often seen, with an occasional rare whooping crane in their midst.

The park occupies the center of a plateau built by volcanism, ringed by mountains, and covered by coniferous forests, alpine lakes, meadows, valleys, marshes, and high, storm-hammered tundra. These peaks and valleys, with all that they hold in their grand embrace, possess a geographic and biologic integrity found in few other regions of this size. In satellite photos, the park appears as a domain of wildness and greenery surrounded by dusky plains. Biologists call it the Greater Yellowstone Ecosystem.

Despite its prominence in satellite photos, the ecosystem almost disappears on a political map. Boundaries have been drawn across it with little regard for natural patterns and rhythms. Three states claim a piece of the Yellowstone area, along with six national forests, two national parks, more than ten wilderness areas, and a crazy quilt of other jurisdictions. Nature pays no heed to these administrative boundaries. The weather moves according to other laws. Plants seek out those places where climatic conditions are right. Migrating animals respond to ancient imperatives, as they always have. Political distinctions serve only to divide the territory according to managerial objectives that often conflict with one another. As in other places throughout the country, the primary environmental challenge here is to recognize that all the various administrative pieces belong to a much greater and enormously beautiful whole.

From a traveler's perspective, Yellowstone divides into three fairly distinct zones. The west side is a land of geysers, hot springs, and warm rivers. The east side is dominated by the cold water of the Yellowstone River, its superb canyon, and the large open spaces of Hayden Valley and Yellowstone Lake. In the north, between two lines of mountains, runs a long, open valley drained by the Lamar River and a lower section of the Yellowstone. Of course, hot springs occur throughout the park, as do rivers, lakes, and mountains; but as a quick overview, these zones make sense.

One word of caution. Perhaps more than other major national parks, Yellowstone requires ample time for a visit. Although richly endowed with natural beauty, it lacks a compelling center of attention like the Grand Tetons, or the sheer granite walls of Yosemite Valley, or the abyss of the Grand Canyon. Here is the most famous national park in the world, and there are so many trees! Since the fires of 1988 there

RIGHT: *Except for eyes and ear tips, snowshoe hares (top left) turn white in winter; amid controversy, the gray wolf (top right) is being reintroduced to Yellowstone to balance the ecosystem; agile and alert, mule deer (bottom right) can jump eight-foot fences; Yellowstone supports a stable population of grizzlies (bottom left), threatened elsewhere.*
OVERLEAF: *Tiers of travertine rise above Minerva Spring at Yellowstone's Mammoth Hot Springs. Two tons of minerals are deposited here daily.*

ABOVE: *On a wintry day, steam rises from Morning Glory Pool (named for the intensely blue flower) in the Upper Geyser Basin of Yellowstone's Old Faithful area. Colorful algae produce the rim's yellow ring.*

are fewer of those, and the scenery is better as a result. Still, the landscape appears somewhat undramatic at first encounter. Nothing could be further from the truth. The park has great power, but it speaks with a quiet voice. To hear it takes time—and solitude, which even in summer can be found by deviating a bit from the beaten path.

The real power of Yellowstone lies in subtle shadings, in smells and sights and sounds that haunt our memories years later: the sound of an elk bugling on a frosty autumn morning; the steam of hot springs rising in the cool of the evening and hanging like banners against the darkening forest; Old Faithful erupting in the moonlight; the shore of Yellowstone Lake on a calm morning, with Yellowstone cutthroat trout dimpling the mirror-smooth surface. Taken together, such experiences create a sense of wild wholeness found in few other places.

Our route comes into the park at South Entrance on Routes 191, 89, and 287. From here, the road climbs a long slope through a virtual tun-

ABOVE: *Offering a welcome change of color each autumn, golden aspens prefer well-drained slopes and quickly pioneer areas cleared by fires or logging. Deer, elk, and moose browse the tree's twigs, foliage, and bark.*

nel of lodgepole pines to the rim of Lewis Canyon, a 600-foot-deep gorge between two rhyolite lava flows. From there, it continues past Lewis Lake, crosses the Continental Divide, and arrives at the shore of Yellowstone Lake. The fine little thermal area here is called the **West Thumb Geyser Basin.** Perched on the edge of West Thumb Bay, the basin is marked by colorful springs and hot creeks bubbling into the lake—a good introduction to Yellowstone's scenic and natural diversity.

At this road junction, travelers must make a decision. The park roads form a rough figure eight 142 miles around. Add to this the five entrance-road spurs, and there is a lot of ground to cover. Two days is an absolute and insufficient minimum. Picking one section and exploring at a slower pace is better than taking the entire drive in a hurry. Our driving route includes both the upper and lower loops of the figure eight, called the Grand Loop Road, but some travelers might choose just the lower one—or part of that.

185

The road running west from West Thumb climbs again through forest, crosses the Continental Divide (twice), and drops into the **Upper Geyser Basin,** home of **Old Faithful Geyser.** Although everyone should see Old Faithful (preferably not from the standard row of benches in front of the visitor center), other features in the basin are in some ways more interesting. Easy paths, some paved, lead past a great

variety of hot springs and geysers of all sizes and shapes. Check at the visitor center for a map and predictions of eruption times, then head out to the likes of Grand, Daisy, Riverside, and Castle geysers. Early morning is the best time because the steam is denser, light angles are low, there are fewer people about, and wildlife is common.

The river here was named the Firehole by fur trappers, not because of the hot ground and steaming vents but because of a forest fire that burned the valley, or "hole," in the early 1800s. Since 1988, the name has once again become appropriate.

ABOVE: *The official flower of Yellowstone, the fringed gentian, grows near geothermal areas, which is reflected in its scientific name:* Gentiana thermalis.

RIGHT: *The 1988 Yellowstone fires opened up the overgrown forests, allowing many sun-loving plants and flowers, such as these yellow arnicas, to thrive.*

From Old Faithful, the road follows the Firehole through several more geyser basins: first Biscuit Basin, then Midway and Lower geyser basins. At Midway, the enormous crater of Excelsior Geyser rumbles with the force of a rolling boil. After a long period of inactivity, it last erupted in 1985 to a height of 80 feet. That impressive sight was only a shadow of its efforts in the 1880s, when eruptions hit 300 feet. Beside Excelsior's turbulent unrest lies the quiet pool of the second largest hot spring in the world—named Grand Prismatic for the vibrant colors of its algae beds.

ABOVE: *Seemingly oblivious to winter, a Yellowstone bison plods through windblown snow. Strong enough to fend off most predators, adult bison face just a few natural threats, including winter starvation.*

A few miles north is the lower basin, and a delightful side road, the Firehole Lake Drive. Visitors who reach **Great Fountain Geyser** near the predicted time of eruption will find even a long wait worthwhile. Also in this area are Firehole Lake, a steamy pool with a hefty overflow, and Fountain Paint Pot, named for its boiling pots of colorful mud, which plop and burp in a revoltingly humorous way.

Why the heat? Beneath Yellowstone is a body of molten rock, or magma, a "hot spot" in the mantle of the earth. This heats the surface of Yellowstone, which in turn heats the water that trickles into the ground. Depending on the underwater plumbing structure, the water returns to the surface as hot springs, geysers, or steam. One interesting feature of the hot spot is that it stays put as the continent drifts westward above it—like a stationary flame with a sheet of plastic passing over it. In time, a line of melted plastic would show where the plastic sheet had passed over the flame. Similarly, the track of Yellowstone's hot spot stretches west across Idaho and into Oregon. Geologists predict that the track will continue moving toward the east and north as the continent moves west.

Occasionally, the magma does more than warm the ground. Some 600,000 years ago, volcanic pressure blew the central part of the park sky high in a cataclysmic explosion. It is one of the largest eruptions known to have occurred anywhere on earth—perhaps a hundred times the scale of Krakatoa's eruption in the last century. After devastating the landscape for hundreds of miles downwind and probably initiating long-term effects on global weather, the Yellowstone volcano collapsed to form a caldera measuring 28 by 47 miles. This event and subsequent smaller eruptions shaped Yellowstone as it appears today.

The tour of thermal areas continues north past Norris Geyser Basin and such strange phenomena as Frying Pan Spring, Roaring Mountain, and Obsidian Cliff to **Mammoth Hot Springs.** Mammoth is different from the other springs, where hot water in the geyser basins brings silica to the surface, depositing broad shields and cones of a silica substance called geyserite. The water at Mammoth is loaded with calcium carbonate, which forms travertine. The calcium carbonate appears to be coming from the limestone of adjacent Terrace Mountain, dissolved underground and then carried up and deposited on the surface—literally a mountain turning itself inside out.

From here, the emphasis changes to mountain scenery as the road heads east to Tower Junction. Although at Tower our route turns south toward Canyon, the road that leads to the northeast entrance and the community of Cooke City is a splendid drive. At the town, travelers will be tempted to follow Route 212 into Montana across magnificent Beartooth Pass or to turn down Route 296 toward Cody. Choosing driving routes in the Rockies is difficult because every road goes somewhere intriguing.

Remaining in the park, our route makes the long ascent to Dunraven Pass on the slopes of **Mount Washburn.** A moderate hike up the shoulder of the mountain leads to a fire lookout offering a panoramic view of Yellowstone. Most of the old caldera is visible, stretching from the far side of Yellowstone Lake to a point directly below. The south side of Mount Washburn forms part of the crater rim.

189

ABOVE: *Lit by a June sunrise, the 308-foot Lower Falls cascades into the spectacular Grand Canyon of the Yellowstone. Originally grayish brown,*

The next step driving south is **Canyon**, where the Yellowstone River has carved a magnificent multihued canyon through thermally altered rhyolite. As it tumbles into this gorge, the river crashes over two large waterfalls: Upper Falls, 109 feet high, and more famous Lower Falls, 308 feet high. Trails lead along both canyon rims and to the brinks of both falls. In this appealing place, it's very easy to get distracted and spend an entire day.

But Yellowstone Lake beckons to the south, beyond wildlife-rich Hayden Valley, which provides more distractions in the form of bison,

190

the canyon's steep rhyolite walls have been transformed by geothermal heat and chemicals into brilliant shades of red, yellow, and orange.

pelicans, swans, and perhaps a grizzly digging roots on the rolling sage-covered hills. Among worthwhile stops is Black Dragon's Cauldron, a thermal area noted for its captivating but revolting black waters.

Not so **Yellowstone Lake**, whose waters are crystal clear and very cold. At 7,733 feet, it is the largest high-altitude lake in the country, and every one of its 110 miles of shoreline is worth exploring. Happily for drivers, the road from here back to West Thumb follows the shore, providing numerous opportunities to stop and walk stony beaches or cast for trout.

ABOVE: *Pilot and Index peaks slice the sky along Yellowstone's north-eastern border. Viewed here from the Beartooth Highway, they are part of a long wall of mountains rising 3,000 feet over the valley.*

Our route, however, turns east toward Cody. For a few miles it follows the shore (where moose, bison, and pelicans can often be seen), before climbing steadily toward Sylvan Pass on the crest of the Absaroka Mountains. This rugged section of Yellowstone features dense forests of lodgepole pine, spruce, and fir and small streams that tumble toward the lake through winding finger meadows favored by moose in summer.

Of the views that open toward the south and east as the road climbs, the best is at Lake Butte Overlook, where a panorama stretches from the Gallatin Range on the northwest corner of the park to the Teton Mountains, some 60 miles south. Between the two lie Yellowstone Lake, several smaller mountain ranges, and mile after mile of superb wild country. Visitors can sit at Lake Butte with a map and plan a lifetime of backcountry excursions.

Near the pass, Sylvan Lake reflects the double summits of Top Notch Peak, while the great smooth bowl of Avalanche Peak looms to the north. At the top of the bowl, prehistoric sheep hunters or vision questers constructed shelter pits in the bare summit rocks. Today, hikers use the pits to escape the wind and enjoy one of the best views across Yellowstone.

Sylvan Pass (8,559 feet) is a stony defile between steep talus fields. The road clings to the slope, and drivers grip their steering wheels a little tighter as they start down the far side. This road is not as steep as the original, which had a corkscrew bend built in.

Beyond East Entrance, administrative responsibility shifts to **Shoshone National Forest❖,** the country's oldest national forest, set aside in 1891 as part of what was called the Yellowstone Park Timberland Reserve. The forest occupies the eastern side of Yellowstone, extending southward along the Absaroka and Wind River ranges. About 50 million years old, the Absarokas are volcanic in origin. The Winds, by comparison, are fault-block mountains with an exposed granite core—very different in appearance, topography, and vegetation.

On both sides of the highway, Routes 14, 16, and 20, the land is largely occupied by the **North Absaroka❖** and **Washakie Wilderness Areas❖.** Both are big timber-covered expanses and superb horse country. Trails are long—up to 80 miles without doubling back or crossing a road. Farther south more designated wilderness, the **Fitzpatrick❖** and **Popo Agie Wilderness Areas❖,** extend along the east slope of the Wind River Mountains.

The road burrows through dense forest until it reaches Pahaska Tepee, the original hunting lodge of Buffalo Bill Cody (1846–1917). The great showman considered this premium country, and it still is. One wonders what changes Cody might notice today if he were plunked down in a wilderness meadow a few miles off the road. It would be nice to think that he would see no difference, until he noticed an airliner leaving a contrail against the sky. A man with his reputation would likely bring it down with a single rifle shot just to see what in blazes it was.

The valley widens as Routes 14, 16, and 20 descend along the North Fork of the Shoshone River, past hoodoos and big forested mountains. The hoodoos are volcanic intrusions that have weathered out from the surrounding softer rock. They stand now like the walls of ruined castles, radiating from a common volcanic center to the north.

The deep forest fades gradually away, replaced by junipers and sagebrush on the dusty, south-facing slopes. The desert plants tell a dry story of life in the rain shadow of the Yellowstone highlands.

193

Around Buffalo Bill Reservoir, there is more rock than vegetation, a far cry from the mossy shore of Sylvan Lake. The dam, wedged into a tight bedrock gorge, is the site of a new visitor center offering exhibits and information about the surrounding area.

Up ahead, that open space spread out under the endless sky is the Bighorn Basin, 10,000 square miles of irrigated farms, oil wells, sagebrush, and badlands. Greeted by this sight, many travelers are tempted to put on the blinders, turn up the music, and head for the next range of mountains. But like the state's other intermontane basins, this one holds a few surprises for those who take time to look around.

BIGHORN BASIN

The Bighorn Basin was once a wintering ground for bison and a hunting area for Indians. Although white settlers brought cattle and ran irrigation canals, the big economic story here is one of oil, in numerous anticlines (arches of stratified rock), that ring the basin. Discoveries were made in the early 1900s, and production continues still. Yet most of the basin remains fiercely undeveloped, an area of badlands and colorful desert and a few rivers that all drain north through the striking canyon of the Bighorn River. The basin is a reminder that despite green, snow-topped mountains, the West is essentially a desert, receiving on average about 15 inches of rain per year. In the few places where water does collect, so do birds and other wildlife.

One such place is **Bighorn Canyon National Recreation Area❖** (take Route 14A from Cody northeast to Lovell), a deep gorge where the muddy Bighorn River once flowed through a cottonwood-lined bottom. The Yellowtail Dam, completed in 1967, changed the river into a winding reservoir 71 miles long. The dam and most of the lake lie across the border in Montana, but access to the spectacular central section is through Wyoming. Just outside Lovell on Route 14A, the Bighorn Canyon Visitor Center offers exhibits and information, including a fine three-dimensional model of the region. A short distance farther, Route 37, the paved access road, heads north, following the canyon rim past

---

RIGHT: *Never shed, the curled horns of bighorn sheep grow from the skin over a concealed bony core. When two rams charge into each other, the force of the impact can break the horns and skulls of smaller males.*

ABOVE: *A wild horse keeps a wary watch on an arid Wyoming hillside. Horses significantly improved the economic life of Plains tribes, and provided more leisure time for spiritual ceremonies and artistry.*

numerous scenic points before dead-ending at Barry's Landing.

For much of that distance, Route 37 traverses a rugged bench separating the sharp escarpment of the Pryor Mountains from the vertical depths of the canyon. Several viewpoints provide glimpses into the terra-cotta–colored gorge. Only desert dwellers thrive at this end of the recreation area. Vegetation thins out to almost nothing in some places. Junipers and mountain mahogany scatter sparsely over the hills, while cottonwood trees line the draws. Sharp-pointed yucca and prickly pear cactus are little interpretative signs saying, "It's dry here." In fact, this is about the shadiest part of the Yellowstone plateau's rain shadow. Horseshoe Bend, in the canyon's upper reaches, averages a mere six inches of rainfall per year.

Along the cliffs, bighorn sheep can sometimes be seen. Although the rams spend their summers high in the Pryor Mountains, ewes and lambs may stay at lower elevations all year. Watch also for peregrine falcons. Young birds have been released here as part of a regional attempt to reestablish the population.

On its way to Barry's Landing, Route 37 passes through part of the **Pryor Mountain Wild Horse Range❖**, a 38,000-acre area administered for the protection of wild horses. Managers keep the herd at about 100 animals; every few years a roundup is held, and the surplus population is offered for adoption. How long these horses have lived in this rugged strip of land between the Pryor Mountains and the canyon is uncertain. They may have been here since the 1700s, a theory supported by their resemblance to early Spanish horses—overall dun or grulla in color, with dark tiger stripes on the legs, a cross on the withers, and skeletal peculiarities. If so, these animals are a direct link to one of the most important events in the history of the American West: Their arrival spawned the great horse cultures of the buffalo plains. To people who had once moved and hunted only on foot, horses brought mobility and power.

Where they enter Bighorn Lake, the Bighorn and Shoshone rivers have created a delta, a 19,424-acre area of wetlands and river bottoms administered as the **Yellowtail Wildlife Habitat Management Unit❖.** More than 35 miles of dirt roads lead through stands of cottonwood trees along the lake and past man-made ponds. Wooded areas support mule deer, white-tailed deer, wild turkeys, rabbits, hawks, and owls. Wetlands are a good place for seeing shorebirds and waterfowl, including great blue herons, white pelicans, Canada geese, and numerous ducks. In all, more than 160 species of birds have been counted here, including the rare spectacle of whooping cranes.

After its junction with Route 37, Route 14A (Medicine Wheel Passage-Scenic Byway) scrambles over the edge of the Bighorn Basin and begins a steep climb of about 5,000 feet to the summit of the Bighorn Mountains and **Bighorn National Forest❖.** This road is one of those fine Rocky Mountain specialties that makes a car feel like an airplane. Up it goes through the cliffs and talus slopes as the flat basin drops away behind. On days when the air is good, one can look clear across the Bighorn Basin to the high peaks of the Beartooth and Absaroka ranges.

The top of the Bighorns is a rolling expanse of alpine tundra and coniferous forest. High meadows stream with meltwater that crashes toward the surrounding lowlands through a network of canyons. The area seems almost like a plateau, whose edges are more spectacular than its center. But this feeling is an illusion. The Bighorns possess a craggy, granitic heart, where glaciers feed high, sparkling lakes: the **Cloud Peak Wilderness Area❖,** part of the national forest. Presiding over it all is Cloud Peak, 13,175 feet high.

Like most of the ranges in Wyoming, these are fault-block mountains with a granite core that rose beneath layers of sediments—the same limestones that form the rim of Bighorn Canyon far below. Up here, the limestone is riddled with caves, one of which, **Natural Trap Cave,** is a sinkhole with an 80-foot vertical drop and a treacherous lip of smooth stone. Over thousands of years, all kinds of animals have fallen to their death here, producing a treasure trove of bones for paleobiologists. Skeletons recovered from the cave include most of the big Pleistocene animals—cheetahs, lions, shortfaced bears, saber-toothed tigers, mastodons, and more. Layered among the bones is a 300,000-year record of pollen, which helps date the remains and shows what sort of plants grew here in the past. Also in the vicinity, **Horsethief Cave** boasts the first **National Underground Recreational Trail,** a designation of interest only to experienced cavers because it is the underground equivalent of a wilderness experience.

More accessible is a mysterious archaeological site called the **Medicine Wheel National Historic Landmark❖,** about 25 miles east of Lovell on Route 14A. The wheel is a rough circle of limestone rocks about 80 feet in diameter with 28 spokes radiating from a central cairn. It was built 300 to 700 years ago on a bare, wind-ripped ridge 10,000 feet high in the northern Bighorns. What was its purpose? Rock alignments suggest that it served as a calendar to mark the movements of celestial bodies through the seasons. Its structure also resembles the medicine lodge where Plains Indians conduct their Sun Dance ceremony (there are 28 spokes in the wheel and 28 lodge poles in a medicine lodge). Even though, sadly, an encircling barbed-wire fence is required to protect the wheel, it remains a sacred and powerful place.

The Bighorns warrant days of wandering. Forest roads lead to secluded lakes and deep canyons. Hiking trails rise above the timberline to the high peaks. Having achieved the cool alpine heights, however, our driving route now leaves them behind. At the town of Burgess Junction, we turn south on Route 14 (Bighorn Scenic Byway). For a few miles, the road stays high; then it plunges back down toward the basin through spectacular **Shell Canyon❖.**

In places, the canyon narrows to a tight gorge. Halfway down are a rest area and visitor center beside a waterfall that thunders through a slot of Precambrian stone. The first shelled fossils were found in this 2.9-billion-year-old rock. A few miles below, on the north wall, the sharp folding of overlying layers is visible in cross-section. They demonstrate, in one glance, the inner structure of the range—a sedimentary blanket still partly covering a hard old uplifted block.

These sediments contain more than oil. North of the town of Shell is the famous Howe dinosaur quarry, where paleontologists in the 1930s unearthed an unusual concentration of dinosaur bones. A group of sauropods seem to have been trapped in a mud hole and died there. Recently, the most complete allosaurus skeleton ever found was recovered from public land a few hundred yards from the old quarry. The allosaurus was a predator similar in appearance to the fearsome *Tyrannosaurus rex.* Called Big Al, the remains are now in the Museum of the Rockies in Bozeman, Montana. A cast of the skull is on display in the Greybull town museum (some 15 miles west of Shell).

From here south, deep canyons have clawed into the tawny limestone hide of the mountains. Rough roads batter their way along the scenic foothills. (One, the **Red Gulch–Alkali National Backcountry Byway❖**, runs from west of Shell south to Hyattville.) Those preferring pavement can get a good sample of this country by taking Routes 16 and 20 from Greybull to Manderson and then turning southeast on Route 31 to the **Medicine Lodge State Archeological Site❖** near Hyattville.

This lovely spot is set among layered cliffs of red and buff that rise above bright-green ranch fields. Down from the looming Bighorns comes Medicine Lodge Creek, a tiny gem of cold water that has attracted people for thousands of years. Now managed by the state, the site protects an elegantly smooth cliff of red rock covered with petroglyphs and pictographs. Walking trails and dirt roads lead into the canyons beneath big cottonwood trees and soaring limestone walls.

Return to Manderson and follow Route 20 south, passing through Worland and turning west on Route 431 about ten miles south of town. Some 15 miles west on Route 431, the **Gooseberry Formations❖** are impossible to miss because these badlands seem about to chew away at the road. They stretch off into the distance, a vast melting landscape where erosion happens before one's eyes. Although it looks like stone, the ground is colorful dried mud soft enough to powder beneath the soles of running shoes. Several resistant layers provide caprocks to protect what lies below, resulting in a fantasy of hoodoos, miniature canyons, gargoyles, and drip castles. The mud shapes would be interesting by themselves, but the broken terrain provides good cover for deer, coyotes, bobcats, and birds of prey. From the Gooseberry Formations, continue west on Route 431 and turn south on Route 120 to Thermopolis.

FROM THERMOPOLIS TO SOUTH PASS

Route 120 hurtles south over rolling grassland toward Thermopolis, where one of the world's largest single hot springs supplies several bathing and swimming pools on the banks of the Bighorn River. Nothing washes away road dust like hot mineral water. Nor is there any quicker way to melt a hurried travel schedule.

ABOVE: *During annual spring mating displays, the male sage grouse inflates huge yellowish air sacs on his neck and performs a ritualized dance at a traditional display site, or lek. The female watches, then chooses her mate.*

RIGHT: *Colorful algae streaks thick deposits of travertine at Thermopolis's Hot Springs State Park, which encompasses the world's largest single mineral hot spring. Groundwater seeps down into deep layers of hot rock, only rising to the surface at the springs.*

When resuming the journey, take Route 20 and then 26 south toward the town of Riverton, noticing which river is alongside. At Thermopolis it is the Bighorn River. A few miles south, it is the Wind River. How could one river become another in midstream? Through a historical accident: The Bighorn was named from its lower end, and the Wind River from its headwaters, by people who thought they were two separate streams. This coincidence is not surprising because for

most of its length the Wind River flows southeast as straight as an arrow before breaking suddenly toward the north. The bend comes at Riverton, on the far side of spectacular Wind River Canyon. Riverton is a fine name for the plain that collects not only the Wind River but also the Little Wind, the Popo Agie, the Little Popo Agie, and all the various forks and creeks that drain the western slope of the mighty **Wind River Range❖,** a shining batch of granite needles that lies straight ahead.

About 15 miles north of Riverton, turn west on Route 134 to the **Ocean Lake Wildlife Habitat Management Unit❖.** The lake is a shallow 6,100-acre puddle filled with the surplus irrigation water that drains from surrounding sugar-beet farms. The result is a haven for wildlife, mostly shorebirds and waterfowl. Because the landscape is as flat as Kansas, and there is little cover for birders, a spotting scope is useful. So is a quick eye: long-billed dowitchers, American bitterns, and Wilson's phalaropes, among other wading birds, blink in and out of the reeds and sedges lining the lake.

Not far away, beneath high limestone walls above the city of Lander (return to Riverton and take Route 138 southwest), the Popo Agie River performs a similar vanishing trick at **Sinks Canyon State Park❖** (on Route 131 about 10 miles south of town). After tumbling out of the high country like any other mountain stream, it disappears underground— swallowed up by a gaping cavern mouth called the Sinks. From there, no one knows precisely what happens to the water, except that it resurfaces half a mile down the canyon in a clear, sand-bottomed pool called the Rise. Tests using dyed water prove that the Sinks and the Rise are indeed connected, but the dye takes about two hours to get from one to the other, indicating that the underground channels are complicated and circuitous. From an observation point above the pool, visitors can toss trout food to huge, fat lunkers drifting like dirigibles in the clear water.

The park occupies about a mile of the sloping canyon bottom, a pleasant area shaded by a mixed forest of cottonwoods, junipers, aspens, and pines. A seasonal forest road extending from Route 131 offers a long, bumpy route to South Pass. The paved alternative leads

---

LEFT: *Sunset emblazons the walls of Flaming Gorge at the confluence of the Blacks Fork and Green rivers. In 1868, John Wesley Powell followed the Green to the Colorado River and explored the Grand Canyon.*

back through Lander, then south on Route 287 to Route 28 south. Crossing South Pass on Route 28 to Farson provides a cross-section view of Wyoming's historic economy, from the sage-covered valley of the Popo Agie, through tilted sedimentary layers, past irrigated alfalfa fields to the Precambrian rock of the alpine zone. The sediments hold oil, gas, and minerals. In the older hard rocks, miners found gold and built the boom towns of Atlantic City and South Pass City. The Oregon Trail passed through this area, as did the other trails leading to the west coast. Fur trappers took beaver from the streams. Indians hunted elk, deer, and sheep. Loggers take trees. Tourists take pictures. That progression sums up Wyoming's modern economy as well.

SOUTHWESTERN WYOMING

Although it clearly belongs in Wyoming's huge inventory of high, cold desert, the southwest looks more like central or southern Utah. Brightly colored rock strata have been eroded into dramatic shapes. Vegetation is sparse, often limited to sage and other scrub. Our itinerary begins at the town of Farson, just a little north of Eden and west of the Winds. Only a crossroads, this tiny community lies in the heart of sage country. Here in 1847, Mormon leader Brigham Young asked mountain man Jim Bridger about the prospects of settlement in the Salt Lake Valley. Apparently Bridger knew more about travel routes than farming, because although he gave good directions, he held out no hope for agriculture. Reportedly, he offered $1,000 for the first bushel of corn grown there. The Mormons proved him wrong, although there is no record of where that first bushel ended up or what price it fetched.

Young and his followers were bushwhacking, finding their own way across the roadless west. Today there are several highways to choose from. Take Route 28 southwest along the Big Sandy River and follow the tracks of westward pioneers. But first, a word about Eden.

Settled by Mennonites who saw great promise in the valley, the town of Eden is just four miles south of Farson and is worth a visit if only to have a few letters postmarked from paradise. Ten miles east of Eden (who can resist that image?) lies one of the strangest landscapes in the Rockies. An enormous dune field stretches more than a hundred miles to the Seminoe Mountains. Dunes rising above grassy valleys top 150 feet in height. The cold climate prevents water from evaporating during the winter, so even on hot summer days it stands in marshy bottoms amid the dunes. Evidence of prehistoric human activities includes petroglyphs and pictographs on cliff faces and hunters' campsites complete with the bones of their prey. This is wild, rarely visited country; from the highway there is no sign that such an interesting place lies just over the horizon.

But that area is handled in more detail in Chapter 6. From Farson, Route 28 heads toward the **Seedskadee National Wildlife Refuge❖**. Strung along a 35-mile stretch of the Green River, the refuge takes its name from a Crow Indian word meaning "river of the prairie hen" (sage grouse). In addition to grouse, birds seen here include Canada geese, pintails, mallards, teal, gadwalls, sandhill cranes, coots, various shorebirds, and birds of prey—more than 200 species in all. There are several great blue heron nesting colonies. Roads open to the public provide good sightseeing, and most of the refuge is open for hiking.

Route 372 southeast beside the Green River leads to the next stop, **Flaming Gorge National Recreational Area❖,** south of Rock Springs (Route 530, which leads from Route 372, skirts the west side of the gorge, while Route 191 south from Rock Springs runs along the east side). A spectacular canyon on the Green River, Flaming Gorge was declared a national recreation area after being filled with water behind the Flaming Gorge Dam. The 91-mile-long lake winds through a variety of landscapes from open, sage-covered hills to deep canyons with cliffs reaching 1,500 feet. The dam, the visitor center, all but two of the campgrounds, and the most rugged section of the canyon are in Utah. The Wyoming end of the reservoir is wilder, providing fewer services and access points, and the highways on either side of the lake are for the most part well back from the edge. Nonetheless, these roads are nothing short of splendid. No one who drives either road (especially Route 191 on the east side) on a calm July evening should ever again think that dry, empty spaces must be bleak.

Nor are such spaces truly empty, a fact long known to geologists and prospectors, who consider soil and vegetation an inconvenient overburden. So do paleontologists, who search the rocks for a different

OVERLEAF: *Lodgepole pines frame Green River Lakes and Squaretop Mountain in the Wind River Range north of Pinedale. The Green River's headwaters rise in the Winds' snow-laden meadows and glaciated basins.*

sort of treasure—fossils. For a look at some of their treasure, return to I-80 from Flaming Gorge and take Route 30 northwest to the town of Kemmerer. About ten miles east of town off Route 30 lies one of the great fossil mother lodes, **Fossil Butte National Monument❖,** which contains the best-known representation of freshwater-fish evolution in America. The butte is 1,000 feet high and consists of sediments deposited 50 million years ago in the bottom of a shallow lake. Today the remains of ancient creatures that lived in and around the lake are found between layers of laminated limestone like flowers pressed and dried in the pages of a book. The fossils, usually dark colors, stand out against the pale limestone like oriental etchings, rock-hard and exquisitely detailed. Skin, scales, fins, and bones are clearly visible, as are the wings of insects and the netted veins of leaves. Because conditions in the lake apparently caused periodic mass dieoffs, great numbers of fossilized remains appear at specific strata in the stone. More than 20 kinds of fish have been found, including gar, stingray, paddlefish, catfish, and others now extinct. Insect fossils, also common, encompass more than a hundred species. Others include bird skeletons in which even the feathers are visible, turtles up to six feet long, the oldest known fossil bat in North America, crocodiles, and more.

The visitor center provides a splendid display of these fossils, along with films showing how they were unearthed. Two interpretative trails lead to inactive fossil quarries. Visitors to this strange and evocative place come away full of images from the deep past, when the landscape was wholly different from the one we see today.

WIND RIVER RANGE, THE TETONS, AND JACKSON HOLE

Returning to Farson, our itinerary heads north toward the Tetons on Route 191. The next 50 miles, driven near sunset on a summer evening when cumulus clouds are sailing over the craggy summits of the Wind River Range, can be among the most beautiful miles on earth. On the other hand, if the wind is howling and snowdrifts are closing ranks across the road in an arctic expanse of white, these 50 miles begin to

RIGHT: *The Snake River curls past the base of Grand Teton, which rises 7,000 feet over the floor of Jackson Hole. Aspens and lodgepole pines grow along the Snake, providing roosts for bald eagles and ospreys.*

ABOVE: *A belted kingfisher perches in an alder. To snare a fish, these birds will hurl themselves into streams, ponds, and even through waterfalls.*

BELOW: *A brood full of young yellow warblers sing for their supper in a willow thicket at Grand Teton National Park.*

feel like an adventure. Never fear: This stretch isn't quite as lonely as it seems. If the car breaks down, some fellow or woman in a pickup truck will be along.

In summer and fall, no one should drive past the Winds without paying a closer visit. Peppered with lakes and alpine meadows and lifting much of its terrain above the tree line, this range provides some of the best hiking in the country. The rock is granite, weathered by time and polished by glaciers. Mountains on the crest commonly exceed 12,000 feet. Anchoring the south end of the range stands Wind River Peak (13,192 feet high). Farther north, in one spectacular congregation of crags, more than a dozen ice-clad summits exceed 13,000 feet. They include Gannett Peak, which at 13,804 feet ranks as the highest point in Wyoming.

Three wilderness areas occupy most of the high country—the **Bridger Wilderness Area**❖ on the west slope, and the Fitzpatrick and Popo Agie wilderness areas on the east. Of the various access points on this side of the range, two stand out: **Elkhart Park** and **Green River Lakes.** The first is just outside the town of Pinedale. Forest Roads 111 and 134 lead north to a high meadow affording good views of the range and excellent day hikes. The second involves a longer drive through the upper Green River Valley to a pair of lakes framed by high peaks (take Route 191 west from Pinedale and turn north on Route 352). The trail from here to Elkhart Park should win a prize—or be kept secret like the treasure it is. Stay here for a bit, relax, and let the madding crowds hurry on to the focal scenic spot in all of Wyoming, the Tetons. After a suitable interval, return to Route 191 and follow it north to **Jackson Hole.**

By definition, mountains and valleys are inseparable. They belong together. Each defines the other, and nowhere more dramatically than in Jackson Hole, where the Teton Range meets its companion valley the way a continent meets the ocean: abruptly, with nothing in between. One is essentially flat while the other is a turmoil of uplifted and eroded rock.

They come together along a fault line, or perhaps it would be better to say that they have come apart along that line. Beginning nine to ten million years ago, and continuing today, the mountain block has risen while the valley has fallen. All told, there has been a displacement of about 30,000 vertical feet, with the valley falling roughly four times as far as the mountains have risen.

Although erosion has stripped off much of the rock that once lay atop

ABOVE: *An American goldfinch feasts on bull thistle seeds. The birds nest late to coordinate their peak feeding demands with the annual seed crops of prairie plants.*

211

what we now call the Tetons, the rampart is still one of the most spectacular in the Rocky Mountains. Besides the famous central peaks
(Grand Teton, Middle Teton, and South Teton) there are numerous others, notably Mount Moran, Mount Owen, and Teewinot. Together with
lower but hardly less imposing summits, they present a ragged crest running in a north-south line, a narrow, compact range that seems to show
exactly how mountains ought to look.

The Tetons are indeed a model range. They come complete with
snowfields, glaciers, cascading creeks, sparkling alpine lakes, dense
forests, high tundra, a nearly complete selection of northern Rocky
Mountain wildlife (of important native species, only the wolf is missing),
and a rich complement of weather patterns. Lightning storms rip the
summer skies. Autumn rain clouds lie dull and heavy over a brown
landscape. Winter brings abundant snow. Yet always between the
storms come periods of generous sunshine.

Bounded by the Tetons on one side and the Gros Ventre Range on
the other, Jackson Hole is a broad open space largely covered by sagebrush, with occasional islands of conifers. (Mountain men used the term
hole to describe just such a valley as this one.) Streams pour off the
mountains and into the Snake River. Rising deep in the wilderness just
south of Yellowstone, the Snake slides through Jackson Hole and drains
southward through a deep canyon. Eventually it swings across Idaho on
its way to the Pacific Ocean.

In its 485 square miles, **Grand Teton National Park❖** encompasses
most of Jackson Hole and the Teton Range. It is buttressed on all sides
by other natural areas, including the **Bridger-Teton National
Forest❖**, the **National Elk Refuge❖, Targhee National Forest❖,** and
several wilderness areas on national forest land. North of the town of
Jackson, the elk refuge is marked by a high fence east of Route 191.
Covering 24,700 acres, the refuge is a haven for 7,000 to 10,000 elk that
migrate each autumn from the surrounding mountains. Until the first
settlers arrived about a hundred years ago, the animals ranged freely
over the entire valley. As ranching and other uses expanded on the
valley floor, the elk lost ground, and their population shrank dramatically. The refuge was established to alleviate those problems. The
range was improved through irrigation to provide better natural forage,
and in midwinter the elk are fed alfalfa like domestic livestock.

Above: *An imposing bull elk bugles to challenge other bulls intent on raiding his harem of cows. Rutting bulls also engage in strenuous shoving matches, and the forest echoes with the clatter of sparring antlers.*

Public access to the refuge is limited, depending on season. The best time to see elk is from October through April, when they are visible in large numbers from the highway. During midwinter, horse-drawn sleigh rides carry visitors close to the herd. Trumpeter swans and other water birds are often seen at Flat Creek, just north of Jackson; on cold mornings, the swans are ghostly figures drifting in dense mist.

At the north end of the refuge, a paved road follows the Gros Ventre River northeast past the town of Kelly to the scene of a great geologic event—**Gros Ventre Slide.** In 1925 the side of a mountain slid into the Gros Ventre River, creating a dam 225 feet high. Two years later the dam gave way, unleashing a tremendous flood that destroyed Kelly and submerged a large area of Jackson Hole. Today, a smaller lake, called **Slide Lake❖,** occupies that part of the valley. Above it the huge scar caused by

Overleaf: *A herd of elk cast long shadows across the snow at the National Elk Refuge near Jackson. The refuge replaces the traditional wintering grounds that once stretched more than 100 miles south to Pinedale.*

the slide is visible for miles around. Beyond the lake, the high peaks are part of the **Gros Ventre Wilderness❖,** a region of open, sometimes flat-topped summits favored by bighorn sheep. Because water drains easily through the sedimentary rock, there are relatively few lakes in the Gros Ventres, but the summer wildflower meadows are among the best in the Rockies.

The attention of most visitors, however, is naturally drawn in the opposite direction, to the Tetons. Once seen, the striking silhouette of these mountains can never be forgotten. Occupying the regal center is Grand Teton, 13,770 feet high. The other peaks, hardly less impressive, array themselves on both sides.

Two roads lead through the national park—combined Routes 191 and 89 and Teton Park Road, which leaves Routes 191 and 89 at the town of Moose Junction. Both are spectacular. Both will make visitors want to stop frequently. Those interested in more than a passing view of the mountains, however, should take the inner road, which provides access to most of the park trailheads and to scenic highlights such as Jenny Lake.

At first, the Tetons seem to reveal everything in a single glance. From certain points, the whole range is visible. One of these points is **Signal Mountain,** a relatively low hill that stands east of Jackson Lake, away from the main Teton Range, and provides a grandstand view of a huge slice of country. Visitors can drive to the lookout (passenger cars only), and after a few minutes of standing there, feel as if they have seen it all.

Yet those who take the time to look closer find rich rewards in the details. Wildlife is everywhere. Moose and deer can be seen any time of the year. The park has a small herd of bison. Elk become highly visible in late summer and fall, while pronghorn roam the sage flats. Waterfowl include ducks, Canada geese, white pelicans, trumpeter swans, and occasionally a common loon. The bottomlands of the Snake River provide superb birding; bald eagles and ospreys are not hard to find.

Those seeking mountain hikes will do well to begin with the classics.

LEFT: *A member of the 1870s Hayden expedition, William Henry Jackson created photographs of the West that fired the nation's imagination. Here he and an assistant have somehow lugged a darkroom high in the Tetons.*

ABOVE: *The glassy waters of the upper Snake River reflect the distant summit of Mount Moran in Grand Teton National Park. Meadows such as*

The most popular is to ride the launch across Jenny Lake and hike up Cascade Canyon. Other easy to moderate hikes include the trails to Leigh Lake, Phelps Lake Overlook, Bradley and Taggart lakes, and several trails along Jackson Lake originating at the Colter Bay Visitor Center.

Longer trails lead high into the mountains. Climbers naturally head for the summits, while vigorous hikers find superb routes that circle the peaks. In doing so, they find that the west side of the range is quite different. The slope is more gradual. There are numerous lakes and long, deep canyons, many of them in the adjacent **Jedediah Smith Wilderness,** administered by the Targhee National Forest. The wilderness is an area roughly 50 miles long by 5 miles wide laid out along the western slope of the Tetons. People come here for the same reasons they visit the other side, with the added benefit of solitude (there are far fewer visitors here). The wilderness area is more accessible through Idaho. (Take Route 22 west from Jackson and turn north on Route 33 at Victor, continuing north

this—broad, moist, with a protective fringe of lodgepole pine for cover— often draw elk, deer, and moose in the evening or early morning hours.

on Route 32. Routes 33 and 32 compose the Teton Scenic Byway; dirt roads run from the highway to various trailheads.)

Heading north from the Tetons, Routes 191 and 89 skirt Jackson Lake and head for Yellowstone. Between the two parks is the **John D. Rockefeller, Jr. Memorial Parkway❖,** a scenic corridor named in honor of the man who contributed so much to the preservation of national park systems throughout the United States, including Grand Teton National Park. By all appearances, the parkway is a continuation of the two national parks, and most visitors pass through without noticing any administrative change. Nor is there a scenic difference: coniferous forests, mountain meadows, views of distant mountains. Just beyond Flagg Ranch resort, Forest Road 261 takes off west toward the Idaho town of Ashton, a rough and dusty 46 miles. This road also provides access to Yellowstone's remote southwestern corner, the Bechler region— an area known (but not well-known; few people visit) for its waterfalls.

219

EASTERN WYOMING

To many travelers, the high plains and deserts of eastern Wyoming seem bleak, monotonous, and nearly barren—a region to pass through as quickly as possible, preferably while turning the pages of a best-seller for distraction. The hundreds of miles of sagebrush flats, arid hills, gravelly ravines, and dried-up creek beds can indeed get tedious. And though the landscape teems with animals, most are hard to see. Still, to those with a bit of patience and an open mind, eastern Wyoming reveals itself as a region of great beauty and astounding diversity.

Grasslands and deserts sprawl over much of the territory as vast, open areas where Swainson's hawks, golden eagles, and prairie falcons ride the thermals and plunge from the sky to nail Uinta ground squirrels, prairie dogs, and desert cottontail rabbits. Pronghorn, often called antelope, turn up just about everywhere, and now and then a coyote trots across a hillside. The terrain varies from seemingly endless ramps and basins of lush grass to rolling hills covered with a mix of sagebrush and bunchgrass; from colorful badlands to rimrocked plateaus and even sand dunes.

Roughly speaking, the grasslands extend from north to south across

LEFT: *Looking south toward Colorado, the glacially carved summit of Medicine Bow Peak provides a splendid panorama of the rolling terrain and the rounded silhouettes of the ancient Medicine Bow Range.*

the state and stretch eastward from the Bighorn and Laramie mountains to the Great Plains of Nebraska and South Dakota. The deserts run along the southern portion of the state, from the western slopes of the Sierra Madre range to the Green River Valley and nearly as far north as the Wind River Mountains. The plants and animals living in these harsh climates have developed special means for coping with the scarcity of water, the extreme temperature variations, the lack of protective cover, and the strong, persistent winds.

Despite all the open country in eastern Wyoming, mountains rarely drop from view. The Bighorns form the western boundary of the Powder River Valley. The Black Hills jut into the state's northeastern corner. In the southeast, three mountain ranges—the Laramie, Medicine Bow, and Sierra Madre—spill across the border from Colorado and contain glacially carved peaks that top 12,000 feet. The spectacular Wind River Range towers over the parched country of the Great Divide Basin, and a host of lesser ranges form the northern rim of the desertlands.

Through the grasslands and between the mountain ranges run some of the most important rivers in Wyoming. The North Platte curls around the northern edge of the southern mountains. The Sweetwater flows east across the central plains and joins the North Platte west of Casper. To the north run the Powder and Belle Fourche (pronounced bell-FOOSH) rivers. All rise in mountainous terrain and sometimes cut impressive gorges and canyons before emerging onto the prairies as sinuous oases for waterfowl, songbirds, and large mammals such as elk, deer, and years ago, bison and grizzly bears.

Our tour of eastern Wyoming encompasses grasslands, mountains, and desert. It begins at Devils Tower, in the northeastern corner, moves west through the Powder River Basin, and then visits the southeastern mountains. West of the mountains, it runs through the southern deserts and returns north through the central plains.

There is little public land in this region, and the evidence of human use is very strong. The buffalo are gone, of course, replaced by domestic cattle and sheep. Oil and gas wells dot the landscape. The North

---

OVERLEAF: *At the foot of Devils Tower, black-tailed prairie dogs venture from their burrows. Living in dense colonies, the closely related dogs have evolved special behavioral adaptations to prevent inbreeding.*

Platte has been dammed in several locations for flood control and irrigation. Large strip mines extract coal from the Powder River Basin, and the state's largest cities were built here.

Even so, eastern Wyoming retains an essential element of the West that more popular areas have lost—a sense of vast emptiness. Of isolation. Of the freedom and peace that come from living far beyond the reach of the fads, the hype, the hustle, the distractions, even the amenities of urban life. There are no cappuccino stands within walking distance of the trailheads here, no traffic jams in the forest, no cheek-by-jowl camping, no one-hour photo shops a stone's throw from the best sights. In this uncrowded, unmarketed area, visitors rarely need to share the river or the hills with anyone, except maybe an osprey or an owl.

ABOVE: *Consummate diggers, badgers burrow faster than all other mammals and excavate rodents, such as prairie dogs, for meals.* **RIGHT:** *The scale of Devil's Tower is hard to grasp until a climber (lower left) is spotted among the columns.*

DEVILS TOWER NATIONAL MONUMENT

Our route through eastern Wyoming starts in the northeastern corner of the state at **Devils Tower National Monument❖**, a stout cylinder of gray rock that rises from the forests of the Black Hills roughly 25 miles northwest of the town of Sundance. The country's first national monument, Devils Tower is a huge flat-topped plug of bare rock scored by hundreds of parallel grooves that sweep its sheer walls from top to bottom. It resembles a petrified tree stump of colossal proportions. Rising 867 feet above a gentle bulge of forested land, it overlooks a rolling landscape of grassy meadows, modest cliffs, and ponderosa-pine forests. The **Belle Fourche River** meanders through the meadows at its base, carving out and exposing high banks of vermilion mud and red sandstone.

The tower seems at once larger and smaller than it actually is. Its girth appears immense, yet one can stroll around the base in half an hour. On

ABOVE: *A great blue heron takes flight. These gangly shorebirds stalk watercourses throughout the Northern Rockies mainly looking for fish, but also for small mammals, frogs, and nestlings of other birds.*

the other hand, its squat, sawed-off shape tends to make it seem shorter than it really is. Visitors don't get a true sense of its height until they pick out some climbers on its walls. Even through binoculars, they look tiny.

The mass of rock that would become Devils Tower formed about 60 million years ago when this portion of Wyoming was relatively flat and overlain with multicolored layers of sedimentary rock. Molten magma forced its way through thousands of feet of these layers and collected in a mass, perhaps buried beneath the surface or lying inside the neck of an ancient volcano. In either case, the magma cooled and solidified into a hard rock known as phonolite porphyry. As it cooled, the rock contracted, fracturing into multisided (usually six-sided) columns that measure roughly four to eight feet in diameter. Over millions of years, the ancestral Belle Fourche River washed away the softer, sedimentary rocks surrounding the mass of cooled magma and slowly exposed the tower as a tightly packed bundle of columns. Its relatively stable rock and virtually infinite array of cracks and faces attract many rock climbers, mostly very good ones. Although some intermediate routes exist, the climbing generally requires advanced skills.

Devils Tower is more than an odd rock and a challenging climb,

ABOVE: *Big ears and a sharply pointed muzzle enable red foxes to locate and catch small rodents moving in thick brush. Omnivorous, red foxes also enjoy berries, insects, frogs, snakes, and birds and their eggs.*

however. Here the rich habitats of mountain, prairie, and river converge, bringing disparate plant and animal species into close proximity. Despite all the bare rock, the tower is home to many plants and animals. Prairie falcons nest at the top of the tower and glide off to hunt rodents on the valley floor. Rock doves (pigeons) nest among the niches and ledges. Western rattlesnakes living at the summit are occasionally seen slithering up the cracks. Least chipmunks, pack rats, and bushy-tailed woodrats also live at the top, finding plenty to eat among various grasses, forbs (herbs other than grasses), and shrubs.

Ponderosa pines circle the base of the tower, forming a pleasant, spacious forest with a breezy canopy of branches and needles high overhead and a roomy floor of sparse grass underfoot. Here and there, the trees open onto a meadow, which usually offers a fine view of the tower. White-tailed deer spend much of the day in the forest or along its fringe, browsing the shrubs and other broadleaf plants.

Larger meadows stretch across the floor of the valley. These open, sunny areas abound with rodents and insects that feast on seeds, roots, and leaves. Mice, northern pocket gophers, shrews, meadow voles, bushy-tailed woodrats, Uinta ground squirrels, and black-tailed prairie dogs reproduce at astounding rates, but a wide variety of predators control their numbers. Coyotes, red foxes, long-tailed weasels, badgers, and bobcats ambush, dig out, or otherwise capture rodents, while hawks, eagles, falcons, and owls mount an around-the-clock air assault.

The clear, swift waters of the Belle Fourche sweep through the bottomlands. Large cottonwoods grow along its current, spreading their limbs over the thick grass and casting broad, cool shadows. In the great, silvery snags of dead cottonwoods, colorful wood ducks, great horned owls, and red-headed woodpeckers build their nests. High banks of red clay and sandstone rise from the sod along the outside curves of the river. Cliff swallows nest against the red banks and dart over the water snatching freshly hatched insects from the air. During migration, great blue herons stop along the river to wade the shore and catch frogs and small fish. Four relatively short loop trails explore the area's various habitats. Two circle the tower. The third makes a circuit of a ridge north of the tower, and the fourth explores the riverbanks and meadows to the south.

The south trail passes a large colony of black-tailed prairie dogs that sprawls over a flat expanse of short grass between the river and the tower. Some of the animals can be seen out in the grass, sitting back on their haunches, watching. They look paunchy and prosperous. Others trundle about on all fours, nosing the grasses and forbs.

The mound at the entrance to each burrow is more than just a pile of debris thrown out of the hole. Measuring at least a foot high and two feet across, it serves as a lookout and as a dike to keep out water. The animals carefully maintain the mounds, occasionally throwing on fresh dirt and packing it into place with their blunt noses. They also cut down tall vegetation to give themselves a clear view on all fronts. Each burrow is an ambling tunnel that drops about 4 vertical feet (though they can be as deep as 16 feet) and runs horizontally for about 30 feet to an emergency exit. It branches off into several chambers—a listening post near the entrance, a toilet, a living area, and an-

---

RIGHT: *Although fanciful, this 1866 engraving does reflect the density of prairie dog towns and the co-tenancy of rattlesnakes and burrowing owls.*
OVERLEAF: *In the foothills of the Medicine Bows, the leaves of cottonwoods and willow shrubs inflame the autumn banks of the North Platte River.*

F.W.KEYL. del.

other chamber that traps air in case of flood.

Although the arrangement of burrow entrances may seem haphazard, prairie dogs live in highly organized communities. Large colonies break down into wards, and each ward contains family groups called coteries. The dogs scrupulously observe the boundaries and defend them with great tenacity. In early spring, though, pups are granted community-wide dispensations to wander wherever they like. Later, they learn to behave properly.

Prairie dogs cooperate for mutual defense. If one dog spots potential danger, it barks a warning and flicks its tail. Instantly, all dogs within earshot sit up and take notice. If the warning seems justified, they too start barking. Soon the alarm spreads throughout the area. If danger is imminent, the dogs bolt into their burrows. If the danger subsides, the dogs signal the "all clear" by throwing up their forepaws, calling loudly, arching their backs, and dropping to all fours. A different, more urgent alarm goes up if a prairie dog spots a hawk. At the sound of this special air-raid warning, all scramble down their holes immediately rather than pause to judge the peril for themselves.

POWDER RIVER BASIN

From Devils Tower, Route 14 winds southwest through a series of small valleys, hollows, and patches of forest adorned with cliffs, open meadows, and narrow streams. This intimate setting offers many ups and downs, twists and turns, and the promise of a new discovery beyond each bend in the road. Suddenly, travelers break out of the pines and there, far below and spreading out for what seems like forever, is a vast plain of grass without a tree on it.

This expanse is the **Powder River Basin,** a largely flat, but sometimes gently rolling, landscape of prairie grass that once rumbled under the hooves of great bison herds. It extends from the western slopes of the Black Hills (some of which are in the **Black Hills National Forest❖**) to the eastern slopes of the **Bighorn Mountains** and from the banks of the **North Platte River** in Wyoming to the **Yellowstone River** in Montana. It has been fought over many times during the last 125 years. Plains Indian tribes tried to keep white miners and settlers out of it during the 1860s and 1870s. Ranchers fought among themselves for control of it starting in the 1880s. More recently, its valuable coal, oil, and uranium deposits have sparked battles between industry and environmentalists. After dropping down to the plain, stop and have a look back at the western lobe of the Black Hills. Measuring 40 miles wide by 80 miles long, they rise like an island off the Great Plains.

Our route through the Powder River Basin follows I-90 to Gillette and then Route 59 south through the heart of the grasslands to Douglas. About a hundred million years ago, a tropical forest covered this part of Wyoming and extended throughout what is now the Great Plains. As the Rocky Mountains rose to the west some 70 to 100 million years ago, they began to force the moist Pacific air that had supported the tropical forest to rise and cool, wringing the air dry of precipitation. As the climate grew colder and drier, the trees died and a newly evolved family of plants—grasses—took their place.

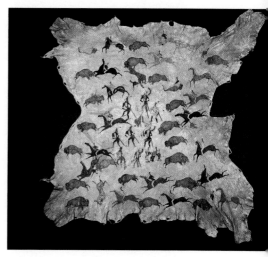

Like all of Wyoming's high plains, the Powder River Basin is a punishing environment. Drought is common. Evaporation rates are high. Temperatures range from the 90s to well below zero. Winds often blast across the flats at 60 miles per hour. Snow tends to blow away or evaporate before it can melt into the soil. Grasses have adapted to such harsh conditions by concentrating a

ABOVE: *Not surprisingly, bison and horses dominate this striking elk-hide painting created by a Shoshone artist about 1900; the images depict the traditional Sun Dance sacred to the Plains tribes.*

large proportion of their biomass underground as roots—a much larger proportion than, say, oak trees. Drought, fire, or, in years gone by, a herd of bison might decimate growth above ground, but with root systems intact grasses can quickly send up new shoots.

Many animals of the prairie also find the key to success underground. Burrows insulate their residents from extreme temperature variations and provide hiding places in an environment where there are few above ground. Other residents, such as the pronghorn and

235

Above: *World-class sprinters that can see up to four miles, pronghorn bolt at the slightest sign of danger, although, ever curious, they could often be*

white- and black-tailed jackrabbits, compensate for the lack of hiding places with keen eyesight, agility, and tremendous bursts of speed.

Often called antelope and sometimes just goats, pronghorn are exotic-looking beasts with a tan body, big black eyes, white stripes across the neck, and oddly shaped black horns. Males also have a broad black stripe that covers the face from snout to horns. Pronghorn are the fastest animals in the Western Hemisphere, capable of exceeding the interstate speed limit. They can sprint at 70 miles per hour for three to four minutes and cruise easily at 30 miles per hour.

For the past century, the Powder River Basin has been one of the world's leading sources of energy. Throughout the region are bobbing oil wells, natural-gas pipelines, and long coal trains rolling slowly eastward. The vast deposits of low-sulfur coal (roughly a trillion tons) that underlie the area are the geologic remains of the dense tropical forest that covered this part of Wyoming before the mountains rose and the grasses took over. The nation's seven largest mines operate in the basin, strip-mining veins as thick as 70 feet. Environmentalists worry that the mines have destroyed grassland habitat for elk and deer and threaten groundwater quality. The companies assert that they obey federal requirements to save and replace the topsoil and rocks they remove to get at the coal.

Thunder Basin National Grasslands❖ lies southeast of Wright off

lured back by hunters waving a colorful rag. Once 20 to 40 million prong-horn roamed the western plains; today there are fewer than 30,000.

Route 59. A hodgepodge of private and public lands, it illustrates the deep and abiding effect of human activity on the semiarid plains of the West. Short-grass prairies, like those of the Powder River Basin, are the driest of all grasslands. A small decline in precipitation can tip the scale from short-grass to desert—as can a little of the wrong sort of human interference. People living in the Thunder Basin area learned that lesson the hard way during the 1920s and 1930s.

Once the bison had been hunted nearly to extinction and the Plains Indian tribes had been forced off the land, overgrazing by livestock, unsound farming methods, and years of drought combined to turn the region into a dust bowl. During the Great Depression, the federal government bought up hundreds of failed homesteads, reseeded the prairie, planted windbreaks, and built dams and ponds. Within about ten years the desert retreated and a new short-grass prairie took hold.

Thunder Basin's landscape is a mix of rolling plains punctuated by knobs and ridges and high plateaus with steep, eroded slopes. Grasses such as blue grama, needle-and-thread, and western wheatgrass cover much of the land, but there are also broad areas dominated by sagebrush and prickly pear cactus. Cottonwoods grow along the river courses, and ponderosa pines and juniper trees claim the high ground.

Wyoming's largest concentration of pronghorn live in the Thunder Basin area, along with mule deer, white-tailed deer, and elk. Mountain lions prey on the grazers. Other predators such as coyotes, bobcats, badgers, and long-tailed weasels feed on a cornucopia of small rodents and rabbits.

Dotted with hundreds of ponds and drained by a handful of rivers and streams, Thunder Basin also supports an abundant array of birds, both wetland and upland. Western grebes, American white pelicans, double-crested cormorants, great blue herons, and many types of ducks share the terrain with such prairie critters as prairie falcons, sage grouse, waxwings, and yellow warblers.

THE SOUTHERN MOUNTAINS: DOUGLAS TO THE SIERRA MADRE

Approaching Douglas Route 59 dips and climbs through the rolling prairie, and suddenly an isolated mountain appears on the horizon. Over each ramp of grass, the mountain seems to shift forward, growing in height and breadth and finally adding a range of other peaks on either side. The mountain is **Laramie Peak❖,** the first summit seen by emigrants on the Oregon Trail and a landmark for overland travelers for thousands of years. It and the mountains around it are the northern front of the **Laramie Range,** a broad welt of stone and forest that runs all the way down to Cheyenne and beyond. The range is one of three that project into southeastern Wyoming from Colorado. Our route follows the eastern slopes of the range to Cheyenne on I-25.

Before we proceed south, the Douglas area offers two attractions. The northern portion of the Laramie Range includes a section of the **Routt/Medicine Bow National Forest❖,** a patchwork of public land that covers much of southeastern Wyoming's high country. Part of the forest includes Laramie Peak, where the summit, elevation 10,272, offers a tremendous view of the plains and nearby mountains. Visitors can hike to it on a steep 5.5-mile trail from Friend Park Campground southwest of Esterbrook (take Route 94 instead of I-25 south from Douglas).

Another attractive spot, **Ayres Natural Bridge,** lies in the foothills of the Laramie Range about a dozen miles west of Douglas off I-25. The

---

RIGHT: *Ayres Natural Bridge spans La Prele Creek in the foothills of the Laramie Mountains. The limestone arch lies in a sensuous amphitheater that the flowing water has hollowed out of the pale red sandstone.*

ABOVE: *An early artist of western wildlife, John J. Audubon did this 1851 portrait of the rare black-footed ferret. Now endangered, these ferrets are being reintroduced into their natural plains habitat.*

bridge is a graceful arch of limestone that protrudes from a high bluff and spans the clear waters of La Prele Creek, which carved the bridge and the surrounding natural amphitheater waved in smooth red sandstone. Box elders, chokecherry bushes, and poplars line the creek and frame various views of the arch. Swarms of cliff swallows flit overhead.

Traveling south on I-25 from Douglas, visitors soon catch a few glimpses of a large reservoir—one of many formed by dams along the North Platte River. This one, the Glendo Reservoir, connects downstream with the smaller Guernsey Reservoir to form a more or less continuous pool from the town of Orin to Guernsey. Two state parks have been built beside the water. **Glendo State Park❖,** a base for powerboaters and anglers, is surrounded mainly by low, treeless hills. **Guernsey State Park❖,** on the other hand, lies in a pleasant canyon. Sandstone cliffs rim the walls of the canyon, and stands of ponderosa pine and juniper grow along the lower slopes.

South of Wheatland, Route 34 follows Sybille Creek west into the Laramie Range. A locals' shortcut to Laramie, the road also passes the **Sybille Wildlife Research and Conservation Education Center❖,** a facility at the heart of efforts to save the black-footed ferret from extinction. These ferrets are the rarest mammals in North America. Their former range extended throughout the Great Plains, mirroring the range of their primary source of food—prairie dogs. As settlers plowed the prairie into farmland, they destroyed vast areas of prairie-dog habitat and exterminated hundreds of thousands as pests. With the prairie-dog population in decline, the ferret population plummeted. By the mid-1970s, many considered the species extinct.

Then in 1981, a small group of ferrets was discovered on a ranch near Meeteetse, about 30 miles south of Cody. Biologists watched and studied them from a distance until 1985, when an outbreak of canine distemper killed nearly all of them. Eighteen were trapped and taken to the Sybille center to form the nucleus of a captive breeding program. By the winter of 1993, 152 ferrets were living at the center and 90 others had been reintroduced to the wild at a prairie-dog colony in the nearby Shirley Basin. Although predators themselves, the ferrets are also prey to owls, badgers, and coyotes. Of the 90 released, about 24 survived in 1993. Biologists plan to release ferrets elsewhere and hope to have 1,500 adult ferrets living in the wild by 2010.

South of Wheatland, I-25 pulls away from the eastern front of the Laramie Range and crosses the **Denver-Julesberg Basin** to Cheyenne. From there, our route heads west over the backs of the three mountain ranges that spill into Wyoming from Colorado. The Laramie Range and the **Medicine Bow Range❖** are both spurs of Colorado's spectacular Front Range. Farther west, the **Sierra Madre Range❖** presents the northern front of Colorado's Park Range.

A long fault line cuts northeastward through all three of the Wyoming ranges. North of the line, each range is composed mainly of rocks older than 2.5 billion years. To the south, each range contains rock about a billion years younger. Geologists report that the seam represents the juncture of two pieces of continental crust that joined together long ago while the North American continent coalesced.

Much later, about 70 to 90 million years ago, a collision between the North American continental and the Pacific oceanic plates began crumpling the continent's western margin. As a result, mountains rose throughout the West. The southeastern Wyoming ranges appeared about 70 million years ago, during a period of mountain-building called the Laramide orogeny.

Broad, rounded, and covered over with thick forests, the Laramie, Medicine Bow, and Sierra Madre ranges seem bland compared with the craggy heights of Wyoming's Wind River or Teton ranges. But there are some pleasant surprises. Odd granite formations crop up in the rolling meadow and forest country of the Laramie Range, and the road across the Medicine Bows climbs above 10,000 feet and jollies along through an open subalpine landscape studded with glacially carved cirques. Perhaps best of all, these mountains draw significantly fewer visitors than those to the northwest, so it's easier to find a private corner of them.

From Cheyenne, Route 210 runs west across the prairie. This road, like the interstate and the railroad, climbs a gentle ramp of gravel and other debris that eroded from the mountains during the last 60 million years. Called the **Gangplank,** it stretches from the plains to the top of the Laramie Range in one long, fairly consistent pitch. Soon the road passes into forested hills and begins to cross the Laramie Range on a broad, rolling plateau. Stretches of open grassland reach off between belts of ponderosa-pine forest. Ravines and gullies cut down into steep valleys. Large hills of granite, overgrown with pine and juniper, rise from the meadows. Oddly shaped hunks of pink granite seem to sprout everywhere. Smooth-sided boulders with rounded corners dot the meadows, and jumbled piles and columns of the same rise over the treetops. The weird appearance of these rocks has inspired many theories, and one of the best clusters is even named Devil's Playground. But they are just chunks of extremely old granite (1.4 billion years) that weathers and fractures easily.

With its mix of open grassland, protective forest, and abundant water, the area makes a fine home for elk and deer. Forest Roads 700, 701, and 707 lead off Route 210, and there are several good trails through the area. A great place for mountain-biking and day hiking, it is also heavily used by off-road vehicles (ORVs).

Route 210 soon connects with I-80 and bombs down the steep side of the mountains into Laramie, where we pick up Route 130 and follow it across the Laramie Plains to the town of Centennial. Scattered sections of the **Routt/Medicine Bow National Forest❖** appear throughout eastern Wyoming, but the heart of the forest and perhaps the best of its country lies just ahead in the Medicine Bow and Sierra Madre mountains. The Medicine Bows are also called the Snowy Range because of the large outcroppings of white quartzite at the crest of some peaks.

A number of the mountains rise well above timberline, and their cliffs tower over dozens of deep glacial lakes. Both ranges collect deep snow every winter and remain snowcapped much of the summer (roads often stay closed through mid-June). Much of the country is densely forested with aspen, lodgepole pine, Douglas fir, and, in the higher elevations, Engelmann spruce and subalpine fir. Wildflowers clog the high country meadows during midsummer. The mountains provide habitat for black bears, bighorn sheep, elk, deer, mountain lions, and legions of smaller mammals and birds.

From Centennial, Route 130 climbs through layers of forest and emerges above timberline in a realm of high cliffs, boulder fields, small lakes, broad meadows, and thickets of stunted trees. Backpackers often hike days to reach such country. Though easily visited here, it is not an easy place to live. Few animals spend the whole year, and plants have had to adapt to an extremely short growing season and the drying effects of both wind and intense sunlight. High-country plants can photosynthesize at very low temperatures. Some, like the glacier lily, grow right through the snow in springtime. Others sport a waxy covering to conserve moisture or grow fuzz on leaves and stems to diffuse the sun's rays. In the highest reaches, the plant community is supremely fragile. A new plant might take as long as 25 years to gather enough energy to flower and reproduce.

Route 130 runs beneath Medicine Bow Peak, elevation 12,013 feet, and tops out at Snowy Range Pass, elevation 10,847 feet. Then it tilts back down through the forest and drops into the semidesert hills of the Saratoga Valley. Four small wilderness areas are easily accessible from the southern end of the valley. The **Platte River** and **Savage Run** wildernesses lie among the foothills of the Medicine Bows. The **Huston Park** and **Encampment River** wildernesses are in the Sierra Madres, south of the small town of Encampment. None of the areas are large enough for extended backcountry travel.

The Platte River Wilderness, just 36 square miles, protects the wild country of the river's **North Gate Canyon** near the Colorado border. Here, the North Platte careens through narrow gorges with rock towers 100 feet high and passes beneath high, arid hills. A foot trail leads downriver for several miles from the **Six Mile Gap Campground.** The Savage Run Wilderness, 23 square miles, includes steep-sided canyons and high, rolling plateaus. A trail follows Savage Run Creek for nine miles.

Huston Park Wilderness comprises 48 square miles of forested high

ABOVE: *Among the very first alpine flowers to appear each spring, glacier lilies blossom in soils soaked by freshly melted snow.*

RIGHT: *Cliffs of two-billion-year-old quartzite rise 1,000 feet over Maries Lake in the Medicine Bow Range; dwarfed subalpine fir trees grow along the shoreline.*

country in the Sierra Madre. Elevations reach 10,500 feet, and a primitive trail marked with rock cairns and tree blazes runs through it. The Encampment River Wilderness, 12 square miles, covers a narrow corridor along the Encampment River. A small herd of bighorn sheep live here.

From Encampment, follow Route 70 over the last of the three mountain ranges of southeastern Wyoming—the Sierra Madres. Around the turn of the century, miners hoped to strike it rich here. Their efforts turned up a lot of dirt and stone, but little paying ore. Evidence of their labors remains in the hills around Battle Pass, elevation 9,915 feet. Another high-country tour, the road leads through mountains a shade less spectacular than the Medicine Bows and is not paved for about 25 miles. After topping the Sierra Madre, the route drops into the desert country of the Washakie Basin and heads north from the town of Baggs on Route 789 into the Great Divide Basin.

THE DESERTS: FROM RAWLINS TO FARSON

Topping the Continental Divide, about a dozen miles south of Creston Junction, visitors catch their first glimpse of Wyoming's desert core and begin a long descent onto a very wide, very flat plain of grass, sagebrush, and small rock outcroppings. This is the southern perimeter of the **Great Divide Basin❖,** an enormous depression that lies at the heart of the state's desert lands. In the distance ahead, two small mountain ranges mark its northern perimeter. They are the **Green Mountains❖,** straight ahead, and the **Ferris Mountains Wilderness Study Area❖,** to

the right. The Continental Divide encircles the basin, running like the rim of an irregularly shaped bowl from Rawlins most of the way to Rock Springs. This topographical curiosity dictates that the pitifully small amount of moisture that falls here drains back into the basin rather than into the Atlantic or Pacific watersheds.

Wyoming's desert extends west from Rawlins to the Green River Valley and north from Colorado to the Green and Ferris mountains. Its vast, skin-puckering territory is given over to sagebrush flats and rim-rocked plateaus, sand dunes and crumbling hillsides, parched river bottoms and dried-up lakebeds. Many people have trouble generating any interest in, much less affection for, this desiccated landscape. They speed through on I-80, giving the desert only a passing glance and perhaps a shudder before steering northwest for Yellowstone.

That's too bad. The desert is a place of great, if unconventional, beauty. The vistas extend forever over a colorful bed of soils that vary among gray, yellow, red, olive, and brown. And the hills, plateaus, and ridgelines have been knocked apart into rugged and interesting shapes largely unobscured by vegetation. The setting is especially beautiful at dawn or dusk, when the angle of light lengthens the shadows, defining every crack in the ground and amplifying the rich colors of rock and soil. Anyone who has seen the twisted form of a juniper growing from a red sandstone cliff at sunset knows how beautiful the desert can be. And anyone who has strolled through a sagebrush flat in the springtime and seen the various types of grasses, the flowering plants, and the blooming cacti knows that the supposed monotony of the desert landscape is a mirage.

Though it can be fascinating, much of the desert's appeal lies hidden beneath the surface or camouflaged among the brush. Many of its unusual animals, for example, live close to the ground or under it and rarely venture out before dark. Those who may never see an Ord's kangaroo rat or a burrowing owl develop an appreciation for the unseen when they learn that the former can hear the air-pressure wave preceding the strike of a rattlesnake and that the latter scares off intruders by mimicking the sound of a rattlesnake's rattle. Similarly, many of the desert's plants at first seem drab and hostile, especially when viewed en masse from the highway. On closer inspection, they reveal remarkable adaptations to their environment.

The desert is, of course, a very dry place. Most of the land receives less than ten inches of precipitation each year, and what does fall tends to evaporate quickly because of the strong winds, high summer temperatures, and intense sunlight. Even in the winter, when temperatures reach well below zero, much of the moisture from snowfall is lost through sublimation (the passage of water directly from solid to vapor). Many plants adapt to the harsh conditions with light-colored, fuzzy leaves that diffuse sunlight. Some, like the sagebrush, sink deep taproots to draw water from moist low-lying soils. Others, like the prickly pear cactus, spread roots close to the surface so they can quickly absorb any trace of moisture. The prickly pear also stores its water in thick-coated, succulent pads covered by sharp barbs that ward off grazers.

Survival here is a challenge for animals too, but many, including big game animals, do quite well. Scattered throughout the desert are pronghorn and mule deer, as well as the state's only herd of desert elk and about 400 wild horses. These grazers feed on grasses, forbs, and various shrubs, including sagebrush. They find cover in dry gulches and depressions and in the lee of the larger plants. Here and there, water bubbles to the surface from springs. Among the sand dunes, snow melts into pools that last the summer. And rainstorms in the early spring fill some of the depressions. White-tailed prairie dogs, Wyoming ground squirrels, kangaroo rats, and other rodents proliferate on the desert floor, providing food for badgers, long-tailed weasels, and the many raptors that ply the skies. Other predators include mountain lions, bobcats, coyotes, and red foxes.

Although much of the desert territory is remote and unpopulated, there are many signs of intense human use. Oil and gas wells dot the basins and hills, and the network of roads built to serve them runs nearly everywhere. Pipelines and power lines crisscross the horizons, and large flocks of sheep and some cattle graze among the sagebrush. Still, this vast and wild landscape is well worth the time to explore.

Our route from Creston Junction heads west on I-80 along the southern fringe of the Great Divide Basin, then turns north at Rock Springs on Route 191 to Farson. Along the way, several dirt roads lead off into the desert. All are suitable for short excursions, but trips of more than a couple of miles are not recommended without good maps, water, and a vehicle made for rugged terrain. A small amount of moisture can transform even the main roads into tremendously slick, virtually impassable sur-

faces. Maps and advice are available at Bureau of Land Management offices in Rawlins and Rock Springs.

One interesting area is **Red Lake❖**, a large dry lakebed about 30 miles north of the town of Table Rock. Sand dunes up to 200 feet high surround it, and bobcats hunt desert cottontails and other small mammals nearby.

Another site worth visiting is **Adobe Town Wilderness Study Area❖**, south of Bitter Creek, which sprawls across a high desert landscape deeply eroded by wind and water into colorfully banded cliffs, haystacks, and buttes. These formations tower over canyons, draws, gulches, and other gashes in the ground.

East of Farson, the **Killpecker Sand Dunes❖** billow across a broad basin within view of the Wind River Mountains. They are part of a band of scattered dune fields extending from Wyoming's Eden Valley all the way to Nebraska, and many dunes are 200 feet high.

ABOVE: *Named for the buff feathers on their head and neck, golden eagles were slaughtered by the thousands in the 1950s by sheep ranchers, despite little evidence of livestock depredation.*

LEFT: *Wind and water acting on soft sandstone and clay stone have produced a spectacular, tortuous landscape at Hell's Half Acre, a chasm of badlands between Casper and Shoshoni.*

Partly visible to the south from the South Pass area (take Route 28 northeast from Farson), the **Oregon Buttes❖** and **Honeycomb Buttes❖** represent outstanding badlands topography. Layers of green, yellow, red, gray, and white sedimentary rock are exposed on their flanks. They rise from low sagebrush flats and reach 8,431 feet at the summit of Continental Peak.

THE CENTRAL PLAINS: FROM FARSON NORTHEAST TO BUFFALO

Route 28 northeast from Farson threads an escalating path between the southern front of the Wind River Mountains and the northern rim of the Great Divide Basin. Broad vistas of the desert appear as the road climbs toward **South Pass,** a droop in the spine of the Rockies that allowed nineteenth-century emigrants to pass through the mountains with relative ease. The pass was the linchpin of the Oregon Trail, which our route traces across the central plains of Wyoming to Casper.

Route 28 climbs farther into the mountains, passing the nearly abandoned gold-mining towns of South Pass City and Atlantic City. It also affords a full view of an open-pit mine where U.S. Steel stripped the mountains for taconite (low-grade iron ore) until 1983. The long descent toward Lander unfolds a more attractive panorama—**Red Canyon❖,** a spectacular embankment of vermilion sandstone.

Several miles south of Lander, take Route 287 east through another set of red-rock cliffs that burst from the olive-drab hillsides. It climbs out of the **Beaver Creek Valley** onto a high badlands escarpment called **Beaver Rim❖.** Visible to the north is the cleft in the Owl Creek Mountains where the Wind River runs into the Bighorn Basin. To the west, there's a grand view of the Wind River Mountains, and straight ahead are the Green and Ferris mountains.

Soon the road tops out in the Sweetwater Valley, a classic high plains landscape with plenty of space, sagebrush, and pronghorn. Closer to the Green and Ferris mountains, bulges of coarse granite appear north of the highway. The **Sweetwater Rocks,** a large expanse of decomposing granite, extend for about 20 miles along the Sweetwater River. Some of the formations were important landmarks on the Oregon Trail: **Split Rock, Devils Gate,** and **Independence Rock** (about ten miles east of Split Rock, turn northeast on Route 220). Also called the Granite Mountains, these humps of stone are the summits of a buried mountain range as spectacular as the Wind River Mountains. Like most of Wyoming's peaks, these rose about 70 million years ago during the Laramide orogeny, a period of mountain building. And like most of Wyoming, they were buried by various sedimentary formations in the millions of years that followed. However, the other mountains were washed clean of their sediments during another period of uplift two to three million years ago, whereas the Sweetwater Hills retained their sedimentary cover. Geologists say the landscape here closely resembles much of Wyoming two million years ago.

A few miles beyond Independence Rock, Route 220 passes an arm of the **Pathfinder Reservoir❖,** one of three impoundments of the North Platte River southwest of Casper. The other two are the **Seminoe Reservoir❖** and the **Alcova Reservoir❖.** To human eyes, Pathfinder—a broad sheet of water among dreary heaps of gravel—seems as dull a body of water as one can find in the West. Seminoe, on the other hand, sprawls at the foot of steep-sided mountains, sand dunes, and immense red hills, while Alcova glimmers beneath a spectacular band of red-rock cliffs. All three provide important nesting and feeding areas for waterfowl and shorebirds. One of the islands in the Pathfinder Reservoir houses a breeding colony of American white pelicans, one of just eight such colonies in the West. Pelicans can be seen on all the reservoirs, as can common loons, western grebes, green-winged teal, ducks, great blue herons, cormorants, and egrets. A loop road starting at the town of Alcova makes a pleasant tour of the area. Before reconnecting with Route 220 near Pathfinder dam, it crosses **Fremont Canyon❖,** a stunning little gorge with vertical cliffs about 75 feet high.

From Alcova, Route 220 crosses a broad plain and drops down to the banks of the North Platte River, which it follows to Casper. Soon the northern spur of the Laramie Mountains appears. On the approach to Casper, a wildlife-viewing sign marks **Jackson Canyon❖,** a good place to look for eagles during the winter. From Casper, a western detour of 40 miles on Route 26 leads to **Hell's Half Acre,** a broad chasm of prickly badlands cut into the ground by wind and rain. Greenish shales, red, pink, and yellow clay stone and sandstone offer heartbreaking vistas at sunset.

Back at Casper, I-25 heads north into the Powder River Basin through rough, broken country. To the east, hundreds of watercourses—dry most of the year—have cut the land into small mesas, gullies, ravines, and gulches. About 20 miles north of Casper, Route 259 dips through the Salt Creek Field, Wyoming's most productive oil field. Beyond the town of Midwest, I-25 jogs to the west and soon enters the foothills of the Bighorn Mountains, which form the western boundary of the Powder River Basin and include one of the highest summits in Wyoming—**Cloud Peak,** elevation 13,166 feet.

At Kaycee, Route 190 turns southwest and follows the course of the **Middle Fork of the Powder River** into one of the Bighorn Range's most beautiful areas. It includes the **Red Wall,** a high red cliff that faces

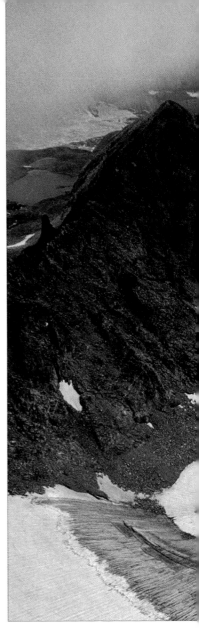

RIGHT: *In the Bighorn Mountains, a series of cascading glacial lakes slip away from the summit of Cloud Peak. The gritty, semicircular icefield clinging to the cliffs above the highest lake is Cloud Peak Glacier.*

west and extends about 20 miles from north to south. Route 190 leads to the **Middle Fork Recreation Area❖** and the **Outlaw Cave Campgrounds**. There, one can look back at the Red Wall and pick out **Hole-in-the-Wall❖,** a famous keyhole in the cliffs that sheltered outlaws around the turn of the century. The campgrounds also overlook **Middle Fork Canyon,** a steep-walled chasm up to 1,000 feet deep. Nearby is the **Bar C Cairn Line,** a prehistoric alignment of stone cairns three quarters of a mile long that marks the best route westward. The Bureau of Land Management office in Buffalo publishes a free guide to the area. From Buffalo, visitors can either return east to the Devils Tower area on I-90 or drive west into the Bighorn Basin on Route 16.

In the Northern Rockies, the mountains tell the big story. The peaks define the region. They set it apart, both aesthetically and physically from the rest of the United States and even from other regions in the mountainous West. The high country draws the eye and the imagination to the crags, the snowfields, and the wildflower meadows where bighorn sheep munch on purple lupine, and pikas stack grass like so many tiny ranchers in a Tolkien fantasy. But the Northern Rockies embrace much more than mountains. Here, too, are spectacular rivers, both thundering and placid, im-

mense crystalline lakes, colorful desert badlands, canyons, prairies, caves, and hot springs—all populated by some of the most exotic animals found anywhere in the world. The roads of Wyoming, Idaho, and Montana open this fabulously rich and varied landscape to those with a bit of time on their hands and an urge to wander beating in their hearts. It's a good place to roll down the window and let your hand wing along on the passing wind.

FURTHER READING ABOUT THE NORTHERN ROCKIES

ALT, DAVID, AND DONALD HYNDMAN. *Roadside Geology of Montana.* Missoula, MT: Mountain Press, 1986. Part of a very useful series for anyone interested in the shape of the land; volumes also available for Idaho and Wyoming from same publisher.

ARNO, STEPHEN F., AND RAMONA P. HAMMERLY. *Northwest Trees.* Seattle: The Mountaineers, 1977. More than an identification guide, this book offers incisive details about how trees adapt to climate and soil conditions and how they have been used by animals and humans.

BENYUS, JANINE M. *The Field Guide to Wildlife Habitats of the Western United States.* New York: Simon and Schuster, 1989. Terrific thumbnail sketches of the major wildlife habitats west of the Mississippi.

BROWN, LAUREN. *Grasslands.* New York: Knopf, 1985. A comprehensive field guide to the plants and animals of the Great Plains.

CARRIGHAR, SALLY. *One Day at Teton Marsh.* New York: Ballantine Books, 1972. A natural history classic describing the rhythms of life at the base of the Teton range.

CONLEY, CORT. *Idaho for the Curious.* Cambridge, ID: Backeddy Books, 1982. 1982. A hefty, engagingly written tome that leaves out no corner or backroad of a surprisingly diverse state; however, some descriptions are outdated.

DOIG, IVAN. *This House of Sky.* New York: Harcourt, Brace, Jovanovich, 1978. The autobiographical story of a Montana boyhood.

EHRLICH, PAUL, DAVID DOBKIN, AND DARRYL WHEYE. *The Birder's Handbook.* New York: Fireside Books, 1988. This book supplies the natural history information about birds that identification guides omit; both encyclopedic and entertaining.

FISCHER, CAROL, AND HANK FISCHER. *Montana Wildlife Viewing Guide.* Helena, MT: Falcon Press, 1990. A survey of wildlife viewing sites in Montana, part of a series that also covers other states in the region.

FRAZIER, IAN. *Great Plains.* New York: Farrar, Straus and Giroux, 1989. The author reveals fascinating details about the Great Plains and the life they support.

KITTREDGE, WILLIAM, AND ANNICK SMITH, EDS. *The Last Best Place: A Montana Anthology.* Helena: Montana Historical Society, 1988. Nearly 1,200 pages of selected stories and writing about Montana, from Native American times to the present.

LAVENDER, DAVID. *Let Me Be Free.* New York: Doubleday, 1992. An excellent history of the Nez Percé War of 1877.

———. *The Rockies.* Lincoln: University of Nebraska Press, 1981. The history of the Rocky Mountain region told primarily from the perspective of the mining industry.

SCHMIDT, JEREMY. *Adventuring in the Rockies.* San Francisco: Sierra Club Books, 1986 (rev. 1993). A guide to parks and wilderness areas in the

Rocky Mountains from New Mexico to northern Canada.

SCHMIDT, THOMAS, AND WIN BLEVINS. *History from the Highways: Wyoming.* Boulder, CO: Pruett, 1993. A guide to the early history of Wyoming, organized along driving routes.

SCHULLERY, PAUL. *Mountain Time.* New York: Schocken Books, 1984. The insightful and highly entertaining story of the author's years as a naturalist in Yellowstone National Park.

ABOVE: *The work of artists on early expeditions helped convince Congress to establish national parks. In 1871 William H. Jackson photographed painter Thomas Moran at Yellowstone's Mammoth Terraces.*

GLOSSARY

'a'a rough, broken lava

anticline stratified rock inclining downward in an arch

aquifer layer of rock, sand, or gravel through which groundwater received from rain or melted snow moves

arête sharp-crested ridge

badland barren, arid area in which soft rock strata are eroded into varied, fantastic forms

batholith large mass of igneous rock that has melted into surrounding strata and lies a great distance below the earth's surface

butte tall, steep-sided tower of rock formed from an eroded plateau; buttes delay inevitable erosional changes because of their hard uppermost layer of rock

caldera crater with a diameter many times that of the vent, formed by the collapse of a volcano's center

cinder cone cone-shaped hill formed from the accumulation of charred lava that builds up around the vent of a volcano

cirque large, bowl-shaped depression in a mountain hollowed by glacial movement

conifer cone-bearing tree of the pine family; usually evergreen

coulee deep ravine, usually dry, worn away by running water

crater bowl-shaped depression or indented area produced by a volcanic expulsion of material from inside the volcano, or by the impact of a meteorite

delta alluvial deposit, often triangular (named for the Greek letter delta), that forms at river mouths or tidal inlets

escarpment cliff or steep rock face, formed by faulting or fracturing of the earth's crust, that separates two comparatively level land surfaces

forb herb other than grass, especially one growing on a prairie or meadow

hoodoo natural column of rock often formed into fantastic shapes; volcanic intrusions found in western North America

horn mountain peak carved by a glacier on three or more sides

hot spring issue of water from the earth that has been heated by the geothermal energy of heated rocks below the earth's surface

kipuka island of vegetation on old lava not overwhelmed by more recent flow; biologically significant

lava tube tunnel formed when the upper crust of a lava flow cools and solidifies, and the molten lava below flows out

magma molten rock material within the earth that becomes igneous rock when it cools

mesa isolated, relatively flat-topped natural elevation more extensive than a butte and less extensive than a plateau

moraine debris (rock, sand, gravel, silt, and clay) carried by a glacier and left along its sides or terminus wherever it pauses or retreats

pahoehoe smooth, satiny, unbroken type of lava

petroglyph carving on rock, especially one made by prehistoric people

pictograph prehistoric painting or drawing on rock created with natural pigments applied with animal-hair brushes

rapids broken, fast-flowing water that tumbles around boulders; classified from I to VI according to increasing difficulty of watercraft navigation

riparian relating to the bank of a natural watercourse, lake, or tidewater

sagebrush North American pale-colored shrub; has a bitter juice and and an odor resembling sage; found on alkaline plains throughout the western U.S.

scarp line of steep cliffs formed by erosion

sedimentary rocks formed from deposits of small eroded debris such as gravel, sand, mud, silt, or peat

sierra high mountain range with jagged, knife-like ridges carved by glaciers (from the Spanish word for saw)

spatter cone cone-shaped formation made of ejected clots of lava built up on the vent of a volcano

subalpine forest upper limit of trees on a mountain; a zone of transition in which conifers decrease in size and number as elevation increases and temperature drops

talus accumulated rock debris at the base of a cliff

tectonic referring to the deformation of the earth's crust, the forces involved, and the resulting formations

timberline boundary that marks the upper limit of forest growth on a mountain or in high latitudes; beyond the boundary, temperatures are too cold to support tree growth; also called the tree line

travertine mineral formed by deposition from spring waters or hot springs, forming (among other deposits) stalactites and stalagmites

tundra treeless region of arctic, subarctic, or alpine regions dominated by lichens, mosses, and low-growing vascular plants

wetland area of land covered or saturated with groundwater; includes swamps, marshes, and bogs

LAND MANAGEMENT RESOURCES

The following public and private organizations are among the important administrators of the preserved and protected areas described in this volume. Brief explanations of the various legal and legislative designations of these areas follow.

MANAGING ORGANIZATIONS

Bureau of Land Management (BLM) Department of the Interior

Administers nearly half of all federal lands, some 272 million acres predominantly in the western states. Resources are managed for multiple uses: recreation, grazing, logging, mining, fish and wildlife, and watershed and wilderness preservation.

Bureau of Reclamation (BR) Department of the Interior

Created by the Reclamation Act of 1902 to revive arid lands in the 17 western states. Projects provide irrigation to more than 10 million acres, municipal and industrial water, hydroelectric power, recreational facilities, and fish and wildlife enhancement.

Idaho Department of Parks and Recreation

Manages 23 state parks. Registers boats, off-road vehicles, and snowmobiles, and administers state recreation areas, boating docks, and trails.

Idaho Fish and Game Department

Responsible for preservation, protection, and management of all wildlife areas within Idaho. Maintains state hunting and fishing areas and licenses.

Montana Department of Fish, Wildlife and Parks

Administers and maintains state parks, wildlife areas, and fisheries. Responsible for hunting and fishing licensing. Includes Division of Conservation Education and Division of Resource Management.

National Park Service (NPS) Department of the Interior

Regulates the use of national parks, monuments, and preserves. Resources are managed to preserve and protect landscape, natural and historic artifacts, and wildlife. Also administers historic and national landmarks, national seashores, wild and scenic rivers, and the national trail system.

U.S. Fish and Wildlife Service (USFWS) Department of the Interior

Principal federal agency responsible for conserving, protecting, and enhancing the country's fish and wildlife and their habitats. Manages national wildlife refuges and fish hatcheries as well as programs for migratory birds and endangered and threatened species.

U.S. Forest Service (USFS) Department of Agriculture

Administers more than 190 million acres in the national forests and national grasslands and is responsible for the management of their resources. Determines how best to combine commercial uses such as grazing, mining, and logging with conservation needs.

Wyoming Game and Fish Department

Conserves and enhances state wildlife and fisheries. Maintains more than 160,000 acres of wildlife management areas, regulates hunting and fishing licenses, and protects and studies state's endangered species.

Wyoming State Parks and Historic Sites

Administers the state parks, state recreation areas, historic sites, petroglyph sites, archaeological sites, markers and monuments, snowmobile program, and state trails program. Part of state Department of Commerce.

DESIGNATIONS

Archaeological Site
Area of significant archaeological interest and resources that may contribute to the study of prehistory. Managed by BLM or individual states.

National Backcountry Byway
Dirt or gravel road designated for its scenic, geologic, or historic attributes. Mainly for sightseeing and recreation via automobile. Managed by BLM.

National Conservation Area
Area set aside by Congress to protect specific environments. Rules for use of land are less restrictive than those in wilderness areas. Managed by BLM.

National Forest
Large acreage managed for the use of forests, watersheds, wildlife, and recreation by the public and private sectors. Managed by USFS.

National Grasslands
Federal land where more than 80 percent of the canopy cover is dominated by grasses or grasslike plants. May encompass private holdings. Managed by USFS.

National Historic Site
Land area, building, or object preserved because of its national historic significance. Managed by NPS.

National Monument
Nationally significant landmark, structure, object, or area of scientific or historic significance. Managed by NPS.

National Natural Landmark
Nationally significant natural area that is a prime example of a biotic community or a particular geologic feature. Managed by NPS.

National Park
Spacious primitive or wilderness area with scenery and natural wonders so outstanding it has been preserved by the federal government. Managed by NPS.

National Recreation Area
Natural area designated for recreation; hunting, fishing, camping and limited use of power boats, dirt and mountain bikes, and ATVs permitted. Managed by NPS.

National Wildlife Refuge
Public land set aside for wild animals; protects migratory waterfowl, endangered and threatened species, and native plants. Managed by USFWS.

Wild and Scenic River System
National program to preserve selected rivers in their natural free-flowing condition; stretches are classified as wild, scenic, or recreational. Also develops hydropower projects. Management shared by BLM, NPS, and USFWS.

Wilderness Area
An area that by law must retain its primeval character and influence, without permanent improvements or human habitation. Recreational use is permitted (hiking, primitive camping, horseback riding), subject to regulation. Designation was created by the Wilderness Act of 1964. Managed by BLM.

Wildlife Habitat Management Unit
State land managed to protect wildlife. Aside from seasonal restrictions, hunting, fishing, and public access are allowed. Managed by individual states.

Wildlife Management Area
Natural area owned, protected, and maintained for recreation; hunting, fishing, trapping, and cross-country skiing permitted. Managed by individual states.

NATURE TRAVEL

The following is a selection of national and local organizations that sponsor nature-related travel activities or can provide specialized regional travel information.

NATIONAL

National Audubon Society
700 Broadway
New York, NY 10003
(212) 979-3000
Offers a wide range of ecological field studies, tours, and cruises throughout the United States

National Wildlife Federation
1400 16th Street N.W.
Washington D.C. 20036
(703) 790-4363
Offers training in environmental education for all ages, wildlife camp and teen adventures, conservation summits involving nature walks, field trips, and classes

The Nature Conservancy
1815 North Lynn Street
Arlington, VA 22209
(703) 841-5300
Offers a variety of excursions based out of regional and state offices. May include hiking, backpacking, canoeing, horseback riding. Contact above number to locate state offices

Sierra Club Outings
730 Polk Street
San Francisco, CA 94109
(415) 923-5630
Offers tours of different lengths for all ages throughout the United States. Outings may include backpacking, hiking, biking, skiing, and water excursions

Smithsonian Study Tours and Seminars
1100 Jefferson Dr. SW
MRC 702
Washington D.C. 20560
(202) 357-4700
Offers extended tours, cruises, research expeditions, and seminars throughout the United States

REGIONAL

Idaho Travel Council
700 West State St.
Boise, ID 83720
(208) 334-2470
Publishes and distributes annual guidebooks containing information on transportation, recreation, and accomodations. Also answers specific travel and lodging questions

Travel Montana
PO Box 200533
Helena, MT 59620
(800) VISITMT [847-4868]
Offers free vacation planning kits containing maps and information on transportation, recreation, and accommodations. Operators can also answer specific vacation planning questions

Wyoming Division of Tourism
I-25 at College Drive
Cheyenne, WY 82002
(800) 225-5996
Offers general information about Wyoming, Yellowstone National Park, Grand Teton National Park, all state parks and historic sites, travel, and accommodations

How To Use This Site Guide

The following site information guide will assist you in planning your tour of the natural areas of Idaho, Montana, and Wyoming. Sites set in boldface and followed by the symbol ❖ in the text are here organized alphabetically by state. Each entry is followed by the mailing address (sometimes different from the street address) and phone number of the immediate managing office, plus brief notes and a list of facilities and activities available. (A key appears on each page.)

Information on hours of operation, seasonal closings, and fees is not listed, as these vary from season to season and year to year. Please also bear in mind that responsibility for the management of some sites may change. Call well in advance to obtain maps, brochures, and pertinent, up-to-date information that will help you plan your adventures in the Northern Rockies.

Each site entry in the guide includes the address and phone number of its immediate managing agency. Many of these sites are under the stewardship of a forest or park ranger or supervised from a small nearby office. Hence, in many cases, those sites will be difficult to contact directly, and it is preferable to call the managing agency.

The following umbrella organizations can provide general information for individual natural sites, as well as the area as a whole:

IDAHO

Bureau of Land Management
3380 Americana Terrace
Boise, ID 83706
(208) 384-3000

Idaho Department of Parks and Recreation
7800 Fairview Ave.
Boise, ID 83704
(208) 327-7407

Idaho Fish and Game Department
600 S. Walnut St.
Box 25
Boise, ID 83707
(208) 334-3700

Idaho Travel Council
700 West State St.
Boise, ID 83720
(208) 334-2470

MONTANA

Bureau of Land Management
222 N. 32nd St.
Box 36800
Billings, MT 59107
(406) 255-2904

Montana Department of Fish, Wildlife and Parks
1420 East Sixth Ave.
Helena, MT 59620
(406) 444-2535

Travel Montana
PO Box 200533
Helena, MT 59620
(800) VISITMT

U.S. Fish and Wildlife Service
100 N. Park, Ste. 320
Helena, MT 59601
(406) 449-5225

WYOMING

Bureau of Land Management
2515 Warren Ave.
Cheyenne, WY 82001
(307) 775-6256

Wyoming Division of Tourism
I-25 at College Drive
Cheyenne, WY 82002
(800) 225-5996

Wyoming Game and Fish Department
5400 Bishop Blvd.
Cheyenne, WY 82006
(307) 777-4600

Wyoming State Parks and Historic Sites
2301 Central Ave.
Barrett Building
Cheyenne, WY 82002
(307) 777-6323

IDAHO

BEAR LAKE NATIONAL WILDLIFE REFUGE
U.S. Fish and Wildlife Service
PO 9, Montpelier, ID 83254
(208) 847-1757   **BW, CK, F, H, I, XC**

BOISE NATIONAL FOREST
U.S. Forest Service
1750 Front St., Boise, ID 83702
(208) 364-4100
Includes North and South Fork of the
Payette River, part of the Idaho
batholith, and Kirkham Hot Springs
    BT, BW, C, CK, F, H, HR,
    I, MT, PA, RC, S, T, XC

BRUNEAU CANYON
Bureau of Land Management, Boise District
3948 Development Ave.
Boise, ID 83705
(208) 384-3300
Very difficult access, no maintained trails
    C, H

BRUNEAU DUNES STATE PARK
Idaho Department of Parks and
Recreation
Star Route Box 41
Mountain Home, ID 83647
(208) 366-7919   **BW, C, CK, F, GS, H,**
    HR, I, MT, PA, RA, T

**C. J. STRIKE WILDLIFE
MANAGEMENT AREA**
Idaho Fish and Game Department
SW Region
3101 South Powerline Rd.
Nampa, ID 83686
(208) 887-6729   **BW, C, CK, F,**
    H, I, MT, PA, S, T

CAMAS NATIONAL WILDLIFE REFUGE
U.S. Fish and Wildlife Service
2150 E. 2340 N.
Hamer, ID 83425
(208) 662-5423   **BW, H, I, XC**

CARIBOU NATIONAL FOREST
U.S. Forest Service
250 South Fourth Avenue
Pocatello, ID 83201
(208) 236-7500
Includes St. Charles Canyon and
Minnetonka Cave; stop at Forest offices

in Montpelier, Pocatello, Malad, or Soda
Springs for information and a travel map
    BT, BW, C, DS, F, H, HR,
    I, MT, PA, RC, T, TG, XC

CHALLIS NATIONAL FOREST
U.S. Forest Service
HC 63, PO 1671
Challis, ID 83226
(208) 879-2285
Includes Lost River Range and the
Salmon River Mountains
    BT, BW, C, CK, F, H, HR,
    I, MT, PA, RC, S, T, TG, XC

CITY OF ROCKS NATIONAL RESERVE
Idaho Department of Parks
and Recreation
Box 169, Almo, ID 83312
(208) 824-5519   **BT, BW, C, GS, H, HR, I,**
    MT, PA, RA, RC, T

CLEARWATER NATIONAL FOREST
U.S. Forest Service
12730 Hwy 12
Orofino, ID 83544
(208) 476-4541
Includes Giant White Pine Campground,
North Fork of the Clearwater River,
Lochsa River   **BT, BW, C, CK, F, H, HR,**
    I, MT, PA, RC, S, T, XC

**CRATERS OF THE MOON
NATIONAL MONUMENT**
National Park Service
PO 29, Arco, ID 83213
(208) 527-3257
Windy and hot in summer; wear sturdy
shoes for hiking; loop road may be
closed in winter due to snow, but information center will be open
    BW, C, GS, H, I,
    MT, PA, RA, T, XC

DEER FLAT NATIONAL WILDLIFE REFUGE
U.S. Fish and Wildlife Service
13751 Upper Embankment Road
Nampa, ID 83686
(208) 888-5582   **BW, CK, F, H, HR,**
    I, MT, PA, RA, S, T, XC

DEVOTO MEMORIAL GROVE
Clearwater National Forest Headquarters
12730 Hwy 12
Orofino, ID 83544
(208) 476-4541   **F, H, I, MT, PA, T**

BT Bike Trails	**CK** Canoeing, Kayaking	**F** Fishing	**HR** Horseback Riding
BW Bird-watching	**DS** Downhill Skiing	**GS** Gift Shop	**I** Information Center
C Camping		**H** Hiking	

FARRAGUT STATE PARK
Idaho Department of Parks and Recreation
3400 Ranger Road, Athol, ID 83801
(208) 683-2425
Includes the Willow Picnic Area, campfire programs, guided hikes, small museum, radio controlled airplane flying field, boat ramp; make reservations for campgrounds **BT, BW, C, CK, F, H, HR, I, MT, PA, S, T, XC**

FRANK CHURCH–RIVER OF NO RETURN WILDERNESS
Payette National Forest
Krassel Ranger District
PO 1026, McCall, ID 83638
(208) 634-0600 **BW, C, CK, F, H, HR, RC, XC**

GIANT WHITE PINE CAMPGROUND
Clearwater National Forest
Palouse Ranger District
Potlatch, ID 83855
(208) 875-1131
Grounds maintained from mid-May to late September; available on a first-come, first-serve basis **BT, BW, C, H, HR, MT, PA, T, XC**

GOODING CITY OF ROCKS AND LITTLE CITY OF ROCKS
Bureau of Land Management
Shoshone District, PO 2-B
Shoshone, ID 83352
(208) 886-2206 **H**

GRAYS LAKE NATIONAL WILDLIFE REFUGE
U.S. Fish and Wildlife Service
74 Grays Lake Road
Wayan, ID 83285
(208) 574-2755
Refuge closed to public April 1–October 9, but can be viewed from surrounding county road; extreme winter climate conditions **BW, I**

GREAT RIFT NATIONAL NATURAL LANDMARK
Bureau of Land Management
Eastern Idaho Visitors Information Center
PO 50498, Idaho Falls, ID 83405-0498
(208) 523-1012; (800) 634-3246
Bring water, sturdy hiking boots, extra gas, 4WD vehicle. Includes Hell's Half Acre Natural Landmark **BW, C, H, I**

HARRIMAN STATE PARK
Idaho Department of Parks and Recreation
8 C66, 500, Island Park, ID 83429
(208) 558-7368
Includes dorm facilities for groups only **BT, BW, F, H, HR, I, MT, T, TG, XC**

HELLS CANYON NATIONAL RECREATION AREA
88401 Hwy 82
Enterprise, OR 97828
(503) 426-4978
Includes Hells Canyon Wilderness, Pittsburg Landing, Heaven's Gate Lookout, Seven Devils, Hells Canyon Dam **BT, BW, C, CK, DS, F, GS, H, HR, I, L, MT, PA, RC, RA, S, T, TG, XC**

HELL'S HALF ACRE NATURAL LANDMARK
Bureau of Land Management
Eastern Idaho Visitors Information Center
PO 50498
Idaho Falls, ID 83405-0498
(208) 523-1012; (800) 634-3246
Part of Great Rift National Natural Landmark **BW, C, H, MT, T**

HEYBURN STATE PARK
Idaho Department of Parks and Recreation
Rte. 1, Box 139
Plummer, ID 83851
(208) 686-1308
Borders on Coeur D'Alene Lake **BT, BW, C, CK, F, H, HR, MT, PA, RA, S, T**

IDAHO PANHANDLE NATIONAL FORESTS
U.S. Forest Service
1201 Ironwood Dr.
Coeur D'Alene, ID 83814
(208) 765-7223
A combination of three forests: Saint Joe, Coeur d'Alene, Kaniksu National Forests; borders of Coeur D'Alene Lake **BT, BW, C, CK, F, H, HR, I, MT, PA, S, T, TG, XC**

JEDEDIAH SMITH WILDERNESS
Targhee National Forest
Teton Basin Ranger District
PO 177
Driggs, ID 83422
(208) 354-2312
Includes caves to explore; must have WY license to fish **BW, C, DS, F, H, HR, I, MT, S, XC**

L	Lodging	**PA**	Picnic Areas	**RC**	Rock Climbing	**TG**	Tours, Guides
MT	Marked Trails	**RA**	Ranger-led Activities	**S**	Swimming	**XC**	Cross-country Skiing
				T	Toilets		

JERRY JOHNSON HOT SPRINGS
Clearwater National Forest
Powell Ranger Station
Lolo, MT 59847
(208) 942-3113   **BW, H, MT, S, XC**

LOCHSA RIVER
Clearwater National Forest Headquarters
12730 Hwy 12, Orofino, ID 83544
(208) 476-4541   **BW, C, CK, F, H,**
I, L, MT, PA, S, T

MALAD GORGE STATE PARK
Idaho Department of Parks and Recreation
1074 East, 2340 South
Hagerman, ID 83332
(208) 837-4504
Includes Niagara Springs, Crystal Springs
Lake; wear sturdy shoes, bring water
BT, BW, H, HR, MT, PA, RA, T, TG

MARKET LAKE WILDLIFE
MANAGEMENT AREA
Idaho Fish and Game Department
804 North 2900 E., Roberts, ID 83444
(208) 228-3131
Make reservations for group tours
BT, BW, CK, H, HR, I, T, XC

MASSACRE ROCKS STATE PARK
Idaho Department of Parks and Recreation
3592 N. Park Lane
American Falls, ID 83211
(208) 548-2672
BW, C, F, GS, H, I, MT, PA, RA, T

MESA FALLS SCENIC AREA
Targhee National Forest
Ashton Ranger District
Ashton, ID 83420
(208) 652-7442
BT, BW, C, CK, DS, F, GS, H, HR,
I, L, MT, PA, RA, RC, S, T, XC

MUD LAKE WILDLIFE
MANAGEMENT AREA
Idaho Fish and Game Department
1165 E. 1800 N., Terreton, ID 83450
(208) 663-4664
Make reservations for group tours
BW, C, CK, F, H, HR, PA, T, TG

NEZ PERCÉ NATIONAL HISTORIC PARK
National Park Service
PO 93, Spalding, ID 83551
(208) 843-2261

Includes Whitebird Canyon Battlefield,
Whitebird Summit, Selway River, Selway
Falls, museum with Nez Percé artifacts
in Spalding   **I, GS, H, MT, PA, RA, T**

NIAGARA SPRINGS
Malad Gorge State Park
1074 E. 2350 S.
Hagerman, ID 83332
(208) 837-4505   **BW, C, CK, F,**
PA, RA, T, XC

OWYHEE UPLANDS NATIONAL
BACKCOUNTRY BYWAY
Bureau of Land Management, Boise District
3948 Development Ave.
Boise, ID 83705
(208) 384-3300   **BW, C, F, H,**
HR, PA, T, XC

PONDEROSA STATE PARK
Idaho Department of Parks and Recreation
Box A
McCall, ID 83638
(208) 634-2164
Includes evening programs and guided
hikes; borders Payette Lake
BT, BW, C, CK, F, H,
I, MT, PA, RA, S, T, XC

PRIEST LAKE
National Forest Service
Priest Lake Ranger District
HCR 5, Box 207
Priest River, ID 83856
(208) 443-2512
Includes Roosevelt Grove of Ancient
Cedars and Granite Falls
BT, BW, C, CK, F, GS, H, HR,
I, L, MT, PA, RC, S, T, TG, XC

ROOSEVELT GROVE OF ANCIENT CEDARS
National Forest Service
Priest Lake Ranger District
HCR 5, Box 207
Priest River, ID 83856
(208) 443-2512
Includes Granite Falls   **B, H, MT, PA, T**

SALMON NATIONAL FOREST
U.S. Forest Service
Box 729
Salmon, ID 83467
(208) 756-2215
Includes Lemhi Range and Beaverhead
Mountains   **BT, BW, C, F, H, HR,**
I, MT, RC, S, T, XC

BT	Bike Trails	**CK**	Canoeing, Kayaking	**F**	Fishing	**HR**	Horseback Riding
BW	Bird-watching			**GS**	Gift Shop		
C	Camping	**DS**	Downhill Skiing	**H**	Hiking	**I**	Information Center

Sawtooth Fish Hatchery
Idaho Fish and Game Department
HC 64, Box 9905, Stanley, ID 83278
(208) 774-3684   I, T

Sawtooth National Forest
U.S. Forest Service Headquarters
2647 Kimberly Road E.
Twin Falls, ID 83301
(208) 737-3200
Includes Smoky Mountains
BT, BW, C, CK, F, H, HR, GS,
I, MT, PA, RA, RC, S, T, XC

**Sawtooth National
Recreational Area**
Sawtooth National Forest
Star Route North
Ketchum, ID 83340
(208) 774-3681
Includes Redfish Lake, Sawtooth
Wilderness Area, Sunbeam Hot Springs,
Boulder Mountains, Big Wood River,
Salmon River, White Cloud Peaks,
Sawtooth Valley
BT, BW, C, CK, F, GS, H, HR, I,
L, MT, PA, RA, RC, S, T, TG, XC

Selway-Bitterroot Wilderness
U.S. Forest Service
Route 2, Box 475
Grangeville, ID 83530
(208) 983-1950
Includes Selway River and Selway Falls;
group of 20 or more requires a permit
to enter
BW, C, CK, F, H, HR, I, MT, PA, S

**Snake River Birds of Prey
National Conservation Area**
Bureau of Land Management, Boise District
3948 Development Ave.
Boise, ID 83705-5389
(208) 384-3300   BT, BW, C, CK, F,
H, HR, PA, T, TG

Targhee National Forest
U.S. Forest Service
PO 208, St. Anthony, ID 83445
(208) 624-3151
Includes Island Park, Big Springs and Big
Springs National Water Trail: (208) 558-
7301; Mesa Falls Scenic Area, Upper and
Lower Mesa Falls: (208)652-7442
BT, BW, C, CK, DS, F, GS, H, HR,
I, L, MT, PA, RA, RC, S, T, XC

Montana

Absaroka-Beartooth Wilderness
Shoshone National Forest,
Clarks Fork Ranger District
1002 Road 11
Powell, WY 82435
Stay on trails, bald rock and alpine
tundra very fragile
(307) 754-7207   BW, C, F, H, HR,
MT, RC, XC

Anaconda-Pintler Wilderness Area
Bitterroot National Forest
1801 North 1st Street, Hamilton, MT 59840
(406) 363-7117   BW, C, F, H,
HR, MT, RC, XC

Bear Trap Canyon
Bureau of Land Management, Butte District
106 N. Parkmont, Butte, MT 59702
(406) 494-5059
BW, C, CK, F, H, MT, RC, T

Beaverhead National Forest
U.S. Forest Service
420 Barrett Street, Dillon, MT 59725
(406) 683-3900
Includes portions of the Anaconda-
Pintler Wilderness, Lee Metcalf
Wilderness, and Pioneer Mountains
Scenic Byway   BT, BW, C, CK, F, H,
HR, I, PA, RC, S, T, XC

**Benton Lake National
Wildlife Refuge**
U.S. Fish and Wildlife Service
PO 450, Black Eagle, MT 59414
(406) 727-7400   BW, T

Big Hole National Battlefield
National Park Service
PO 237, Wisdom, MT 59761
(406) 689-3155
BW, F, GS, H, I, MT, PA, RA, T, TG

Big Hole Valley
U.S. Forest Service
Wisdom Ranger District
PO 238, Wisdom, MT 59761
(406) 689-3243   BT, BW, C, F, GS,
H, HR, L, MT, PA, S, T, XC

**Bighorn Canyon
National Recreation Area**
(*See* Wyoming section
of Site Guide)

L	Lodging	**PA**	Picnic Areas	**RC**	Rock Climbing	**TG**	Tours, Guides
MT	Marked Trails	**RA**	Ranger-led Activities	**S**	Swimming	**XC**	Cross-country Skiing
				T	Toilets		

BITTERROOT NATIONAL FOREST
U.S. Forest Service
1801 N. 1st Street, Hamilton, MT 59840
(406) 363-7161   **BW, C, F, H, HR,**
MT, PA, RC, S, XC

BLACKLEAF WILDLIFE MANAGEMENT AREA
MT Dept. of Fish, Wildlife and Parks
4600 Giant Springs Rd., PO 6610
Great Falls, MT 59406
(406) 454-3441   **BW, H, MT, RC, XC**

BOB MARSHALL WILDERNESS
National Forest Service
1935 3rd Ave. E.
Kalispell, MT 59901
(406) 755-5401   **B, C, F, H, HR, MT, RC, S**

BOULDER MOUNTAINS
Deerlodge National Forest
Ranger District, PO 400, Butte, MT 59703
(406) 287-3223
Portions located in Helena National
Forest   **BT, BW, C, F, H, HR, MT, PA, T**

BOWDOIN NATIONAL WILDLIFE REFUGE
U.S. Fish and Wildlife Service
HC 65, PO 5700, Malta, MT 59538
(406) 654-2863   **BW, I, MT, XC**

CANYON FERRY LAKE
Bureau of Land Management
Canyon Ferry Project
7631 Canyon Ferry Road
Helena, MT 59601
(406) 475-3319   **BW, C, CK, F,**
H, I, PA, S, T

CHARLES M. RUSSELL NATIONAL WILDLIFE REFUGE
U.S. Fish and Wildlife Service
PO 110, Lewistown, MT 59457
(406) 538-8706   **BW, C, CK, F, H, HR**

CUSTER NATIONAL FOREST
U.S. Forest Service
PO 2556
Billings, MT 59103
(406) 657-6361   **BW, C, CK, DS, F, GS, H,**
HR, I, MT, PA, RC, S, T, XC

EARTHQUAKE LAKE
U.S. Forest Service
PO 520, West Yellowstone, MT 59758
(406) 646-7369
B, CK, F, GS, H, HR, I, L, MT, T, TG, XC

ELK ISLAND
MT Dept. of Fish, Wildlife and Parks
PO 1630, Miles City, MT 59301
(406) 232-4365
BW, C, CK, F, H, HR, PA, S, TG

FLATHEAD NATIONAL FOREST
U.S. Forest Service
1935 3rd Ave. E.
Kalispell, MT 59901
(406) 755-5401
Beware of grizzly bears and mountain
lions   **BT, BW, C, CK, DS, F, H,**
HR, I, L, MT, PA, RC, S, T, TG, XC

FREEZEOUT LAKE WILDLIFE MANAGEMENT AREA
MT Dept. of Fish, Wildlife and Parks
4600 Giant Springs Rd.
PO 6610
Great Falls, MT 59406
(406) 454-3441   **BW, C, CK, H, PA, T**

GALLATIN NATIONAL FOREST
U.S. Forest Service
PO 130
Bozeman, MT 59715
(406) 587-6747
Includes part of Absaroka-Beartooth
Wilderness   **BT, BW, C, CK, DS, F, H,**
HR, I, MT, PA, RC, T, XC

GATES OF THE MOUNTAINS WILDERNESS
Helena National Forest
PO 478
Helena, MT 59624
(406) 458-5241   **BW, C, CK, F, GS, H,**
I, MT, PA, S, T, TG

GLACIER NATIONAL PARK
National Park Service
Park Headquarters
West Glacier, MT 59936
(406) 888-5441
Includes scenic boat tours and Native
American programs
BW, C, CK, F, GS, H, HR, I,
MT, PA, RA, RC, S, T, TG, XC

GOLDEN SUNLIGHT MINE
453 Montana Hwy.,
2 EastWhite Hall
MT 59759
(406) 287-3257
Make tour reservations 24 hours in advance   **TG**

BT	Bike Trails	**CK**	Canoeing, Kayaking	**F**	Fishing	**HR**	Horseback Riding
BW	Bird-watching			**GS**	Gift Shop		
C	Camping	**DS**	Downhill Skiing	**H**	Hiking	**I**	Information Center

GRANT MARSH WILDLIFE MANAGEMENT AREA
MT Dept of Fish, Wildlife and Parks
2300 Lake Elmo Dr.
Billings, MT 59105
(406) 252-4654   **BW, C, CK, F, PA**

GREAT BEAR WILDERNESS
U.S. Forest Service
1935 3rd Ave. E.
Kalispell, MT 59001
(406) 755-5401   **BW, C, F, H, HR, MT, S**

HAILSTONE NATIONAL WILDLIFE REFUGE
U.S. Fish and Wildlife Service, PO 110
Lewistown, MT 59457
(406) 538-8706   **BW, H**

HEBGEN LAKE
U.S. Forest Service
PO Box 520
West Yellowstone, MT 59758
(406) 646-7369   **BW, CK, F, GS, H, HR,
I, L, MT, S, T, TG, XC**

HOWRY ISLAND
Bureau of Land Management
Powder River Resource Area
Miles City Plaza
Miles City, MT 59301
(406) 232-7000
    Access via car most of the year; day use;
    motorized vehicles prohibited to explore
    island; bring insect repellant
                   BW, CK, F, H, HR, PA, S

HUMBUG SPIRES PRIMITIVE AREA
Bureau of Land Management, Butte District
106 N. Parkmont
Butte, MT 59702
(406) 494-5059   **BW, C, F, H, HR,
I, RC, T, XC**

JAMES KIPP RECREATION AREA
Bureau of Land Management
1160 Airport Road
Lewistown, MT 59457
(406) 538-7461
                        **BW, C, CK, F, H,
HR, I, PA, S, T, XC**

JEWEL BASIN HIKING AREA
Flathead National Forest
1935 3rd Ave. E.
Kalispell, MT 59901
(406) 755-5401   **BW, C, F, H, MT, RC, XC**

KOOTENAI NATIONAL FOREST
U.S. Forest Service
Headquarters
506 US Hwy 2 West
Libby, MT 59923
(406) 293-6211
    Includes Cabinet Mountain Wilderness,
    Ten Lakes Scenic Area, Ross Creek
    Scenic Area, Kootenai Falls, Rocky Mtn.
    Trench, Lake Koocanusa, and the
    Whitefish Range
                        **BT, BW, C, CK, F, H,
HR, I, MT, PA, RC, S, T, TG, XC**

LEE METCALF NATIONAL WILDLIFE REFUGE
U.S. Fish and Wildlife Service
PO 257
Stevensville, MT 59870
(406) 777-5552   **BW, F, H, MT, PA, T**

LEE METCALF WILDERNESS AREA
Beaverhead National Forest
Gallatin Supervisor Area
10 E. Babcock Ave.
PO 130, Federal Bldg.
Bozeman, MT 59771
(406) 682-4253
    Bring bear-proof food containers
                  BW, C, F, H, HR, MT, RA, TG, XC

LEWIS AND CLARK CANYONS STATE PARK
Montana Department of Fish,
Wildlife, and Parks
PO 949
Three Forks, MT 59752
(406) 287-3541 (main office)
(406) 287-5424
(summer information number)
    Two-mile walking tour available; camp-
    ing cabins available   **BT, BW, C, CK,
F, GS, GT, H, I, MT, PA, RA, T**

LEWIS AND CLARK NATIONAL FOREST
U.S. Forest Service
PO 869
Great Falls, MT 59403
(406) 791-7700   **BT, BW, C, DS, F, H,
HR, I, L, MT, PA, S, T, XC**

LITTLE BIGHORN BATTLEFIELD NATIONAL MONUMENT
National Park Service
Box 39
Crow Agency, MT 59022
(406) 638-2621   **I, T, TG**

L	Lodging	**PA**	Picnic Areas	**RC**	Rock Climbing	**TG**	Tours, Guides
MT	Marked Trails	**RA**	Ranger-led Activities	**S**	Swimming	**XC**	Cross-country Skiing
				T	Toilets		

MADISON RIVER CANYON EARTHQUAKE AREA
U.S. Forest Service
PO 520, West Yellowstone, MT 59758
(406) 646-7369
Includes Cabin Creek Campground
BW, C, CK, F, H, HR, I, MT, PA, RC, S, T, XC

MAKOSHIKA STATE PARK
Montana Department of Fish,
Wildlife, and Parks
PO 1242, Glendive, MT 59330
(406) 365-6256   **BW, C, GS, H, I, MT, PA, T, TG, XC**

MEDICINE LAKE NATIONAL WILDLIFE REFUGE
U.S. Fish and Wildlife Service
223 N. Shore Road
Medicine Lake, MT 59247
(406) 789-2305
Noted for its pelicans and piping plovers; stop by refuge headquarters for information and regulations
BW, CK, F, H, HR, I, PA, T, XC

MEDICINE ROCKS STATE PARK
MT Dept. of Fish, Wildlife and Parks
PO 1630
Miles City, MT 59301
(406) 232-4365   **BW, C, H, HR, MT, PA, T, XC**

MISSION MOUNTAIN WILDERNESS
Flathead National Forest
1935 3rd Ave. E.
Kalispell, MT 59901
(406) 755-5401   **BW, C, F, H, HR, MT**

MISSOURI RIVER HEADWATERS STATE PARK
MT Dept. of Fish, Wildlife and Parks,
Bozeman Office
1400 S. 19th St.
Bozeman, MT 59715
(406) 994-4042   **BW, C, CK, F, H, MT, PA, T**

MOUNT HAGGIN WILDLIFE MANAGEMENT AREA
MT Dept. of Fish, Wildlife and Parks
1400 S. 19th
Bozeman, MT 59715
(406) 994-4042   **BT, BW, C, F, H, HR, PA, XC**

NATIONAL BISON RANGE
U.S. Fish and Wildlife Service
132 Bison Range Road
Moiese, MT 59824
(406) 644-2211
Self-guided auto tour available; marked foot trails
BW, F, GS, I, MT, PA, T

PAINTED ROCKS STATE PARK
Montana Department of Fish,
Wildlife and Parks
3201 Spurgin Road
Missoula, MT 59801
(406) 542-5500
Fees for day use and camping
BW, C, CK, F, MT, PA, S, T, XC

PIROGUE ISLAND STATE PARK
Montana Department of Fish,
Wildlife and Parks
PO 1630, Miles City, MT 59301
(406) 232-4365
Possible to drive to the island from mid to late summer   **BW, C, CK, F, H, HR, PA, S, XC**

PRYOR MOUNTAIN WILD HORSE RANGE
Bureau of Land Management,
Billings Resource Area
810 East Main
Billings, MT 59105
(406) 657-6262
Some roads are only passable with high-clearance, 4WD vehicles   **BW, H, HR**

RATTLESNAKE NATIONAL RECREATION AREA AND WILDERNESS
Lolo Forest Headquarters
Building 24, Fort Missoula
Missoula, MT 59801
(406) 329-3814   **BT, BW, C, F, H, HR, MT, RC, T, XC**

RED ROCK LAKES NATIONAL WILDLIFE REFUGE
U.S. Fish and Wildlife Service
Monida Star Route, PO 15
Lima, MT 59739
(406) 276-3536   **BW, C, CK, F, H, I, PA, T**

SAPPHIRE RANGE
Deerlodge National Forest
Philipsburg Ranger District
PO 4, Philipsburg, MT 59858
(406) 859-3211   **BW, C, F, H, HR, PA, RA, RC, S, T, XC**

BT Bike Trails	**CK** Canoeing, Kayaking	**F** Fishing	**HR** Horseback Riding
BW Bird-watching		**GS** Gift Shop	
C Camping	**DS** Downhill Skiing	**H** Hiking	**I** Information Center

Scapegoat Wilderness
Flathead National Forest
1935 3rd Ave. E.
Kalispell, MT 59901
(406) 755-5401   **BW, C, F, H, HR, MT, S**

Selway-Bitterroot Wilderness Area
Bitterroot National Forest
1801 N. 1st Street
Hamilton, MT 59840
(406) 363-3131
   Mechanized vehicles prohibited
                      **BW, C, CK, F, H,
                      HR, MT, RC, S, XC**

Sun River Canyon
Lewis and Clark National
Forest Headquarters
PO 869, Great Falls, MT 59403
(406) 791-7700   **BW, C, CK, F, H, HR,
                  MT, PA, RC, T, TG, XC**

Terry Badlands
Bureau of Land Management
Big Dry Resource Area
Miles City Plaza, Miles City, MT 59301
(406) 232-7000   **B, H, HR, XC**

**Upper Missouri Wild
and Scenic River**
Bureau of Land Management
PO 1160, Lewistown, MT 59457
(406) 538-7461
   Visitor center located in Fort Benton, MT
   (406) 622-5185   **BW, C, CK, F,
                    H, I, S, T, TG**

Wild Horse Island
Montana Department of Fish,
Wildlife and Parks
490 N. Meridian Road
Kalispell, MT 59901
(406) 752-5501
   Day use only; access by personal boat,
   some tour vessels available **BW, F, H, S**

Wyoming

Adobe Town Wilderness Study Area
Bureau of Land Management
PO 880, Rawlins, WY 82301
(307) 324-4841
   Extremely remote, isolated area; use
   maps; no water; need high-clearance
   4WD vehicle; roads impassable when
   wet; primitive camping; wild horse
   viewing   **C, H**

Alcova Reservoir
Bureau of Reclamation
705 Pendell Avenue
PO 1630
Mills, WY 82644
(307) 261-7600
   Part of this area is a county park; weather extremes; scorpion and rattlesnake
   precautions; paleontology trail; ice fishing; wind surfing   **BT, BW, C, CK, F,
                  GS, H, I, MT, PA, RC, S, T**

Beaver Rim
Bureau of Land Management
PO 589
Lander, WY 82520
(307) 332-7822
   Scenic area of geologic interest;
   raptor nesting   **BW**

**Bighorn Canyon National
Recreation Area**
National Park Service
PO 7458
Fort Smith, MT 59035
(406) 666-2412
   Large portion is on the Crow Indian
   Reservation; limited access on private
   land; visitor center in Lovell, WY and
   Fortsmith, MT   **BT, BW, C, CK, F, H,
                 I, MT, PA, RA, RC, S, T, XC**

Bighorn National Forest
U.S. Forest Service
1969 South Sheridan Avenue
Sheridan, WY 82801
(307) 672-0751 **BT, BW, C, CK, DS, F, GS,
             H, HR, I, L, MT, PA, RC, T, TG, XC**

Black Hills National Forest
U.S. Forest Service
RR 2, Box 100
Custer, SD 57730
(307) 283-1276
   Call game warden, Sundance or local
   chambers of commerce. Covers large
   area including national and state parks;
   tread lightly program
                **BT, BW, C, DS, F, GS,
             H, HR, I, MT, RC, S, T, XC**

Bridger-Teton National Forest
U.S. Forest Service
PO 1888
Jackson, WY 83001
(307) 739-5500
   White-water rafting; snowmobiling; call

L	Lodging	**PA**	Picnic Areas	**RC**	Rock Climbing	**TG**	Tours, Guides
MT	Marked Trails	**RA**	Ranger-led Activities	**S**	Swimming	**XC**	Cross-country Skiing
				T	Toilets		

for special program messages
BT, BW, C, CK, DS, F, GS, H, HR, I, MT, PA, RA, RC, S, T, TG, XC

BRIDGER WILDERNESS AREA
Bridger-Teton National Forest
PO 1888, Jackson, WY 83001
(307) 739-5500; (307) 367-4326
BW, C, CK, F, H, HR, I, L, MT, RC, S, TG, XC

CLOUD PEAK WILDERNESS AREA
Bighorn National Forest
1969 South Sheridan Avenue
Sheridan, WY 82801
(307) 672-0751
No vehicles; no bicycles; camping for small groups only **BW, C, CK, F, H, HR, MT, RC, XC**

DEVILS TOWER NATIONAL MONUMENT
National Park Service
PO 8, Devils Tower, WY 82714
(307) 467-5283
Especially good bird watching, crossover between west and east flyways; technical rock climbing, need ropes and hardware; monument open to public 365 days a year
BW, C, F, H, HR, I, MT, PA, RA, RC, S, T, XC

FERRIS MOUNTAINS WILDERNESS STUDY AREA
Bureau of Land Management
PO 880, Rawlins, WY 82301
(307) 324-4841
Steep, rugged terrain; 4WD vehicles needed; use maps; frequent weather changes
BW, C, H, HR

FITZPATRICK WILDERNESS AREA
Shoshone National Forest
808 Meadow Lane, Cody, WY 82414
(307) 527-6241
Rough, rugged area; for experienced backpackers or horsepackers
BW, C, F, H, HR, MT, RC, XC

FLAMING GORGE NATIONAL RECREATIONAL AREA
Ashley National Forest
1450 Uinta Drive
Green River, WY 82935
(307) 875-2871
Known for big lake trout and sailing
BT, BW, C, CK, F, H, HR, I, PA, S, T

FOSSIL BUTTE NATIONAL MONUMENT
National Park Service
PO 592, Kemmerer, WY 83101
(307) 877-4455
Weather extremes; if hiking, bring drinking water; seasonal guided hikes
BW, GS, H, HR, I, MT, PA, RA, T, TG, XC

FREMONT CANYON
Bureau of Reclamation
705 Pendell Avenue
PO 1630, Mills, WY 82644
(307) 261-5682
Known for rock climbing and eagle viewing **BW, H, MT, PA, RC, T**

GLENDO STATE PARK
Wyoming Department of Commerce
386 Glendo Park Road
Glendo, WY 82213
(307) 735-4433
Primitive camping; sailing and powerboating; ice fishing **BW, C, CK, F, GS, I, MT, PA, S, T**

GOOSEBERRY FORMATIONS
Bureau of Land Management
Worland District
Grass Creek Resource Area, PO 119
Worland, Wy 82401
(307) 347-9871
No potable water; heavy boots recommended due to snakes and cacti
BW, C, H, HR

GRAND TETON NATIONAL PARK
National Park Service
PO Drawer 170
Moose, WY 83012
(307) 739-3600 (automated information)
(307) 737-3399 (visitor center)
Trail system (220–230 miles) not free of snow until July 1; be aware of altitude; swimming in pools at lodges, other water too cold
BW, C, CK, F, GS, H, HR, I, L, MT, PA, RA, RC, S, T, TG, XC

GREAT DIVIDE BASIN
Bureau of Land Management
1993 Dewar Drive
Rock Springs, WY 82901
(307) 362-6422
High arid desert; bring water; very changeable weather; rough roads
BW, C, H, HR, RC

BT Bike Trails	**CK** Canoeing, Kayaking	**F** Fishing	**HR** Horseback Riding
BW Bird-watching	**DS** Downhill Skiing	**GS** Gift Shop	**I** Information Center
C Camping		**H** Hiking	

Green Mountains
Bureau Of Land Management
PO 589, Lander, WY 82520
(307) 332-7822
    4WD vehicle recommended
                    BW, C, F, H, HR, PA, T

Gros Ventre Wilderness
Bridger-Teton National Forest
PO 1888, Jackson, WY 83001
(307) 739-5500
    Call for special program messages
                    **BT, BW, C, CK, F, H, HR,
                    MT, PA, RC, S, T, TG, XC**

Guernsey State Park
Wyoming State Parks and Historic Sites
Department of Commerce
PO 429, Guernsey, WY 82214
(307) 836-2900 Museum (seasonal)
    Entrance fee to park
                    BT, BW, C, CK, F, H, I, MT, PA, S, T

Hole-in-the-Wall
Bureau of Land Management
189 North Cedar
Buffalo, WY 82834
(307) 684-5586
    Primitive historic site; public access not
    generally available; contact BLM

Honeycomb Buttes
Bureau of Land management
Highway 191 North
Rock Springs, WY 82902
(307) 382-5350
    Wilderness study area; no vehicles

Jackson Canyon
Bureau of Land Management
PO Drawer 2420, Mills, WY 82644
(307) 261-7500
    Contact BLM before visiting; large groups
    could disturb the wintering bald eagles
                    BW, H, HR

John D. Rockefeller, Jr. Memorial Parkway
Grand Teton National Park
PO Drawer 170 , Moose, WY 83012
(307) 739-3600 (automated)
(307) 739-3399 (visitor center)
(307) 543-2401 (district ranger)
    Prime grizzly bear territory
                    **BT, BW, C, CK, F, GS,
                    H, I, L, MT, PA, RA, T, XC**

Killpecker Sand Dunes
Bureau of Land Management
Highway 191 North
Rock Springs, WY 82902
(307) 382-5350
    On eastern side, dune buggies and 4WD
    vehicles are allowed; large herd of elk
    year-round

Laramie Peak
Routt/Medicine Bow National Forest
Douglas Ranger District
809 South Ninth Street, Douglas, WY 82633
(307) 358-4690
    Remote area   **BW, C, F, H, HR,
                    MT, PA, RC, T, XC**

Medicine Bow Range
Routt/Medicine Bow National Forest
Laramie Ranger District
2468 Jackson Street
Laramie, WY 82070-6735
(307) 745-2300
                    **BT, BW, C, CK, DS, F, GS, H, HR,
                    I, L, MT, PA, RA, RC, T, TG, XC**

Medicine Lodge State Archeological Site
Wyoming State Parks and Historic Sites
2301 Central Avenue
Cheyenne, WY 82002
(307) 469-2234
    Drinking water is available; nearest gas 30
    miles; nearest medical facility 50 miles
                    BT, BW, C, F, H, HR, I, PA, T

Medicine Wheel National Historic Landmark
Bighorn National Forest
1969 South Sheridan Avenue
Sheridan, WY 82801
(307) 672-0751
    Walk up to monument, 1 to 2 miles, fair-
    ly steep grade; information center sum-
    mer only   **I, T, TG**

Middle Fork Recreation Area
Bureau of Land Management
189 North Cedar Street
Buffalo, WY 82834
(307) 684-5586
    Includes Outlaw Cave Campgrounds, Bar
    C Cairn Line, and Rock Art Cave; rough
    roads; high-clearance vehicle recommend-
    ed; area generally accessible May 15 to
    November 15; camping is primitive; bike

L	Lodging	**PA**	Picnic Areas	**RC**	Rock Climbing	**TG**	Tours, Guides
MT	Marked Trails	**RA**	Ranger-led Activities	**S**	Swimming	**XC**	Cross-country Skiing
				T	Toilets		

trails are for mountain bikes

BT, BW, C, F, H, HR, MT, PA, RC, T

NATIONAL ELK REFUGE
U.S. Fish and Wildlife Service
PO C, Jackson, WY 83001
(307) 733-9212
Horse-drawn sleigh rides to view win-
tering wildlife; information center open
October through April **BW, F, I, T, TG**

NORTH ABSAROKA WILDERNESS AREA
Shoshone National Forest
808 Meadow Lane, Cody, WY 82414
(307) 527-6241
Includes 200 miles of hiking trails

BW, C, F, H, HR, MT, XC

OCEAN LAKE WILDLIFE HABITAT MANAGEMENT UNIT
Wyoming Game and Fish Department
5400 Bishop Boulevard
Cheyenne, WY 82006
(307) 332-2688 **BT, BW, C, CK, F, H, HR, PA, S, T**

OREGON BUTTES
Bureau of Land Management
Highway 191 North
Rock Springs, WY 82902
(307) 382-5350
Wilderness study area; no vehicles

PATHFINDER RESERVOIR
Bureau of Reclamation
705 Pendell Avenue
PO 1630, Mills, WY 82644
(307) 261-7600
Weather extremes; scorpion and rattlesnake precautions; ice fishing; wind
surfing; sailing; marina
BT, BW, C, CK, F, GS, H, I, MT, PA, RC, S, T

POPO AGIE WILDERNESS AREA
Shoshone National Forest, Washakie
Ranger District, 333 Hwy. 789 South
Lander, WY 82520
(307) 332-9071; (307) 332-5460
BW, C, F, H, HR, MT, RC, XC

PRYOR MOUNTAIN WILD HORSE RANGE
Bureau of Land Management
Miles City District, Billings Resource area
810 East Main, Billings, MT 59105
(406) 657-6262
Entrance in Lovell, WY; Rough, rugged
area; bear precautions **BW, C, H, HR, I**

RED CANYON
Bureau of Land Management
PO 589, Lander, WY 82520
(307) 332-7822
Scenic area for wildlife viewing **BW**

RED GULCH–ALKALI NATIONAL BACKCOUNTRY BYWAY
Bureau of Land Management
Worland District Office, PO 119
Worland, WY 82401
(307) 347-9871
Usually closed in winter

BT, BW, C, H, HR, I

RED LAKE
Bureau of Land Management
Highway 191 North
Rock Springs, WY 82902
(307) 382-5350
4WD vehicle needed; roads hazardous
in bad weather

ROUTT/MEDICINE BOW NATIONAL FOREST
U.S. Forest Service
2468 Jackson Street, Laramie, WY 82070
(307) 745-2300 (information all areas)
(307) 745-2307 (TTY for hearing impaired)
Semi-primitive camping; vault toilets
BT, BW, C, CK, DS, F, GS, H, HR, I, MT, PA, RC, T, TG, XC

SEEDSKADEE NATIONAL WILDLIFE REFUGE
U.S. Fish and Wildlife Service
PO 700, Green River, WY 82935
(307) 875-2187
Remote station; weather extremes; roads
often closed in winter
BW, CK, F, H, I, T, XC

SEMINOE RESERVOIR
Bureau of Reclamation, 705 Pendell Avenue
PO 1630, Mills, WY 82644
(307) 324-7171
Part of this area is a state park; weather
extremes; scorpion and rattlesnake precautions; bighorn sheep viewing; ice
fishing; wind surfing
BT, BW, C, CK, F, GS, H, I, MT, PA, RC, S, T

SHELL CANYON
Bighorn National Forest
1969 South Sheridan Avenue
Sheridan, WY 82801
(307) 672-0751

BT Bike Trails	**CK** Canoeing, Kayaking	**F** Fishing	**HR** Horseback Riding
BW Bird-watching		**GS** Gift Shop	
C Camping	**DS** Downhill Skiing	**H** Hiking	**I** Information Center

Bighorn sheep viewing
BT, BW, C, CK, DS, F, GS, H, HR, I, L, MT, PA, RA, RC, T, XC

SHOSHONE NATIONAL FOREST
U.S. Forest Service
808 Meadow Lane, Cody, WY 82414
(307) 527-6241
Bear precautions; call to check for road closures **BT, BW, C, CK, F, H, HR, I, MT, PA, RC, T, XC**

SIERRA MADRE RANGE
Routt/Medicine Bow National Forest
Brush Creek-Hayden Ranger District
204 West Ninth Street, PO 187
Encampment, WY 82325
(307) 327-5481 **BT, BW, C, CK, F, GS, H, HR, I, L, MT, PA, T, XC**

SINKS CANYON STATE PARK
Department of Commerce,
State Parks and Historic Sites
2301 Central Avenue, Cheyenne, WY 82002
(307) 332-6333 (state park)
(307) 332-3077 (visitor center seasonal)
(307) 777-7284 (Cheyenne year-round)
Trout watching from platform above the rise **BW, C, F, H, I, MT, PA, RC, T**

SLIDE LAKE
Bridger-Teton National Forest
PO 1888, Jackson, WY 83001
(307) 739-5500
Snow machining **BT, BW, C, CK, F, H, HR, MT, PA, RC, S, T, XC**

SYBILLE WILDLIFE RESEARCH AND CONSERVATION EDUCATION CENTER
Wyoming Game and Fish Department
PO 8101 Bosler Route
Wheatland, WY 82201
(307) 322-2784
Group tours available with one week notice; open April through October
I, MT, T, TG

TARGHEE NATIONAL FOREST
U.S. Forest Service
PO 208, St. Anthony, ID 83445
(208) 354-2312
Includes Jedediah Smith and Winegar Hole Wilderness Areas. Call to check trail conditions before starting out with motorcycle or ATV; scenic byways
BT, BW, C, CK, DS, F, H, HR, I, MT, PA, RC, S, T, XC

THUNDER BASIN NATIONAL GRASSLANDS
U.S. Forest Service, Douglas Ranger District
809 South Ninth Street, Douglas, WY 82633
(307) 358-4690
Limited travel in winter; information center at ranger district; 14-day camping limit
BT, BW, C, F, H, HR, I

WASHAKIE WILDERNESS AREA
Shoshone National Forest
808 Meadow Lane, Cody, WY 82414
(307) 527-6241
BW, C, F, H, HR, MT, XC

WIND RIVER RANGE
Bridger-Teton National Forest
PO 220, Pinedale, WY 82941
(307) 367-4326
Usually closed in winter; bear precautions
BW, C, CK, F, H, HR, I, MT, PA, RC, T, XC

YELLOWSTONE NATIONAL PARK
National Park Service
PO 168
Yellowstone National Park, WY 82190
(307) 344-7381
Includes Old Faithful Geyser, Mammoth Hot Springs, West Thumb Geyser Basin; park usually closed Nov. 1 to mid-Dec. and mid-April to mid-May
BT, BW, C, F, GS, H, HR, I, L, MT, PA, RA, T, TG, XC

YELLOWTAIL WILDLIFE HABITAT MANAGEMENT UNIT
Wyoming Game and Fish Department
5400 Bishop Boulevard
Cheyenne, WY 82202
(307) 527-7125
35 miles of roads, 24-hour access
BT, BW, C, CK, F, H, HR, I, PA, T

L	Lodging	**PA**	Picnic Areas	**RC**	Rock Climbing	**TG**	Tours, Guides
MT	Marked Trails	**RA**	Ranger-led Activities	**S**	Swimming	**XC**	Cross-country Skiing
				T	Toilets		

INDEX

Numbers in **bold** indicate illustrations; numbers in **bold italics** indicate maps.

The Northern Rockies

The Northern Rockies

92: New York Public Library, Rare Books Division, New York, NY
93, 96: Art Wolfe, Seattle, WA
99: David Muench, Santa Barbara, CA
100: Art Wolfe, Seattle, WA
101: Alan and Sandy Carey, Bozeman, MT
104: Library of Congress, Washington, D.C.
105: David Muench, Santa Barbara, CA
106: Alan and Sandy Carey, Bozeman, MT
111: Art Wolfe, Seattle, WA
112: Dean Sauskojus, Bozeman, MT
113: Art Wolfe, Seattle, WA
114–115: Thomas D. Mangelsen/Images of Nature, Jackson, WY
117: Annie Griffiths Belt, Silver Spring, MD
118: Tom and Pat Leeson, Vancouver, WA
119: Art Wolfe, Seattle, WA
122–123: John Hendrickson, Clipper Mills, CA
124: David Muench, Santa Barbara, CA
125: Rob Outlaw, Bozeman, MT
126: Tom and Pat Leeson, Vancouver, WA
127: Art Wolfe, Seattle, WA
128: John Hendrickson, Clipper Mills, CA
130–131: Art Wolfe, Seattle, WA
132: Carr Clifton, Taylorsville, CA
134: Art Wolfe, Seattle, WA
136–137: Alan and Sandy Carey, Bozeman, MT
138: Rob Outlaw, Bozeman, MT
142–143: Tom and Pat Leeson, Vancouver, WA
145, 146: Rob Outlaw, Bozeman, MT
147: Bates Littlehales, Arlington, VA
148–149: Pamela Spaulding, Louisville, KY
150: Art Wolfe, Seattle, WA
153: Alan and Sandy Carey, Bozeman, MT
154–155: David Muench, Santa Barbara, CA
157: Yale Collection of Western Americana, Beinecke Rare Book and Manuscript Library, New Haven, CT
158, 160: Art Wolfe, Seattle, WA
161: Keith Szafranski, Livingston, MT
164–165: Tom and Pat Leeson, Vancouver, WA
168: Yale Collection of Western Americana, Beinecke Rare Book and Manuscript Library, New Haven, CT
170–171: David Muench, Santa Barbara, CA
172–173: Erwin and Peggy Bauer, Livingston, MT
174: Art Wolfe, Seattle, WA

178–179: Susan G. Drinker, Snow Mass Village, CO
181, Top Left, Top Right, Bottom Right: Art Wolfe, Seattle, WA
181, Bottom Left: Michael H. Francis, Billings, MT
182–183: Jeff Gnass, Sisters, OR
184, 185: Art Wolfe, Seattle, WA
186: Jeff Foott, Jackson, WY
187: Dean Sauskojus, Bozeman, MT
188: Art Wolfe, Seattle, WA
190–191: Jeff Gnass, Sisters, OR
192: Pamela Spaulding, Louisville, KY
195: Art Wolfe, Seattle, WA
196: Tom and Pat Leeson, Vancouver, WA
200: Bates Littlehales, Arlington, VA
201, 202: Art Wolfe, Seattle, WA
206–207: Jeff Gnass, Sisters, OR
209: Art Wolfe, Seattle, WA
210, 211, 213: Thomas D. Mangelsen/Images of Nature, Jackson, WY
214–215: Art Wolfe, Seattle, WA
216: Denver Public Library, Western History Department, Denver, CO (Neg. # 6775)
218–219: Dick Durrance II, Snow Mass Village, CO
220: Art Wolfe, Seattle, WA
224–225: John Gerlach/Dembinsky Photo Associates, Owosso, MI
226: Tom and Pat Leeson, Vancouver, WA
227, 228, 229: Art Wolfe, Seattle, WA
231: New York Public Library, New York, NY
232–233: Art Wolfe, Seattle, WA
235: Courtesy of The National Museum of the American Indian/Smithsonian Institution (#23/6400)
236–237: Mike Barlow/Dembinsky Photo Associates, Owosso, MI
239: Art Wolfe, Seattle, WA
240: The New-York Historical Society, New York, NY
244: Jeff Foott, Jackson, WY
245, 248: Art Wolfe, Seattle, WA
249: John Hendrickson, Clipper Mills, CA
252–253: David Muench, Santa Barbara, CA
255: National Park Service, Harpers Ferry, WV
Back Cover: Art Wolfe, Seattle, WA (cougar, sheep); Dean Sauskojus, Bozeman, MT (wildflowers)

ACKNOWLEDGMENTS

The editors gratefully acknowledge the professional assistance of Susan Kirby and Patricia Woodruff.

The following consultants also helped in the preparation of this volume: John E. Grassy; Clyde M. Lockwood; Paul Schullery, president Yellowstone Grizzly Foundation; and Dallas Rhodes, Professor and Chair of Geology, Whittier College, CA.